Economic Theory and Natural Philosophy

Physiology and physics are spurious models in the social sciences because they are concerned with a reality man finds, not with one which he makes.

Werner Stark

The cost of believing in equilibrium - of seeing the study of economics as a search for improved knowledge of a fixed and final subject matter and thus as a hard science like physics or chemistry - is to be in an ineluctable march to obsolescence.

John Kenneth Galbraith

Economic science has about the same relation to science as Beethoven's Moonlight Sonata has to moonlight.

Thomas Crump

Economic Theory and Natural Philosophy

The Search for the Natural Laws of the Economy

Charles Michael Andres Clark
Associate Professor of Economics
St John's University
Jamaica, New York

Edward Elgar

Published by
Edward Elgar Publishing Limited
Gower House
Croft Road
Aldershot
Hants GU11 3HR
England

Edward Elgar Publishing Company
Old Post Road
Brookfield
Vermont 05036
USA

A CIP catalogue record for this book is available from
the British Library

A CIP catalogue record for this book is available from
the US Library of Congress

Printed and Bound in Great Britain by
Hartnolls Limited, Bodmin, Cornwall.

ISBN 1 85278 445 8

Contents

Foreword

This is a book about the power of an idea - in this case, its power to obfuscate, not to clarify, our understanding of society's workings. The idea is that the regularities that form the basis of economic analysis are not the products of social forces, but of subsocial, natural ones, whether these be the imperturbable workings of nature or the unchanging structure of the human psyche. What Charles Clark has done is to trace the permutations of this idea from its earliest beginnings in philosophy and science, through an astonishing series of permutations, down to its present incarnation as the presence of a rational maximizing impulse that enables us to perceive a 'choice theoretic' underpinning the decisions of human agents, in many, perhaps even in all endeavors - most unmistakably in the field of economics.

There is certainly some reason for the persistence of this remarkable idea. Were there not regularities of human behavior there would be no possibility of establishing, much less understanding, the dependable actions of its members on which society relies for its very existence. This is as true for primitive society as for industrial capitalism, but the difference between the two is worth noting. The regularities of behavior that give dependability to the first emerge from the visible and openly encouraged process by which individuals are transformed into members of a tribe, a group, a social unit. Hence there are few mysteries to be investigated in accounting for the continuity of the social order, whatever inscrutable purposes may have brought about its existence in the first place.

In more complicated and technologically advanced societies, typically assuming the organizational form of kingdoms, the means for the regularization of life are equally transparent. Now, in addition to the practices of socialization that always and everywhere shape the raw material of infancy into the ordinary behavior of men and women within the larger state, we can see the coercive hand of kingly or priestly power establishing the norms and requirements of daily life. Here, too, there are no mysteries to penetrate in explaining why society runs along its regular tracks, although there is always the lurking problem of explaining the rightfulness of the ruling power in whose name discipline is exercised.

It is only when we reach the form of social organization characteristic of capitalism that the matter of explaining the origins and tracing the consequences of behavioral regularity becomes important. For it is part of the very constitutive nature of capitalism that the steady hand of traditional socialization loses much of its influence, especially as individuals are encouraged, or forced, to fend for themselves on a society-wide 'market' that establishes the conditions of access to subsistence itself; and it is also part of the constitutive element of the new system that the coercive power of government is greatly compressed as a consequence of its wholesale exclusion from direct control over production and distribution.

Hence, the overwhelming puzzle, not to say the omnipresent anxiety, that presents itself to members of capitalist societies has always been to find assurance that order would assert itself despite the greatly reduced effects of tradition and direct command. As 'economic' behavior becomes the means by which social continuity has been achieved, a search for the roots of its underlying regularity naturally becomes a pivot point on which social understanding is based.

Clark takes us on a tour of the explanations and rationalizations that have sought to provide this vital assurance. The search for such understanding has two possible directions. One is to probe the manner in which capitalist society develops its own standards of normal behavior and its own means of instilling social discipline, to fill in the vacuums left by the retreat of tradition and direct command. This carries the disturbing consequence that capitalist society is thus in charge of its own destiny, in so far as these regulative means could be changed, if the outcomes of the existing standards and means do not seem satisfactory.

Alternatively, it offers the possibility of ascribing the order-bestowing influence of market pressures to presocial, or natural forces, whether these be biological, psychological, rational, or whatever. It is this second path that the theorists of capitalism have chosen, and it is Clark's task to make us see both the temptations of ascribing behavioral regularity to unalterable forces, and of the social consequences of doing so. Thus we examine the changing face of the concept of Natural Law, beginning with Adam Smith's conception of an economy that mirrors the intentions of a benign Deity, through the wholly undeistic, but equally omnipresent influence of general equilibrium theory. As Clark writes: 'Much of the history of economic thought is an attempt to explain economic phenomena as natural phenomena, as determined by natural causes' (p. 18). Running through that history is therefore a persisting effort to evade the responsibility that would have to be squarely faced, were the idea of Natural Law to be consigned to history, once and for all.

In the end, as Clark shows convincingly, this amounts to a renunciation by economics of its social parentage. The economy becomes a great machine; history and the future are reduced to the timelessness of graphs and functions; and self-governance, the great gift that economics has the possibility of awarding to society, is abandoned for subservience to myth and mystery. If there is to be an awakening from this subservience it will have to come from a clear understanding of the fascination and power, as well as the misconceptions and fallacies in the idea of Natural Law. Towards this end, Charles Clark's book makes a signal contribution.

Robert L. Heilbroner
Norman Thomas Professor Emeritus
New School for Social Research
New York, New York

Acknowledgements

This book is based on my doctoral dissertation, *The Natural Law Outlook and Economic Theory*, submitted to the New School for Social Research in 1989. Robert Heilbroner supervised the dissertation and his influence on this work should be quite apparent. I went to the New School specifically to study the history of economic thought under Robert Heilbroner and my debt to him, and to the New School as an institution, although not as great as Reagan's and Bush's contribution to the national debt, is substantial. I must also acknowledge the assistance of Ross Thompson, now of the University of Vermont, and Ed Nell, both of whom served on my dissertation committee, and to Reiner Schürmann and Janet Abu-Lughod, who served as outside readers and who encouraged me to pursue this topic. Of the eight chapters in this book, three are from the dissertation, with many of the other additions having their origins in comments made by Drs Schürmann and Abu-Lughod at my dissertation defense.

Much of my research in the past five years has been stimulated by conversations with my colleague Gary Mongiovi, who always provides the perfect blend of criticism and encouragement. Christine Rider, also of St John's, Ted McGlone, Warren Samuels, Marc Tool, Jerry Evensky, Marco Guidi and Stephen Worland provided useful comments and suggestions on earlier versions of many of these chapters.

I owe a great debt to Michelle Garafolo who read the entire manuscript, preventing numerous violations of the norms of English grammar, and forcing me to make my argument as clear as possible. More than just an editor, Michelle encouraged this project as if it were her own, often making me feel guilty (most likely unintentionally) if I seemed to be making no progress. Her encouragement and friendship are greatly appreciated.

I have received the help of many at St John's, particularly from the Faculty Support Center, who provided much-needed computer assistance, and the Library's Reference Department.

An earlier version of Chapter 4 was published under the title 'Adam Smith and Society as an Evolutionary Process'. It is reprinted from the *Journal of Economic Issues* by special permission of the copyright holder, the Association for Evolutionary Economics. Also, part of Chapter 3 is based on an earlier article 'Natural Law Influences on Adam Smith' in

Quaderni di Storia dell'Economia Politica.

Lastly, I must thank my wife Lisa, and my children: Meghan Julia, Kaitlin Virginia, and Charles Robert Thorstein, for enduring all that goes into writing a book, and John and Carol Clark for passing on to me a set of values that forced me to view economics, not as a branch of mathematics, but as something that affects people.

1. On the Creation of Social Theory

It has been over twenty years since the 'crisis in economic theory' - the widespread disenchantment with the grand neoclassical synthesis. The Keynesian policies which were so successful in the post-war period proved to be inadequate for the new economic environment of the 1970s, particularly the simultaneous existence of inflation and unemployment. Many prominent economists publicly expressed reservations of the ability of economic theory to adequately come to grips with the pressing economic troubles. The reaction to the inability of neoclassical economic theory to explain and offer workable policy suggestions came in two forms. One group of economists, John Kenneth Galbraith the most prominent, suggested that the inherent defect of modern economic theory was its lack of realism; it had not adjusted to the changing economic circumstances and thus did not effectively represent what were the real forces driving the economy. Simply put, the economy changed and economic theory did not. This was the minority opinion held mostly by dissenters from the mainstream tradition. The young economists within the neoclassical school, particularly those influenced by the perspective held at the University of Chicago, saw the principal defect in economic theory as an incompatibility between the neo-Walrasian theory of general equilibrium which was used to explain the behavior of individuals and firms, mircoeconomics, and the macroeconomics loosely derived from the writings of John Maynard Keynes, which was used to explain economic aggregates and upon which fiscal economic policy was based. The two divisions of economic theory (micro and macro) contradict each other: mircoeconomics is based upon the idea that all markets clear, while macroeconomics is based on the reality that all markets do not clear. General equilibrium theory is comprehensive in scope, axiomatic, individualistic (following methodological individualism) and in almost all ways resembles a hard science. Macroeconomics was the result of the Great Depression, an adaptation to intolerable economic events, bounded by historical circumstances and social context. In the ensuing twenty years, the practical economics inspired by Keynes has all but been fully replaced by pre-Keynesian notions and theories updated with modern and sophisticated mathematics. The idea that economic theory

1

should reflect the economy and that as the economy evolves, so also should the theory, smacks of relativism and thus is considered unscientific.

The abandonment of Keynes's economic theory, which reflected the historical realities of his time, for a theory that was independent of history and society, reflects a trend which was carried out in almost all fields of economics. Areas of economic research which were notable for their institutional and historical richness, such as Labor, Industrial Organization, Business Cycles (especially as developed by Wesley Mitchell) and, most perversely of all, Economic History, were emptied of their historical and institutional content, and reformulated to fit the axiomatic nature of the hard core of neoclassical economics. In the case of Economic History, emphasis was now placed on quantitative history; in many cases neglecting or ignoring the qualitative nature of historical change.

These developments in economic theory are firmly rooted in the origins of economics as a discipline. The aim of this book is to demonstrate how and why economic theory has been progressively moving away from history and society in an attempt to find the natural laws of the economy. This objective will be accomplished by examining the historical development of economic theory, particularly with respect to the role that history and society have played in the creation of economic theory. It is the implicit premise of this book that an economic theory which lacks historical content, and does not reflect the economy or society it seeks to explain, cannot avoid being irrelevant. Just as we come to understand economic phenomena by investigating its historical development and its social context, so also our comprehension of economic theory. The necessity of a historical approach to economic theory has been deftly asserted by Joseph Schumpeter (1954a, pp. 12-13):

> First, the subject matter of economics is essentially a unique process in historic time. Nobody can hope to understand the economic phenomena of any, including the present, epoch who has not an adequate command of historical facts and an adequate amount of historical sense or of what may be described as historical experience. Second, the historical report cannot be purely economic but must inevitably reflect also 'institutional' facts that are not purely economic: therefore it affords the best method for understanding how economic and non-economic facts are related to one another and how the various social sciences should be related to one another. Third, it is, I believe, the fact that most of the fundamental errors currently committed in economic analysis are due to the lack of historical experience more often than to any other shortcoming of the

economist's equipment.[1]

Any exposure to neoclassical economic theory[2] will readily show a lack of interest in matters of historical and social context. This antipathy was clearly displayed in a recent investigation (Klamer and Colander 1987) into the opinions of graduate economic students at the leading institutes of economic orthodoxy. In this study the students were asked what factors they thought were important for success in the field of economics. Not surprisingly 98% (Ibid. p. 100) of the respondents indicated that knowledge of mathematics was very important or moderately important to the success of an economist. Only 3% stated that knowledge of the economy was very important and 22% thought that it was moderately important, with 68% stating that it was unimportant. A lack of historical sense is further demonstrated by the fact that only 10% stated that knowledge of economic's literature was very important. Astonishingly, the study also showed that only 34% of graduate students surveyed strongly agreed with the statement that neoclassical economic theory was relevant for understanding the economic problems of today. Many of the interviews with the students indicated their belief that success came from concentrating on technique rather than substance. This study should be seen as reflecting the socialized and institutionalized views of mainstream economic theory and not student's pre-graduate school viewpoints and preferences. The students are merely adapting to the requirements of economic orthodoxy.[3]

The sterility of neoclassical economic theory stems from its approach to understanding economic phenomena. By choosing the natural laws of the economy as its object of inquiry, economic theorists have developed a method which is unhistorical and unsocial. The argument can be simply put; economic theorists' search for the natural laws of the economy has caused them to treat economic phenomena as if they were natural phenomena and thus caused by natural forces, and not social phenomena,

1. Schumpeter also writes that 'in economics ... modern problems, methods, and results cannot be fully understood without some knowledge of how economists have come to reason as they do' (Schumpeter 1954a, p. 6). It is interesting to note that Schumpeter, in his *History of Economic Analysis* (1954a), presents a strong case for relating economic theory to historical factors, yet he views the history of economic analysis as the progressive realization of the concept of general equilibrium and views Walras, who had little historical sense, as the greatest economist and an intellectual figure on a par with Newton.

2. The term neoclassical economic theory is meant to refer to modern mainstream economics based on general equilibrium theory which forms the hard core of current economic orthodoxy.

3. In fact, many of the students expressed in the interviews their dismay over this state of affairs.

the result of social institutions. Therefore, economic phenomena would be best understood by utilizing the methods of the natural sciences, emulating their models and adopting their metaphors. This process leads to the eventual emptying of the historical and social elements in economic theory and analysis.

The approach of the book is as follows. First the question of how an historical investigation of the evolution of ideas should proceed is considered, paying particular attention to the methods of rational reconstruction and historical reconstruction. Following this the relationship between social systems, nature, social theories and natural theories, and particularly the role played by analogies and metaphors in the development of new theories will be examined.

In Chapter 2 the above mentioned method will be employed to understand the relationship between conceptions of nature and the realm of nature and conceptions of society and its realm. Chapters 3 and 4 explicate the role of natural law philosophy and historical and social investigation, respectively, in the work of Adam Smith. In Chapter 5 the rise and fall of scientific history and John Stuart Mill's efforts in constructing a 'scientific' economics based on his conception of social laws and the role of history and nature in their determination will be analyzed. As will be seen in this chapter, the changing conception of what constitutes history and the results of history, together with a changing conception of what is nature leads to an uneasy relationship between economic theory and historical and social context. The marginal utility revolution, with its retrogressive conception of nature, heightens the conflict between economic theory and history and society. Chapter 6 looks at how the search for natural laws of the economy by the marginalists leads to the false division of pure economic theory and political economy. The final separation between economic theory and history and society is seen in the rise of 'scientific' economics, which is examined in Chapter 7. The final chapter examines the consequences of this loss of historical sense in economic theory.

1. Approaches to The History of Economic Theory

In *The History of Economics in its Relation to Social Development*, Werner Stark (1944, p. 1) writes that there are two ways to view the history of economic thought:

> [O]ne is to regard it as a steady progression from error to truth, or at
> least from dim and partial vision to clear and comprehensive perception;
> the other is to interpret every single theory put forward in the past as a
> faithful expression and reflection of contemporary conditions, and thus
> to understand it in its historical causation and meaning.[4]

That the first approach has dominated economic historiography can be
clearly seen in three aspects of how neoclassical economics treats the
history of economic thought.[5]

Much historiography of economic thought, particularly as produced by
neoclassical economists, perceives the economic theories of the past
exclusively from the perspective, and with the attitude, of the present. The
past theorists and theories which are investigated are those which, partially
or wholly, are in agreement with the neoclassical vision of the economy.
Frequently this is only accomplished by a creative reading of the particular
text, imputing much which was not and could not have been intended by the
author. An example of this is Spiegel's (1975) essay on the concept of
equilibrium, where he argues that Plato and Aristotle, in their recognition
of economic interdependence, have discovered the idea of economic
equilibrium. Certainly the interdependence that Plato and Aristotle wrote
about had nothing in common with the idea that individual self-interested
actions, in a market setting, generates economic order. Yet if one views
economic equilibrium as the natural order, that is, the result of natural
laws, then any utterance which can be interpreted as a glimpse of
equilibrium is seen as a step on the march towards universal truth.

The adoption of the philosophy of science as a valid framework to discuss
the history of economic thought and methodology is another expression of
the former view of the history of economic thought. In the past thirty years
historians have increasingly used the methods of the philosophy of science
to explain and evaluate the history of economic theory and methodology.
The goal of the philosophy of science is to provide an answer to the
question of how should science be carried out. Although the natural
sciences were the primary target for the investigations of the philosophers

---

4. Stark's views on how the history of economic thought has developed as a discipline are fully
developed in his posthumously published *History and Historians of Political Economy*
(forthcoming).

5. It is no accident that with the growing dominance of general equilibrium theory as the economic
orthodoxy, the study of the history of economic thought has greatly suffered. An unhistorical
theory is not likely to be interested in history, even its own.

of science, many, such as Karl Popper, suggested that their approach could be extended to the social sciences, particularly economics, with fruitful results. The willingness of historians of economic thought to jump on the philosophy of science bandwagon is rooted, I believe, in the perspective that economic theory, like physics, is attempting to expose universal laws, hence the similarity between economic theory and the natural sciences. Under this perspective, the history of economics must be viewed as the development of progressively better tools for understanding the economy, with its evolution and subsequent changes as the result of these new and improved tools, and not from changes in the economy.

The third expression of this perspective is the use of rational reconstruction as economic historiography. As Marc Blaug has recently written: 'Rational reconstructions analyze [the ideas of past economists] in our terms in order to locate their "mistakes" and to verify that there has been rational progress in the course of intellectual history' (Blaug 1990, p. 28). Blaug feels that inevitably, historical reconstructions must 'at some point lapse into a rational reconstruction for the simple reason that there *is* progress in economics - progress in the tools and analytical techniques of the trade and, occasionally, even progress in our understanding of the workings of the economy' (Ibid.). Here is a clear example of the lasting influence of natural law preconceptions, for the view that the history of economic thought's aim is to find the progress in the development of economics presupposes that the object of economic analysis - the economy - never fundamentally changes. Assuming the existence of natural laws in the economy, the history of our discipline must be a continued progress towards discovering these laws. However, if this were truly the case, one would not have to rely on rational reconstructions to show such progress, an examination of the historical record would suffice. Yet if the economy is evolving, then economic theory, and thus its history, should reflect such evolution. Under rational reconstruction, the emphasis is on how economic theory should have logically developed, emphasizing the independence of economic theory and the economy. This is a modern version of conjectural history, a topic we will return to in our discussion of Adam Smith.

The basic assumption of this approach to the history of economic thought is that economic theory is separate from the economy and society, that it is a branch of logic or mathematics, able to be developed independent of any relation with actual economic phenomena. Carried to its logical conclusion, one is left with an economic theory which attempts to understand the economy without recourse to either history or society.

A contrary approach is based on the fundamental tenets of the sociology of knowledge; that is that ideas are the product of social groups and they reflect the reality or the perception of the reality of social groups, and they can only be appreciated in the context and history from which they originate. Of utmost importance for the creation of economic theory is the material conditions contemporary to the theorists and the intellectual milieu within which they operate. The material conditions provide the phenomena to be explained and the problems to be solved. Conversely, the intellectual milieu, that is, the preconceptions, viewpoints and vision of the theorists and their community, provides the framework with which to categorize and analyze the phenomena in question. In addition, the intellectual milieu establishes the criteria as to what is to be accepted as a valid explanation and what is to be deemed quackery. The vast array of possibilities arising from such a situation attest to the freedom inherent in the process of theory creation. These two factors allow us to explain the development of economic theory but it is not a closed deterministic causality. These are the dominant and persistent forces, the two constant influences on the creation of social theory, yet human free will operates in the construction of social theories as it does in all human endeavors. Furthermore, the current preconceptions can be such that concern for explaining the material conditions can be at a minimum, or even non-existent, thus leading to an economic theory which is divorced from economic reality. This is the case with the development of neoclassical economic theory. Their natural law preconceptions increasingly convince the neoclassical economist of the necessity of divorcing theory and reality (history and society) thus producing a path of development in which the influence of material conditions seems to be insignificant. This allows historians of economic thought, such as George Stigler (1965), to discount the influence of events on economic theory. Stigler is correct if our understanding of the development of economic theory is the path taken by neoclassical economic theory, yet, following Werner Stark (1966) this should be seen as an indictment of neoclassical economic theory, for the sociology of knowledge is not only a vehicle for understanding the development of social theory, it also allows for its evaluation.

2. The Formation of Social Theories

Recently Philip Mirowski (1988) has developed a conceptual framework for understanding the complex factors which go into the formation of social theories. Mirowski's scheme, called the DMD thesis, is based on the work of sociologists Emile Durkheim and Marcel Mauss and the anthropologist, Mary Douglas. It investigates the interaction between society and its conceptions of nature and society in the formation of theories. In their *Primitive Classification* (1903) Durkheim and Mauss argue that primitive societies classify their environment based on their social structure, 'the first logical categories were social categories; the first classes of things were classes of men, into which these things were integrated' (Durkheim and Mauss 1963, p. 82). The origin of the philosophy of nature and science is the imposition of order upon nature through classification. 'Such classifications' they argue, 'are thus intended, above all, to connect ideas, to unify knowledge; as such, they may be said without inexactitude to be scientific, and to constitute a first philosophy of nature' (Ibid. p. 81). The Durkheim-Mauss thesis has been succinctly summarized by Rodney Needham:

> They [Durkheim and Mauss] believed that the human mind lacks the innate capacity to construct complex systems of classification such as every society possess, and which are cultural products not to be found in nature, and they therefore ask what could have served as the model for such arrangements of ideas. Their answer is that the model is society itself. The first logical categories were social categories, they maintain, the first classes of things were classes of men; not only the external forms of classes, but also the relations uniting them to each other, are of social origin; and if the totality of things is conceived as a single system, that is because society itself is seen in the same way, so that logical hierarchy is only another aspect of social hierarchy, and the unity of knowledge is nothing else than the very unity of the social collectivity extended to the universe. (Ibid. pp. xi-xii).

To this Mary Douglas has suggested that in developed societies, conceptions of the natural universe play a fundamental role in the construction of social theories. This tendency is particularly evident in Western Social Thought where the aim since the Enlightenment has been to construct a 'scientific' theory of society, with the conception of science being that of the natural sciences. The DMD thesis looks at the interactions between social concepts and influences such as those studied in the sociology of science (see Barnes 1974) and those concepts in the natural sciences. To quote Mirowski (1988, p. 110):

> Theories of the physical world are shaped by the social relations within the culture that generates them, and these are used in turn to express in reified format the essence of that culture's ideal of order. This ideal of order consequently molds the expression of social concepts and

classifications, eventually transforming the original notions of mastery and control in the social sphere. The circuit is completed by the persistent projection of anthropomorphic concepts onto 'Nature,' and the intended demonstration of the efficacy and legitimacy of structure in the social sphere through its purported success in the mastery of personified nature.

The next chapter illustrates how this interrelation has worked in constructing concepts of nature and society.

Analogies and metaphors play a key role in this process of theory formation, for it is in the application of analogies and metaphors from one sphere (social or natural) to another that theories are developed. The conventional wisdom perceives analogies and metaphors as mere literary embellishments or, at best, as a method of illustrating unfamiliar concepts in a manner that can be better understood by those new to the subject matter. Thus when economists state that market prices gravitate towards long-run equilibrium prices, all those familiar with the concept of gravitation will have a sense of what the economist is saying. Only occasionally have scientists recognized the constructive role of analogies and metaphors in providing new insights or perspectives. Yet even in these rare cases, the role of analogies and metaphors is thought to terminate with the genesis of the new concept, performing no active role in its subsequent development.

This dismissal of the role of analogies and metaphors in the construction of knowledge and theories has blinded the historiography of ideas to their correct role.[6] In *Invention and the Evolution of Ideas*[7] (Schon 1967) Donald Schon demonstrates the great contribution of analogies and metaphors to theory development, and convincingly argues that theories could be created in no other way.[8] Schon labels analogies and metaphors 'displaced concepts'; the application of ideas and concepts from a well developed and fully understood field of knowledge to a new situation, or

---

6. Ted Cohen has noted that 'there has been a very strong line in Western Philosophy, especially in that strain running from British empiricism through Vienna positivism, which has denied to metaphors and their study any philosophical seriousness of the first order' (Cohen 1979, p. 1). These are the philosophical traditions which we see dominating the development of economic theory in the period covered in this study.

7. Originally published under the title of *The Displacement of Concepts*.

8. There is a very large literature on the role of metaphors and analogies. The complexities and full implications of the role of metaphors in theory creation is beyond the limited scope of this book. The interested reader would be well served by consulting the following: Hesse (1967), Black (1962), Ortony (1979) especially the Boyd and Kuhn chapters, and Ricoeur (1977).

utilized in a field for which the current theories are inadequate. Although Schon's analysis is mostly concerned with the displacement of concepts in the physical sciences, a brief summary of his findings will help to illuminate a central aspect of the relationship between social and natural theories.

Schon's central question is: where do new ideas come from and how do they develop? Unfortunately such a compelling topic has been grossly underdeveloped. According to Schon, the neglect of this topic is caused by philosophers constructing two large barriers around the question of where theories originate. For the most part, philosophers and scientists have either shrouded the formation of new ideas and concepts in mystery (i.e. inspiration), or have taken the position that there are no genuinely new ideas, merely a rearranging of the old. Schon's analysis allows us to see not only the origins of ideas, but the genuine novelty of new ideas as well.

At the heart of the quest for knowledge of the unknown is the desire to control our environment, even if this control is only at a psychological level.[9] The first step in any attempt of understanding is the naming and classification of the new phenomena. As seen previously, one would expect the naming and classification system to reflect already existing names and systems, and the new or unknown phenomena would be described with concepts already in existence and well known, that is, with analogies and metaphors. Schon (1967, p. 60) writes:

> metaphors are ways of naming aspects of the new situation and therefore fixing and controlling them. This function should not be underestimated. In every displacement of an old theory to a new situation there is a feeling of transition from helplessness to power. Before, we were aware only of what was puzzling and disturbing; now, suddenly, there is something like clarity and a basis for action. ... These metaphors, however appropriate or inappropriate they may be, name, fix and structure what might otherwise be vaguely troubling situations.

It is only through the displacement of concepts that knowledge can be advanced and that new theories can be developed in order to explain new situations. They are the link between the past accumulation of knowledge, the present situation and the future evolution of our knowledge. Once the singular importance of the displacement of concepts is recognized, three questions naturally arise: 1) where do the displaced concepts come from; 2) why are some concepts chosen over others; and 3) what is the lasting

---

9. An example of this would be Adam Smith's idea that the motivation behind natural philosophy is to 'allay this tumult of the imagination' (Smith 1979, p. 45).

effect of the displacement of concepts.

The answer to the first question is that metaphors come from our culture, in the widest sense of the word. Schon (Ibid. p. 65) asserts:

> Our culture provides the materials from which our metaphors are made. Our technology, our social system, and, in the informal sense of the term, our theories of the world, provide us with concepts for displacement. They are our 'given'. When we come to form theories of business organization, we derive our metaphors from the games we know, from the church and the army as we know them, from our understanding of machines. Our psychologies are based in part on the physics of a few generations ago. Our science takes its metaphors from concepts current in the same or related disciplines.

More problematic is answering the question regarding the selection of metaphors to be adopted, for selection involves choice and choice presupposes a criteria. Schon's analysis is drawn from his experiences working in research and development, therefore his examples of displaced concepts are drawn from the physical sciences and within the context of problem solving. In his analysis, the selection process is guided by what enhances the solution of the problem at hand. Many concepts could be attempted but only those that prove most useful for the problem under scrutiny will survive. 'Metaphors that come to mind and are selected result from the interaction of what is given or imposed by the culture with the demands of the situations confronting us. Theories are chosen from among the culture's store, on the basis of their ability to meet these demands - to give rise to metaphors which will explain these troubling situations or allow them to be changed' (Ibid. p. 68). A change in the problem could lead to the adoption of a different concept for displacement. Schon notes that the analogous relationship between the field from which and to which concepts are displaced is not apparent at the time of displacement, but only becomes apparent as the analogy or metaphor develops. Already existing metaphors, which have served as the foundation of our existing theories, frequently play an important role in the selection process.

The selection process for the social sciences is more complex. Social theory serves two functions: on the one hand it is an attempt to explain social phenomena with the goal of increasing our control over it; and on the other hand it is an attempt to legitimate or challenge the existing situation. In the social sciences one cannot overlook the role of ideology and value judgments. In fact, no social theory has ever existed, nor could exist, free of these normative elements. Thus the choice of metaphors and analogies, and the theories which develop from them, always involves an element of ideology. Social theories thus serve both an instrumental and a ceremonial role, either striving to be useful for solving problems or serving a purpose other than problem solving, this frequently being the legitimation of the current social order. In Werner Stark's analysis of the sociology of knowledge, theories are shaped by the real, which constitutes what we aspire to explain, and the ideal, that is our conception of how things should be. Frequently, the ideal is buried in the preconceptions of the times, yet it is always there and always important. Choice of metaphors and analogies is typically based on both aspects of social theory, although under the Natural Law Outlook the theorist is frequently unaware of this.

The last question is the most important for this study: what is the lasting influence of the displacement of concepts? Schon notes two aspects of the displacement of concepts: a radical and a conservative. The radical aspect has already been noted. By displacing a concept, using an idea or theory to explain a new situation, we are in effect looking at the situation from a fresh perspective. This perspective is what yields the resulting theory or insight that gives us a certain degree of understanding and control.

The conservative function, writes Schon (Ibid. pp. 111-12):

> is to be seen most clearly in the development of theories. Old theories underlie new ones. When old theories are displaced to new situations, all aspects of the old theories tend to locate themselves projectively in the new situations. Epaminondas-like, aspects of the old theory may be taken as projective models for the new situation without being changed themselves in the process. They become fixed as assumptions about the new situation, often unrecognized, carried over uncritically from the old theory. Aspects of the new situation maybe overlooked or misconstrued in a way that damages action or explanation based on the displacement.

The displacement of concepts provides a projective model with which to view new phenomena, with the hope that new insights will be developed from this new perspective. However, the projective model often constrains the subsequent development of the new theory. Builtin biases develop based on the preconceptions of the displaced concept, directing the development of the new theory in a particular direction. Once a concept is displaced into a new field, the direction of the subsequent inquiry frequently follows the pattern set by the concept before its displacement. The adoption of the metaphor of equilibrium from physics on to the problem of price determination in a market setting, as we see in Chapter 7, directs the inquiry towards questions of the balances of forces, as well as conjuring up images of natural laws bringing about a natural order. Furthermore, following the atomistic view of phenomena in physics, the economist develops a mechanistic and atomistic view of society.

Schon's analysis of the displacement of concepts is not only insightful in our understanding of theory formation, but also furnishes a very powerful tool for the historian of ideas. Metaphors and analogies become clues for how theories developed, of what the preconceptions of the theorists were and why theories evolve along specific paths. Schon writes (Ibid. pp. 112-13):

> The actual language of a theory contains metaphors which are vestiges and signs of the old theories whose displacement helped to form the new one. These metaphors are clues to the identity of the old theories. ... In order to discover whether the new theory is actually a displacement from this old one, we look for assumptions transposed from the old theory uncritically to the new situation. If these assumptions are found in the new theory, particularly if their presence is undefended and unexplained, then a presumption is established that the old theory does underlie the new one.

3. On The Nature of Social Laws

There seems to be general agreement that the purpose of all theoretical activity, regardless of the field, is to explain the observed regularities and uniformities. The belief that there are regularities may stem from the preconceptions, derived from the Natural Law Outlook, that a rationally ordered universe must have regularities and uniformities. This theoretical preconception greatly influences the generation of theories, particularly in the social sciences, for it sets up the presumption of a natural order in the social realm somehow analogous to that supposed in the natural.

With the supposition of regularities and uniformities, the quest then becomes to uncover the regularities and uniformities, their origins and the forces which bring them about. These are not unrelated activities for our belief in the source of the regularities can greatly influence, if not determine, not only how we will search for the regularities and uniformities, but what we will consider to be a regular and uniform phenomenon. Our preconceptions as to the source of the regularities and uniformities will, to a large extent, determine what we will consider to be classified as permanent features to be explained and temporary aberrations to be abstracted.

There are two answers to the question as to the source of the observed regularities and uniformities in social life: they are the result of the workings of nature; or they are the creation of society. This book argues that the presumption of economic theory has been, and continues to be, that nature is the ultimate determinant of the regularities and uniformities observed in the economic aspects of human existence. This presumption explains much of the evolution of economic theory, particularly its treatment of history and social factors.

If one adopts the view that society is the ultimate source of the observed regularities and uniformities of social life, which includes economic phenomena, then one's theories would adopt different phenomena to explain, and would rely on different metaphors and analogies with which to develop theories to explain these phenomena. The presumption of nature as the final cause leads to natural metaphors and natural (non-social and historical) phenomena to be explained and thus to an unhistorical and socially contextualless explanation - exactly what underlies much modern economic theory.

The creation of a natural social science, an explanation of social activities based on the operation of nature and determined by natural laws, was clearly the aim of the Enlightenment. The Enlightenment assumed a constant and universal human nature, that societies were based on a natural order, that social activity was determined by natural laws, and that the development of man was the working out of a universal history. The Enlightenment was left with, as Robert Solomon has described it, 'an impossible task, which we are still trying to carry on today: to develop a theory of society without first taking the concept of society seriously' (Solomon 1979, p. 31).

Ultimately, the failings of modern economic theory stem from this erroneous belief, for the role of nature in the determination of social phenomena and social laws is minimal and negative. As Werner Stark has exhaustively demonstrated in his tragically neglected five volume magnum opus, *The Social Bond* (Stark, 1976-1987), nature establishes certain minimum conditions which all societies and individuals must meet (the necessity for food, clothing, shelter and sex) and certain natural factors which determine what humans cannot achieve, i.e., our ability to fly being limited by the laws of gravity. Yet the range of how these necessities can be, and have been, met is so wide and diverse, that we can only conclude that how nature's requirements are satisfied stems from a humanly created culture and customs and not from natural laws. Moreover, the innate ingenuity of humanity has produced the ability to counter the few laws of nature which place limits on our activities. Thus nature, for example gravity, has severely limited humanity's ability to fly, yet this has been overcome by the human generation of knowledge and a technology which can surmount this limitation. The role and influence of nature decrease as societies develop, so much so that nature itself is now greatly influenced, and indeed threatened, by human activities and mastery over it.   The possibility of sociality stems from society's control and suppression of the animalistic instincts nature has embedded in mankind: self-preference and the sex drive. Both, if unchecked by culture and customs, necessarily lead to conflict in society, threatening any possibility for social order. Society is not the reflection of natural propensities, as Adam Smith assumed, but requires their suppression. In this sense, Hobbes was right.

2. Nature and Society

The word 'nature' is seminal for Western Thought. As a concept, nature's power and influence derive from its lucidity and paradoxically its ambiguity. That the word 'nature' has a multitude of meanings and connotations (over a page of the Oxford English Dictionary is devoted to the word nature, not to mention the space used up by its derivatives, such as natural) was noted as early as the seventeenth century when Robert Boyle, a natural philosopher, 'enumerated eight senses of the word as used in philosophy and natural sciences' (Willey 1940, p. 2).[1] Derived from the Latin 'natura', meaning birth, constitution, character, course of things (Oxford English Dictionary, 1971, p. 1900), nature's primary English meanings are: the essential qualities or properties of a thing; the vital or physical powers of man; the inherent dominating power or impulse (in men or animals) by which action or character is determined, directed or controlled; and the creative and regulative physical power which is conceived of as operating in the material world and as the immediate cause of all its phenomena (Ibid.). Originally juxtaposed with the concept of grace, the eighteenth century saw the divinization of nature (Becker 1934) and by the nineteenth century nature replaces God and religion as the ultimate source of human understanding and meaning. By the end of the nineteenth century, nature becomes juxtaposed with artificial, that is, socially or humanly created.

The diversity of meanings of 'nature', instead of creating ambiguity, clarified the use and implications of the term. The power and authority associated with 'nature' stemmed from the ubiquitous acceptance of the view that the universe was a natural order and was, therefore, regulated by natural laws. One of the primary tenets of the Natural Law Outlook is that all phenomena are under one system, what is often called the principle of design. This held for social as well as for natural phenomena. It is thus

---

1. Aristotle listed seven different meanings for φύσις: origin or birth; their seed; source of movement or change; primitive matter; essence or form of natural things; essence or form; and the essence of things which have a source of movement in themselves (Collingwood 1960, pp. 80-82).

quite reasonable to use the same word to refer to the origin of a phenomena, its essence, its structure and the force which brings it to change. All are aspects of the same design. The smooth progression from the theological view of the universe of the middle ages to the scientific view of the nineteenth century was facilitated by the intermediate stage of natural theology, in which nature replaced revelation as the source of our knowledge of God and His creation: the universe. The transition was extremely gradual, owing to the fact that science, as the initiator of much of this change, confirmed the view of the existence of God. Additionally, many clerics played important roles in the conversion from a revelation-based faith to one based on nature.[2] Nature becomes the basis of a new world outlook, a new religion as comprehensive and dogmatic as that which it replaced. The diversity of nature's meanings and applications added to its new role.

The ambiguity in the meaning of 'nature' added to its political value. Robert C. Solomon (1979, p. 31) enumerates this aspect of the word 'nature' in the following passage:

> The word 'nature' played a huge role in Enlightenment ideology, and that alone should make us suspect that it too, like 'Reason,' was as much a weapon as a concept. Sometimes, 'nature' meant the cosmic order, within which human affairs were governed by 'natural laws' just like the stars and the planets. It was this concept the philosophers used when they spoke of 'human nature' and 'natural laws,' their message being that human societies should be run as smoothly and efficiently as the heavens. ... But humans also had a distinctive 'nature,' and this was above all to be rational. Thus 'natural' would also mean 'rational' (as it had in the 'natural law' of the medieval theologians), and an appeal to nature was tantamount to an appeal to universal reason - an appeal which, in Enlightenment ideology, could not be challenged.

One of the ambitions of this book is to demonstrate how malleable the concept of nature and the path to understanding nature has been over its use in economic theory. Much of the history of economic theory is an attempt to explain economic phenomena as natural phenomena, as determined by natural causes. This aspiration is uniform, from the Mercantilists, the Physiocrats and Adam Smith, up to and including modern general equilibrium theory, the hard core of neoclassical economics. The conception of what nature is changes; even more importantly, so does the

---

2. For an in-depth look at natural theology see Chapter 3.

method of how knowledge of nature is acquired. Yet the belief, implicit or explicit, that economics has some affinity with natural science, is somehow grounded in nature, and is regulated by natural laws towards a natural order, is a constant. In agreement with Solomon, we find that in the final analysis, the appeal to nature as the source and structure of economic phenomena is an appeal to authority.

1. Conceptions of Nature

As we clearly see above, defining nature, if we are looking for exact, narrow meanings, is a messy job. The question of the essence of nature is certainly one of the oldest, if not the oldest, humans have contemplated. Both science and philosophy (there is no valid separation of the two until the Enlightenment) owe their origins to man's attempts to understand nature.   Although it is well beyond the scope of this book to offer a comprehensive and complete history of the various conceptions of nature, a brief examination is necessary to see how the different conceptions of nature have influenced social theory.

In the history of philosophy there have been three conceptions of nature, each drawn from different analogies.   These have been nature as an organism; nature as a machine; and nature as a process (evolution). Along with each of these conceptions has also been 'a movement in which the focus of interest shifted from nature to mind' (Collingwood 1960, p. 5).

Early Greek philosophers' (presocratic) search for an understanding of the nature of things and of the natural world led them to the idea that nature and all its phenomena were composed of a single substance. This is the famous system of the Ionians. Socrates, however, altered Greek philosophy towards the conception of nature as an organism, adopting the analogy of the human by which to explain nature. After Socrates, as Collingwood has noted, 'Greek natural science was based on the principle that the world of nature is saturated or permeated by mind. Greek thinkers regarded the presence of mind in nature as the source of that regularity or orderliness in the natural world whose presence made a science of nature possible' (Ibid. p. 3). As argued in the first chapter, following the DMD thesis and the discussion of displaced concepts, it is to be expected that attempts to comprehend nature would be through the use of analogies. In fact, it could be no other way. Furthermore, as Durkheim and Mauss (1963) noted, primitive and early societies use their own reality as a key to unlock the mysteries they find around them. Thus, as already stated, primitive classification systems frequently emulate the social system, or an aspect of the social experience, of the classifiers. In a similar way, the Greeks used themselves, specifically the individual Greek, as a model for the universe of nature. This Collingwood (1960, p. 8) perceptively notes:

> The Greek view of nature as an intelligent organism was based on an analogy: an analogy between the world of nature and the individual human being, who begins by finding certain characteristics in himself as an individual, and goes on to think of nature as possessed of similar characteristics. ... The world of nature as a whole is then explained as a macrocosm analogous to this microcosm.

The Greek conception of nature as an organism is carried over into the middle ages, with one notable addition - purpose. Medieval philosophy was heavily influence by Greek philosophy, particularly Aristotle. Much of Medieval philosophy is Aristotelian, supported and enlarged by the Arabian commentators through whom Aristotle came to Medieval philosophy, and supplemented with Christian theology. Medieval philosophy, particularly the Scholastics, interpreted Aristotle in such a way that his system did not conflict with divine revelation.[3] Moreover, medieval philosophers were primarily theologians and were much more interested in the relations between, and among, humans, than in the relationship between man and things. Furthermore, the Greek organic view of nature was further supported by the organic nature of medieval society, where the individual was defined by his position in society.

The second basic conception of nature comes from the Renaissance's reaction to Medieval thought. Whereas the Greeks had given nature intelligence and a mind, the Renaissance view was that nature was composed of dead matter, 'devoid both of intelligence and of life' (Ibid. p. 5). The movement which the natural world exhibited was the result of natural laws operating on inert matter; laws which were imposed on the universe from above. Nature to them was not an organism but a machine: 'a machine in the literal and proper sense of the word, an arrangement of bodily parts designed and put together and set going for a definitive purpose by an intelligent mind outside itself ' (Ibid.). The order in nature was the result of an intelligence, but it was not that of nature but of nature's designer.

---

3. For a more detailed examination of the relationship between Aristotle and Medieval philosophy, especially with regard to the conception of nature, see Andrew G. Van Melsen's *The Philosophy of Nature*, pp. 52-70.

This principle of design view of the universe was in many ways an extension of what the Medieval philosophers had added to Aristotle's system: the idea that the universe was created by a benevolent God. This idea, as Arthur Lovejoy has so expertly demonstrated in his *The Great Chain of Being* (1936), is one of the oldest conceptions of man, and a very useful one at that. The belief that there is a purpose in nature, and that this purpose is aligned somehow to human happiness is almost a necessity for the human psyche, eliminating the possibility of meaningless existence. This belief legitimized the status quo, for if the present order is the result of a divine plan, there is a strong presumption in favor of it, and thus it is difficult to question. The principle of design has also been of great importance in the development of human knowledge for it gave an answer to the question: what is the goal or aim of nature? This in hand, the philosopher had only to concern himself with efficient causes, how this goal is achieved.

The Renaissance view is in many ways a more consistent application of this overall preconception of the principle of design, for it is the design which is the efficient cause. The Renaissance was a period when man discovered himself and his environment, clearly evident in the great art of the period. Much like the Greeks, the art of the Renaissance was a glorification of man, yet for the Renaissance it was man as he really was, not gods in human form. The emphasis was on empirical reality (Hauser 1957), man as he is and nature as it is. This rebirth of interest in man and in nature, however, took place in a drastically different environment from that of the Greeks and Romans, for in the Renaissance man was beginning to achieve mastery over nature; no longer helplessly subjected to the forces of nature, man was now controlling and manipulating these forces. Nowhere was this new relationship between man and nature more evident than in the creation of the machine, an apparatus which increased the strength and abilities of the human, allowing him, at least to some extent, to hold his own in the fight between man and nature.

> The Renaissance view of nature as a machine is ... analogous in its origin. ... [I]t is based on the human experience of designing and constructing machines. ... Everyone understood the nature of a machine, and the experience of making and using such things had become part of the general consciousness of European man. It was an easy step to the proposition: as a clockmaker or millwright is to a clock or mill, so is God to Nature. (Collingwood 1960, pp. 8-9)

The analogy of the machine would have been of little value to a Greek or Medieval audience, because, as we have seen in the previous chapter, in order for a concept to be displaced it must first be well developed and understood. Furthermore, the rigid social structure of the middle ages was, by the sixteenth century, almost completely replaced by societies where laws were of increasing importance for the maintenance of social order. The view of the universe as regulated by natural laws fits in well with these emerging societies, where human actions were increasingly regulated by laws and less by custom and convention.[4] This is particularly true for the new forms of economic activity emerging in the fifteenth to eighteenth centuries.

This mechanical view of nature becomes an essential element of the Enlightenment's search for the laws of nature, for in many ways the Enlightenment is the application of the science of the Renaissance to the social world. The Enlightenment is typically characterized as a time of the freeing of the intellect, the result of the release of human reason and the human spirit from the chains of a dogmatic theology and rigid social systems. This is certainly how the Enlightenment philosophers viewed themselves. One can also characterize the Enlightenment as a desperate search for non-relativistic moral laws to fill the void left by the fall from secular power of the Catholic Church. This search placed all its hopes on discovering in nature the basis of human morality and sociality, and thus provide the laws which would not only determine how men live, but also, of equal importance, how they should live. As Alasdair MacIntyre has recently demonstrated in *Against Virtue* (1984), the Enlightenment's search for the basis of human morality in reason must be considered a failure. Furthermore, as Werner Stark has convincingly argued in his *The Social Bond*, particularly Volume 1, the roots of sociality cannot be found in nature, but, contrarily, sociality is the conquering of the 'natural' aspect of humans, the animalistic instincts, by society.

The apex of the mechanical view of nature is certainly Newton's mathematical system of the world. Newton's *Principia* went through many editions and his ideas were popularized by no less a figure than Voltaire. The Newtonian method became the accepted method for all investigations and philosophical inquiries. As John Herman Randall stated: 'Newton's name became a symbol which called up the picture of the scientific machine-universe, the last word in science, one of those uncriticized preconceptions which largely determined the social and political and religious as well as the strictly scientific thinking of the age. Newton *was*

---

4. This new type of social regulation has its origins in the towns and cities of the middle ages, separated from the rigid structure of medieval life, by necessity developing laws and regulations to ensure social order. On this see Werner Stark's *The Social Bond*, Vol. 3.

science, and science was the eighteenth-century ideal' (Randall 1926, p. 260).

By the end of the Enlightenment, the word nature stood for the rational order of things (Ibid. p. 274). Newton had most successfully demonstrated this order, yet this outlook is not wholly Newtonian. The influence of Descartes, especially his view of the universe as a mathematical system, and his faith in rationalism over empiricism, never fully disappears, and reemerges whenever the scientific strictures of Newton's rules of reasoning become increasingly hard to adhere to.[5] As stated before, empirical reality can be very inconvenient, and scientific investigations began to show the limitations of Newton's system. One major weakness is that Newton's system had no place for time. 'One great difference marks off this Newtonian world from the world of modern science: in such a machine, time counted for nothing. Processes rolled on their way in cyclical fashion, completing themselves, like the orbits of the planets, in recurrent definite intervals; but there was no real change. The world had always been such an order, and always would be; of growth, of development, of evolution ... there was not the slightest idea' (Ibid. pp. 275-6).

The mechanical view of nature searched for universal laws which regulated both the physical and social universes. These were laws which applied at all times and in all places. Such a view necessitates a static system of fixed laws. Deviations can be explained by temporary interferences; in the social universe these would be non-natural human institutions, in the physical universe the intervention of God: comets, miracles, earthquakes. In the long run, the natural laws enforce themselves and the world is brought back to its natural order. Such a system has no room for growth and development. Yet human experience at the time was being overwhelmed by examples of growth and development. By the end of the eighteenth century the phenomenon of change could no longer be abstracted as a temporary aberration; it had to be considered a dominant and persistent force. It became increasingly difficult to analyze all reality under the machine-universe world view, this being particularly true for the social sciences. Change, growth and development were now the norm.

This brings us to the third conception of nature: nature as a process or, as it is more commonly referred to, evolution. For the Greeks, knowledge

---

5. Just as the Greek view of nature started with nature and ended with the mind of nature, the Renaissance philosophy of nature starts with the scientific investigations into principles and laws of nature by Copernicus, Galileo and Newton; its highest form can be found in Descartes and Kant, where attention is once again shifted to the mind. Descartes's separation of mind and matter allowed the search for the natural laws, both physical and social, to progress unhampered by the messy actualities of observed nature.

was only possible if one assumed that there was no change. The Renaissance-Enlightenment view was that observations of nature were based on our senses, yet underneath the observed surface phenomena existed a natural order which was unchanging and universal. If one followed Newton, then observation was a tool to arrive at the natural laws, while those who followed Descartes trusted only the rational method. Both views of nature, organic and mechanical, by necessity excluded change as part of the natural order. Change was omitted by either abstracting changeable aspects of phenomena or by concentrating on permanent unchanging relations (Collingwood 1960). The permanency of change by the eighteenth century thus required a new cosmology.

Just as the Greek and Renaissance cosmologies were based on analogies, so too was what Collingwood refers to as 'modern cosmology'. Here the analogy is with human history, especially as studied by the historians of the late eighteenth century and early nineteenth century, who will be discussed in Chapter 5. As Collingwood has observed: 'Modern cosmology could only have arisen from a widespread familiarity with historical studies, and in particular with historical studies of the kind which placed the conception of process, change, development in the centre of their picture and recognized it as the fundamental category of historical thought' (Ibid. p. 10). This new cosmology took root well before Darwin, yet it is the seminal work of Darwin, like that of Newton, which gives scientific credence to this view of nature and helped to spread its influence in all directions.

This new evolutionary view had broad consequences for how nature was conceived. Most importantly, change was included as a fundamental factor to be explained. Furthermore, change was now seen as progressive or cumulative, and not as cyclical; nature was no longer considered as mechanical and could not as a whole be described in mechanical terms; teleology was reintroduced giving the progress in nature at least a direction if not a meaning; questions of time had to be admitted into the analysis (they were excluded from mechanical theories) for if change was to take place, then a period of time had to elapse;[6] and lastly, substance and function were no longer separated, substance is resolved into function leaving no distinction between structure and function (Ibid. pp. 13-27).

The above brief history of the conceptions of nature is very much out of the mainstream of the philosophy of science, a perspective which has influenced the study of the history of economic thought greatly if not prodigiously. Following the perspective of Collingwood and those held by

---

6. As Whitehead (1934, p. 48) said 'There is no nature at an instant'.

the sociologists of science (Barnes 1974) and the sociology of knowledge approach (Stark 1958), we see that science is not a detached and autonomous search, unaffected by social and historical developments. In fact, it is quite the contrary. As Collingwood concludes in *The Idea of Nature* (1960, p. 171):

> I conclude that natural science as a form of thought exists and always has existed in a context of history, and depends on historical thought for its existence. From this I venture to infer that no one can understand natural science unless he understands history: and that no one can answer the question what nature is unless he knows what history is.

The importance of history for the social sciences, a less controversial point than that just stated by Collingwood, is paramount. Economic theories only exist in their historical context and lead to nonsense when applied beyond that context.[7] Social theories are expressions of the historical epochs from which they emanate, and one important factor of each and every epoch is its cosmology. The view of what nature is, and what science and scientific method are, has always played an important role in forming social theories. Just as conceptions of nature drew heavily on analogies from everyday experience to explain that which was not understood, social theories frequently draw upon conceptions of nature and of science to explain the enigma of society. It is to this question we now turn.

2. Conceptions of Society

Following the work of Werner Stark, particularly *The Fundamental Forms of Social Thought* (1963), it is useful to differentiate among three basic forms of social thought, each based on a different conception of the nature of society. The varieties of social theory are derived from the three ways society has been viewed in Western Thought: as a unity, as a multiplicity, and as a process.

The conception that society is a unity leads to the view that 'the social order is an organism' (Stark 1963, p. 17). This view, adopting

---

7. This, of course, has not prevented economists from applying economic theories developed to explain market economies, or industrialized market economies, to non-market societies. Much of the new economic history consists of this.

philosophical realism,[8] alleges that society is a single entity and not a collection of entities. All individual action is viewed from the perception of how it fits into the unified social order.[9]

Organicism can have a positive or normative form, that is, the social theorists can believe that society actually is an organism, or contend that ideally society is an organism. In both cases, the perception of society, social action and social phenomena, is holistic. Adoption of the organic view of society frequently leads to the use of biological or physiological analogies. Individual social actors are like parts of the body, diligently performing their functions to promote the health and survival of the social body.

The second form of social thought is the view that society is a multiplicity, a collection of individuals. Here we see the adoption of philosophical nominalism, namely that the individual is real, but that society is merely a mental fiction, having no existence beyond being a collection of individuals. As Stark writes, this form maintains 'that society is a mechanically, not an organically, ordered and coherent entity: an equilibrium system rather than a kind of body, a multiplicity rather than a unity' (Ibid. p. 109).[10] In this form, society is the result of individual actions, not an independent entity. Social behavior is thus atomistic.

As organicism lends itself to biological and physiological analogies, the mechanism view typically adopts analogies from physics and mechanics. Stark (Ibid. p. 10) writes, 'it (mechanicism) ... regards the social cosmos as essentially an equilibrium system. If only the individual is real, then the coherence of society - or rather, the coherence of individuals in society - must be due to the balancing of individual forces. [Thus] social institutions are to them - nay, must be to them - objective resultants of subjective

---

8. Philosophical realism, in its medieval guise, stated that universals have a real, objective existence. For modern philosophy, it generally refers to the view that material phenomena have an existence independent of human perception. In social theory it would hold that society and social phenomena are independent and separate from the individuals that make up society and individual social phenomena.

9. The question of what provides the social order is important for distinguishing between a nature-derived organic society and a created social order. According to Stark, all societies are the creation of humans and not nature, thus those which claim to be established by nature are hiding the necessary value judgments upon which society and social order are based.

10. The important question for any social theory is where social order comes from. For individualistic theories this order is the equilibrium which results from the balancing of the actions of the individuals which comprise the society in question, hence the affinity between individualistic theories and the equilibrium concept.

energies.' Since the individual is the basic building block for mechanistic social theories, supra-individual forces must be explained in terms of individual behavior or must be excluded. Thus the impact of social norms and mores on the individual must be excluded, for this presupposes that society, and not the individual, is real.

Stark (Ibid. pp. 56-7) elucidates the 'striking disagreements between' organicism and mechanism:

> If the social order is likened to an equilibrium system, to the kind of tension between independent energies of which the balance of a pair of scales is the simplest exemplification, then it is almost certain to be interpreted in a non historical and unhistorical spirit. An equilibrium has no history; its laws do not change with the centuries. The formal equations in which it can be described are of timeless validity, as all purely quantitative propositions must be. Rational mechanics is a branch of mathematics and its students glory in the fact: those social theorists who wanted to model [social theory] on rational mechanics were quite unwilling to admit the reality of developmental change.

Both organicism and mechanism yield insights into certain aspects of society. At a certain level of analysis, society does resemble a coherent whole, a unity, whereas it is also true that society is made up of individuals, and these entities are more than just parts of the whole. Clearly, individual behavior is influenced by and can be better understood in its social setting, and yet individuals in possession of free will, can adopt or reject social norms and act either in conformity with them or contrary to them. Different societies, or different aspects of a given society, can seem more organic or mechanistic. The more homogeneous and orderly a society or institution, the more fitting is organicism, and the more individualistic-atomistic is a society, the more applicable are mechanistic theories.[11] Yet both exclude essential elements of the social order and social relations, and thus the adoption of one viewpoint will lead the theorist to exclude significant factors of human existence. As Werner Stark has stated, 'each and every social formation is at the same time a multiplicity and a unity. We cannot speak of a society unless there are before us several human beings, and unless the lives of these human beings are in some way interconnected and interrelated, i.e. constitute a unity of some

---

11. It can be argued that each conception can have great value as a heuristic, and thus according to the cohesiveness of society, we would choose organicism or mechanism according to which heuristic yielded the most insight. However, the conception of society adopted by a particular social theorist is most often, if not always, part of their preconceptions, and thus unexamined. This is particularly true for economists.

kind' (Ibid. p. 1).

Both viewpoints are necessary for an adequate understanding of society, for both society and the individual are conceptions which become meaningless without the other.[12] Societies must have individual members. Yet the same necessity holds for the individual; outside of society the individual ceases to be a human being. Robinson Crusoe was socialized by society before he was shipwrecked, thus his existence was not independent of society. If we take society fully away from human beings, we must take away the community's history, culture, education and most damaging of all, its language. With language gone, the individual's ability to speak and think is gone, since 'thought is clad in linguistic forms' (Ibid. p. 3). 'Natural' man (man in a state of nature) or man independent of society is fundamentally different from the individuals which make up any society a social theory is seeking to explain. Stark (Ibid.) contends:

> The truth is that individual and society are not separate or even separable realities: where the one is, the other must needs be as well, if we use the words in their full and, so to speak, empirically validated sense. And for this reason both philosophical nominalism and philosophical realism are sound, if one-sided, philosophies. The real task before us is, not to decide between them, but, on the contrary, to preserve, and, if possible, to reconcile the two.

This brings us to the third conception of society, society as a process. Stark describes it as 'a definition of social life which does justice, both to the real integration of social order and to the real independence of the individuals comprised by it' (Ibid. p. 1). Such an approach thus tries to understand the interaction between individuals and society, cognizant of the fact that the resultant behavior is something quite different from what is observed in the natural sciences. Stark (Ibid. pp. 12; 218) asserts:

> Physiology and physics are spurious models in the social sciences because they are concerned with a reality which man finds, not with one which he makes....[what is needed is] [L]iberation from the erstwhile voluntary bondage to the natural sciences. Society ... is neither a creation of the laws of mechanics nor a reflection of the laws of biology: it is man's own work, sprung from his will, sustained by his will,

---

12. 'A separate individual,' Charles Cooley, one of the founders of the cultural sociology school wrote, 'is an abstract unknown to experience, and so likewise is society when regarded as something apart from individuals. The real thing is Human Life which may be considered either in an individual aspect or in a social ... but is always, as a matter of fact, both individual and general' (quoted in Stark 1963, p. 223).

perfectible through his will.

The society as a process approach defines society as the creation of the interaction between the individuals and social institutions, both of which adjust to the influence of the other. A social theory which takes as a premise that society is a process must concern itself with explaining the socialization process of institutions on individuals, as well as the adjustment of social institutions to changes in individual behavior.

The preceding two sections have shown how the conception of what nature is and what society is have evolved, and this dual evolution highlights their similarities. Both nature and society have been conceived of in three basic categories: organicism, mechanicism and process. Social factors, as we have seen, and as the DMD thesis suggests, have played an important role in initiating the transfigurations of the concept of nature. The attempt to study society scientifically, with the conception of science being that of the natural sciences, has led to the treatment of society as a natural phenomenon, adopting the conceptions of nature for the study of society and using the metaphors, analogies, models and concepts of current natural sciences for developing social explanations. With the conception of society as a process, there arises the possibility of a truly human social science, for there is no need for the process to be a natural one, although many social theorists past (Sumner) and present (Hayek, Wilson) have attempted just that. The one consistent element in this history is the assumption that society is a function of nature, based on natural principles and functionally or ideally ruled by a natural order. This we shall call the Natural Law Outlook.

3. The Natural Law Outlook

The attempt to explain society, and thus also the economy, as a natural system originates in the natural law philosophy of the Renaissance and the Enlightenment. Philosophers and social theorists began to construct theories which were independent of theology, yet which were not all that different from, and reached most of the same conclusions as, medieval thought. In an attempt to move away from revelation and toward reason as the basis of theories, it is to be expected that the new theories of society would rely heavily on the developing natural sciences as a source of concepts to be displaced in the construction of these new theories. Common to all theorists of this age is the Natural Law Outlook, the idea that the social universe is ordered and regulated in a manner similar to that of the natural. The adoption of displaced concepts from the natural sciences helped to reinforce this perspective; so successfully that it eventually became entombed in the preconceptions of Western Social Thought. Although most modern economists would claim that their theories and systems are quite independent from the natural law systems of the Enlightenment, the continuing influence of natural law philosophy on economic theory is evidenced by the fact that till this day much of modern economic theory is implicitly based on the Natural Law Outlook.

One of the major goals of this book is to demonstrate the lasting influence of the Natural Law Outlook, thus, in order to proceed with this task with as much clarity as possible, the Natural Law Outlook must first be defined.[13] The natural law tradition is as old as Western philosophy, and as diverse. It is the diversity of the ideas and theories that claim to elucidate natural laws which creates much of the ambiguity surrounding the phrase 'natural law'. Yet, even with the many differences and contradictions within natural law philosophies, a common thread runs through the tradition. This I shall call the Natural Law Outlook. Implicit in the term 'natural law' is the universality and sacrosanctity of the theory being advocated. With the success of the Newtonian revolution in science, derived from Newton's claim to having discovered the 'natural laws' in the physical universe, all science, physical and social, sought to do the same. Thus, by the eighteenth century, natural law theories gained a scientific connotation and the search for universal laws became synonymous with being scientific.

The Natural Law Outlook has three essential elements: a belief in a social physics; naturalism; and the derivation of a natural moral theory. A belief in a social physics constitutes the belief that the social universe, like the physical, is subject to a set of universal laws. As Taketoshi Nojiri has written, it 'presupposes the existence and recognizability of the universal "nature" of persons, society, state and the like. So it is properly based upon the epistemological realism which takes the universal being as a reality' (Nojiri 1972, p. 42). In this view, both the individual and society are under the influence of laws that explain human behavior and the origin

---

13. Achieving clarity when one is dealing with a vision or perspective is often difficult, especially with a vision that has persisted as long as the Natural Law Outlook, and which has evolved with changes in societies and with changes in the conception of what nature is. The concentration on the three essential elements of this perspective will, I hope, elucidate connections not frequently noted.

and form of society as manifestations of these laws. The belief in a social physics has its origins in the principle of design, the idea that the social and physical universe are ordered according to God's blueprint. This idea goes back to the Greek philosophers, particularly the Stoics.

Second, natural law theories attempt to determine natural outcomes based on natural causes. Nature, whether human nature or mother nature, is the final cause in all theoretical explanation. Natural law theories with a theological underpinning have God (the Great Architect, Divine Providence, Author of Nature) as the ultimate, or final, cause. Yet, with the Enlightenment's movement away from theological explanations and from any reliance on revelation, natural law theories tend to end their explanations at 'nature', although it was almost always made explicit that nature itself was God's creation. This tendency is the element of naturalism in natural law theories, and one of its most lasting influences has been the prevalence of 'state of nature' explanations (Clark 1991).

Third, the motivation behind social inquiry in the Enlightenment was to improve the understanding of the natural laws so that the happiness of mankind could be improved. There was a great need, not just politically but philosophically, for a non-relativistic moral theory. This antagonism to relativism is one of the great weaknesses of Western Social Thought, shackling theories to the quest for universals, which, in social life, are rare. This desire to understand the laws of nature so that man can live better by them, and thus improve human happiness, was essential to Greek philosophy and Thomas Aquinas. Natural laws were the manifestations of God's intentions on earth; the rules He set up to regulate the universe. Being a benevolent God, natural laws were created to promote human happiness. The discovery of, and obedience to, natural law was essential to the welfare of society. Therefore, all natural law theories have, explicitly or implicitly, the purpose of developing a natural moral theory. Moreover, such theories are teleological for they impute purpose to social phenomena itself, not merely to the individuals who create the phenomena.

The importance of natural law theories and philosophers for the development of economic theory is certainly a well recognized point. Joseph Schumpeter (1954a, p. 107) typifies standard analysis:[14]

> the first discovery of every science is the discovery of itself. Awareness of the presence of a set of interrelated phenomena that give rise to 'problems' is evidently the prerequisite of all analytic effort. And in the

---

14. See also Taylor (1929; 1930); Schumpeter (1954a; 1954b); Bonar (1893); Raynaud (1936); Veblen (1899-1900) and O'Brien (1975).

case of the social sciences, this awareness shaped itself in the concept of
natural law.

Other historians of economic thought have added to this the influence of
particular theories of economic phenomena developed by the natural law
philosophers concerning the development of economic theory. Yet the
importance and influence of natural law on economics has been grossly
underestimated. With few exceptions, historians of economic thought have
distanced economic theory from the natural law philosophy from which it
developed.[15]

Schumpeter's fundamental point was that a 'scientific' study of the laws
of nature in social phenomena led to the recognition of regularities and
uniformities in economic phenomena, and thus to a 'scientific' study of
economics. Certainly these regularities and uniformities are of utmost
importance to any serious analysis of the economic aspects of a society.
However, the influence of natural law goes well beyond the discovery of
regularities in economic phenomena.

The modeling of social phenomena as 'natural' was determined by the
Natural Law Outlook as well as by the political agenda of the theorists.
Acceptance of this method elevates certain aspects of human society to the
realm of natural phenomena and thus beyond social influence and
meddling.[16] Thus the logic of the market becomes a force at an
epistemological level equivalent to gravity and the morality of the market,
or of market outcomes, becomes an 'unscientific' topic of normative
economics and of greatly less importance. In fact, it is outside the proper
field of investigation.

A good way to understand natural law explanations is to look at their
converse. Natural law theories search for the cause of regularities and
uniformities in nature. An alternative approach places society, its history
and its institutions, as the source of these regularities. Take, for example,
the standard assumption regarding human behavior in economics - self-
interest. A natural law theory must explain this as the expression of some

---

15. The earliest example of this type of scholarship is Taylor's study of natural law and economics
(1929; 1930). After demonstrating the influence of natural law on the development of economic
theory, he proceeds to argue that economic theory quickly left behind its metaphysical baggage
and became scientific.

16. On the conservative side we can see this in the work of John Bates Clark (see Chapter 6), but
it can also be easily seen in the work of many post-Marx Marxists, a good example being Nicholi
Bukharan's work, where conformity with nature is used as a justification of radical changes (they
would happen eventually anyway).

force in human nature. An alternative explanation would have such behavior, if it is indeed observed, as the result of the individual's socialization in a particular community. In fact the market can be viewed as one of the social institutions which reinforces and encourages this type of behavior, by rewarding those who are more selfish with greater income. Social explanations are different from natural explanations, in that they stem from historical, cultural and social influence, as well as human free will. In order to develop an economic theory which contains these important elements, we must free inquiry from the Natural Law Outlook.[17]

---

17. The question comes down to whether society is mechanically or organically determined by universal natural laws or is a creation of human choice and activity. See Stark (1963), and (1975-87).

3. Adam Smith's Natural Law Outlook

For all practical purposes, the Natural Law Outlook becomes part of preconceptions of economic theory through the work of Adam Smith. This is not to downplay the importance of the Natural Law Outlook for the Mercantilists, or particularly the Physiocrats, but merely to note the paramount influence of Smith on the subsequent development of economic theory. With Smith, the Natural Law Outlook becomes synonymous with a scientific approach to the study of society. Therefore, to get an adequate understanding of the Natural Law Outlook on the development of economic theory it is essential to see exactly how this viewpoint influences Smith and the effect of it on his ideas.

The first part of this chapter examines the relationship between Adam Smith and natural law philosophy to see to what extent he was influenced by this tradition; to what extent it affected his method and theories. It will be clearly demonstrated that Smith's work grew out of the natural law tradition; that Smith's belief in natural theology led him to a belief in a natural order; and that the influence of Newton reinforced his Natural Law Outlook. After these influences have been demonstrated, we will explore how Smith's natural law views manifest in his theories.

Adam Smith's system of natural law rests on a trio of natural law influences: Newton, Natural Theology, and the natural law philosophers. All three are distinct influences on Smith, however, as would necessarily be the case for a member of the Scottish Enlightenment,[1] all three are interwoven, reinforcing each other, as three aspects of one outlook. We will thus take a detailed look at each of these influences on the Natural Law Outlook of Adam Smith, seeing how Smith's method, the purpose of his analysis, and results he achieved were the consummation of this outlook.

---

1. See Brown (1979b) and Stein (1982) for these influences on the Scottish Enlightenment.

1. Newton and Smith

Isaac Newton's influence on intellectual history would be hard to exaggerate, particularly his influence on the Enlightenment.[2]   From Newton the Enlightenment received a model to emulate in its pursuit of a science of society and a science of ethics. Newton gave the Natural Law Outlook its 'scientific' credentials and thus legitimated the search for natural laws, and at the same time, the work of the natural law philosophers. Furthermore, his discoveries supported Natural Theology. Yet Newton's influence on Smith was more than just the effect Newton had on the eighteenth century, or on Smith as a member of the Enlightenment. Smith studied Newton and his method, and was directly influenced by him. Smith's natural law system and outlook are in many ways an extension of Newton's, and thus an understanding of the Newtonian system, outlook and method will increase our understanding of Smith's.[3]

Newton emphasizes both the importance of the supreme being in the workings of the universe and the independence of scientific discoveries from theology and metaphysics. For Newton, and for the believers in Natural Theology, faith in God was as much a conclusion of research as it was a starting point. Newton's theories dealt only with efficient causes and Newton himself claimed that the only possible final cause is a supreme being. Yet it is clear that a belief in a divine order, the creation of a benevolent God, was an important part of Newton's, as well as Smith's, vision of the universe. The scientific flavor of their theories comes not from their independence from theological or metaphysical content, but in their avoidance of theological or metaphysical beliefs as active forces in their models and their independence from revelation as a tool in science.

---

2. For the relationship between classical economic theory and classical mechanics, see Adolph Lowe's 'On the Mechanistic Approach in Economics' (Lowe 1951, pp. 403-5), as well as Sebba (1953) and Schmitt (1986).

3. In *The Social Physics of Adam Smith*, Vernard Foley has argued that Smith was really a Cartesian in an age where one had to be a Newtonian to be taken seriously. In terms of the Natural Law Outlook, this in no way affects the thesis of this section, for both Newton and Descartes shared the Natural Law Outlook. The major difference between the two, for our purposes, was an epistemological issue; namely, how one investigates the laws of nature, and on this issue Smith follows Newton, however imperfectly, and not Descartes.

Both concentrated mainly on efficient causes, although both state that the final cause is God and that the purpose of understanding the efficient causes is to gain knowledge of God and His design. Roger Cotes, in his preface to the second edition of Newton's *Principia* writes: '[t]he business of true philosophy is to derive the nature of things from causes truly existent, and to inquire after those laws on which the Great Creator actually chose to found this most beautiful Frame of the world' (Newton 1934, p. xxvii). Yet, as so often happens, conclusions are used for confirming preconceptions. In a letter to Richard Bentley, Newton states that he intended his *Principia* to have theological implications: 'When I wrote my treatise about our system, I had an eye upon such principles as might work with considering men for the belief of a Deity; and nothing can rejoice me more than to find it useful for that purpose' (Newton 1953, p. 46).

The Newtonian Method

Newton summed up his method as such: 'Natural philosophy consists in discovering the frame and operation of nature, and reducing them, as far as may be, to general rules or laws - establishing these rules by observations and experiments, and thence deducing the causes and effect of things' (Ibid. p. 1). Newton's method is based on his four rules of reasoning which can be briefly summarized as follows. First, one establishes 'universal qualities' of natural phenomena by observation and/or experiment (rule 3). From this data base one then constructs a proposition 'inferred by general induction' (rule 4) which is both simple and empirically correct (rules 1 & 2). When these propositions have been established, they are to be expressed mathematically, thus establishing the 'rational' operation of the universe. Once mathematically expressed, these propositions become theories with which one then proceeds to explain the observed phenomena under consideration. As Robert Black has observed, 'Newton's method ... involves both inductive and deductive reasoning, and the deductive reasoning occurs in the form of mathematical demonstrations' (Black 1963, p. 7). Newton held that reasoning, particularly 'mathematical reasoning, applied to observation and experiment could lay bare the underlying structure of nature and discover an order and system which was accessible to human understanding' (Ibid. p. 38).

It is important that the deductive reasoning is done through mathematics, for mathematics is rational, and for Newton and his contemporaries and followers, God is reason and his creation, the universe, a manifestation of his reason. Hence the synonymy between rational and natural.[4] Newton himself refers to his physics as rational mechanics (Ibid. p. 19). It seems clear that for Newton 'rational' means the creation of a supreme being.

Newton stressed the importance of following his method, not only for the advancement of science, but for moral philosophy and salvation.

> [I]f natural philosophy in all its parts, by pursuing this method, shall at length be perfected, the bounds of moral philosophy will be also enlarged. For so far as we can know by natural philosophy what is the first cause, what power he has over us, and what benefits we receive from him, so far our duty toward him, as well as that toward one another, will appear to us by the light of nature. (Newton 1953, p. 179)

Clearly, Newton is searching for the natural order and the natural laws, and his method, both its empirical aspects and in its use of mathematics, is designed for this purpose. If God did not order the universe rationally, then mathematics is useless, and similarly, if God's design does not manifest itself in the workings of nature, there is no need for observation or experiment.[5]

Smith is not as explicit as Newton on the proper methodology to be followed for philosophy, but he did not leave us in the dark as to his methodological convictions, which can be ascertained from his scattered remarks on method contained in his philosophical essays and from the method he employs. Our present concern, however, is first with Smith's views on Newton's method, and second with the question of whether he follows Newton's example.

There can be no doubt that Smith had a high opinion of Newton's method and theories. In his *Lectures on Rhetoric and Belles Lettres* (Smith 1983, pp. 145-6) Smith states:

---

4. The extensive use of mathematics in modern economics is a source of much pride within the profession and the basis of the claim that economics is more 'scientific' than the other social sciences. To equate scientificness and mathematics is evidence of the influence of the natural law idea that both the natural and social universes are rationally ordered, and thus since mathematics is the language of rationality, it is the only valid language for economics. We will return to the role of mathematical formalism in Chapter 7.

5. Newton was extending the Cartesian revolution, the adoption of a mathematical view of the universe. Randall's comments on Descartes's outlook are particularly enlightening (1976, p. 236): '[The] external necessity of law is fundamentally mathematical; hence by mathematics alone we can penetrate to them, and by reason of this mathematical constitution of the world, our mathematical knowledge can be applied to experience. ... [M]athematics unlocks the true secrets of nature. ... The whole economy of the world is physical, quantitative, mathematical.'

There are two methods in which a didacticall writing containing an account of some system may be delivered; Either 1st we Lay down one or a very few principles by which we explain the severall Rules, or Phaenomena, connecting one with the other in a natural order, or else we beginn with telling that we are to explain such and such things and for each advance a principle either different or the same with those which went before. ... [T]he 1st method ... is without doubt the most philosophicall one. In the same way in Nat[ural] Phil[osophy] or any other Science of that Sort we may either like Aristotle go over the Different branches in the order they happen to cast up to us, giving a principle commonly a new for every phaenomenon; or in the manner of Sir Isaac Newton we may lay down certain principles known or proved in the beginning, from whence we account for the severall Phenomena, connecting all together by the same Chain. This Latter which we may call the Newtonian method is undoubtedly the most Philosophical, and in every scien[c]e w[h]ether of Moralls or Nat[ural] Phi[losophy] etc., is vastly more ingenious and for that reason more engaging than the other.

There are many inferences to be drawn from the above passage. First, Smith refers to the Newtonian method as 'accounting for the several Phenomena, connecting all together by the same Chain'. Smith himself defines philosophy as the science of the connecting chains of nature (Smith 1980, p. 45). Thus we can infer that, in Smith's opinion, the Newtonian method is synonymous with philosophy itself. Second, Smith tells us that the Newtonian method aims at connecting phenomena into a 'natural order'. The importance of this phrase, and its implications for Smith's time, can only mean that science aims at discovering the design of the Author of Nature. Third, Smith states that the Newtonian method is applicable for natural and moral philosophy, confirming the view that both are under the same natural order. And fourth, Smith tells us, in typical Smithian fashion, that the Newtonian method is superior because it is more pleasing to the human mind; nature in her infinite wisdom has implanted in humans a natural predisposition towards the correct method of philosophy, thus increasing our happiness.

Smith equated the Newtonian method with proper scientific inquiry.[6] How well did Smith follow the Newtonian method? As closely as the difference in subject matter would allow, it would seem. In his major

---

6. For a Newtonian interpretation of Smith see Campbell (1970; 1975). Campbell writes: 'Adam Smith's Theory of Moral Sentiments is to be interpreted and admired principally as a pioneering venture in the scientific study of morality. ... Most critics of Smith's moral theory have failed to appreciate the extent to which he saw himself as applying the methods of Newtonian Science to the study of morals' (1975, pp. 68; 69). See also Thompson (1965).

works Smith follows the method of first laying out some principle derived from nature. Although these principles are not derived only from experiment, which, given Smith's subject matter (social phenomena and morals) would not have been possible, Smith does attempt to demonstrate his principles by observation. He then constructs a theory based on these basic principles and proceeds to offer an explanation of events based on the theory.

Smith's theories seem to evolve. This happens because of the interaction between his theory and the observations he uses to support them. Frequently, the observations run contrary to his theory and he thus adjusts the theory to account for such cases. Smith employs both inductive and deductive reasoning, a point that will be argued at the end of this chapter in our analysis of Smith's theory of value, which starts out as a pure labor theory of value and ends up as a cost-of-production or 'adding up' theory. T. D. Campbell (1975) has argued that Smith's moral theory follows the Newtonian method, explaining morals from the simple principle of sympathy. As we will see in our analysis of Smith's theory of morals in Chapter 4, Smith starts with natural principles, illustrated with examples and observations to offer empirical support. With the use of the natural principles and observations of actual events we see how moral rules evolve from the interaction between individuals and society. Thus, again we have the combination of induction and deduction.

There are two major differences between the Smithian and the Newtonian methods. First, a crucial intermediate step for Newton is missing in Smith, who has no role for mathematical reasoning. In fact, he seemed to be quite hostile to its use in political economy.[7] Second, Smith's subject matter did not lend itself to experimentation to check the reliability of the observations.

Newton's and Smith's Systems

A full account of Newton's system is obviously beyond the scope of this book, but it is useful for our comparison of Smith's and Newton's systems to have at least a brief summary of it. Robert Black (1963, pp. 49-50) has characterized Newton's system as consisting of seven major attributes:

---

7. Evidence of this is Smith's low opinion of Political Arithmetic: 'I have no great faith in political arithmetic' (Smith 1976, p. 534). In general the Scottish Enlightenment did not eschew mathematical reasoning (see Bryson 1968, pp. 21-23). However, the Scottish Enlightenment did not limit its reasoning patterns to mathematical structures and concepts (Dow 1990).

1. [T]here is an order and structure beyond appearances in nature, which are accessible to the human mind.

2. [T]here are isolable systems or subsystems in the structure of nature, and that nature may be known piece meal in terms of such isolable or self-contained systems.

3. [T]he structure of nature runs in terms of universal properties and propensities attributed to anonymous atoms or elements; that results in the large flow from the properties of the elements.

4. [T]he results in the large are predominantly systematic, orderly, and harmonious.

5. [T]his order is maintained through the operation of regular, opposed principles or tendencies.

6. Irregular or disturbing forces or factors exist; their irregular action modifies, or disturbs, the workings of the system but does not disrupt it.

7. The system is self-adjusting or self-equilibrating. The systematic tendencies or principles are so articulated that, when disturbed, they lead to a flexible adjustment which tends to re-establish and preserve order through the re-establishment of balance.

When we compare Smith's general mode of conceptualizing with Newton's system we find many similarities, enough for us to conclude that Smith used Newton's system as a model to emulate. Black (Ibid. p. 92) notes these similarities:

> Smith projects an interpretation of society as a natural system that in conception is strikingly parallel to that of the natural system of the world as displayed by the Newtonian analysis. The atoms of the social system are human individuals; they act according to universal propensities with which they are endowed. These propensities may be classified in a manner comparable to the propensities of inertia and gravitational attraction. The operation of the system is explained in terms of the blind mechanical action and interaction of the elements, the social atoms, according to their assigned propensities. Analytical interest focuses on explaining appearances, and the order and harmony of the system in terms of the underlying propensities... Unsystematic action occurs but the system is so articulated that, though its action be modified, balance is reestablished, and the system persists. ·

Smith's contrast in *The Theory of Moral Sentiments* (TMS) of the original nature (self-interest) and social nature (sympathy) of man is analogous to

Newton's inertia and gravitational attraction, opposing forces that keep the system in equilibrium. We see similar examples in *The Wealth of Nations* (WN), the most prominent being the balancing of self-interested actions of individuals in the marketplace, leading to gravitation of market prices to natural (equilibrium) prices. In fact, on the broad scale of Smith's system, which includes both TMS and WN, Smith's use of self-interest and sympathy as opposing forces to create a social order out of the autonomous actions of individuals is clearly a Newtonian type of system. It seems quite clear that Newton's theories of the laws of motion of physical bodies and his concept of mechanical equilibrium were displaced by Smith on to social phenomena, in both ethics and economics. Smith uses the metaphor of equilibrium as developed by Newton to explain the movement of physical bodies as a heuristic to guide his investigations into social actions.

There are differences between the two systems which seem to show that Smith was aware that the differences in subject matter, preventing him from merely copying Newton's system. Although both systems have disturbing factors, in Smith's these are man himself and manmade institutions, whereas in Newton's, man is powerless to affect the laws of nature. In Smith's system, moreover, not only can man interfere, but his interference can persist (Smith 1976, pp. 378-80), although Smith feels that in the long run the natural laws prevail.

The ability for human intervention leads to another difference in the two systems. Newton is much more optimistic as to the harmonious outcome of the natural order than is Smith. As Jerry Evensky has shown, Smith was an acute observer of human nature and realized 'that human frailty gives rise to less than perfect private virtue, which in turn leads to less than perfect social virtue' (Evensky 1987, p. 464).

From the above analysis we can see that Newton had a great influence on Smith, both directly and indirectly. Newton's discoveries confirm the validity of the natural law perspective, including the Natural Theology aspect which was so important to the Scottish school of moral philosophy. Smith's work was Newtonian because that was the best way of discovering the natural laws and God's design - the natural order.

2. Smith and Natural Theology

Natural Theology is the bridge by which the Enlightenment philosophers crossed over from religion to 'science'. It allows them to uphold the standard Christian moral principles, yet to construct them on a foundation independent from revelation. Its importance, not only for Smith but for Western Thought in general, is typically underestimated or ignored. Not only does it allow an environment which will accept Smith's system, but it provides the justification for it. It is Natural Theology which connects the 'scientific' approach of Newton with the philosophic speculations of the natural law philosophers; it provides the foundation for Smith's theories, the justification for his method, and the moral foundation for his conclusion. Natural Theology extends the Natural Law Outlook into the social sciences with the same claim of 'scientificness' as the natural sciences.

Natural Theology

Natural Theology is the theological manifestation of the search for natural laws. The dominant trend of the Enlightenment, both intellectually and politically, was to seek independence from organized religion, above all, the once secularly powerful Catholic Church. In the intellectual realm this implied that knowledge be based on sources other than revelation, a trend that was, in fact, started by St Thomas Aquinas. This quest freed science, both natural and social (moral), from the restrictions of biblical revelation, and the necessity for theories to be in agreement with 'revealed truths'. Yet this was not an abandonment of the belief in God,[8] or even a Christian God, or basic Christian morality; it was a reaction against secularly powerful organized religion. The Enlightenment replaced organized religion, derived from revelation, with Natural Theology, in which knowledge of God and His intentions was to be discovered from the study of God's creation - the Universe - and thus confirmed independently of revelation.

A main purpose of Natural Theology (sometimes referred to as rational theology) was to derive universal moral principles from nature, particularly human nature. As Voltaire states, 'I understand by natural religion the principles of morality common to the human race' (quoted in Randall 1976, p. 287). All science, under the Natural Law Outlook, was seen as unified. The natural and social realms were just different aspects of His design. Natural Theology explained the existence of an ordered universe as God's design, natural philosophy explained the laws of the same order as they pertained to the movements of physical bodies and moral philosophy explained the natural laws of social actions as they fitted into the overall

8. See Carl Becker's classic *The Heavenly City of the Eighteenth Century Philosophers*.

natural order. The paramount importance of Natural Theology is that natural and moral philosophy were subordinate to it. Natural Theology gave the vision with which natural and moral philosophers viewed the universe. This relationship came full circle when the results of natural and moral philosophy confirmed the natural order that Natural Theology presupposed, thus giving Natural Theology its claim of being based on scientific conclusions and methods. This is clearly expressed by the great Scottish disciple of Newton, Colin MaClaurin:

> Natural science is subservient to purpose of a higher kind, and is chiefly to be valued as it lays a sure foundation for Natural Religion and Moral Philosophy; by leading us, in a satisfactory manner, to the knowledge of the Author and Governor of the universe ... To study Nature is to study into His workmanship; every new discovery opens up to us a new part of his scheme (quoted in Randall, p. 275).

Since the moral and physical universe were two aspects of one overall design, a similar method to discover this plan should be adopted. This, of course, is the foundation upon which methodological monism rests, and without this implicit belief the presumption of the similarity of the social and natural sciences is greatly weakened.

In *The Nature of Social Laws*, Robert Brown (1984, pp. 10-11) shows how the idea of a similarity between the origins and functions of social and physical laws affected social theory:

> Because the two sets of laws were supposed not to differ in their essential features, the physical laws which regulated the course of Nature were thought of as moral commandments issued to an obedient Nature, and moral laws as the natural regularities which Society both should, and largely did, obey. This assimilation of natural and social laws to the directives laid down by a Divine Legislator, in pursuit of His scheme of salvation for mankind, made it difficult to discuss the features of Society without moralizing; or to discuss the features of Society without mistaking them for aspects of eternal Nature. Thus the interpretation both of natural regularities and of social observations as being embodied commandments had the effect, well recognized and much supported by religious belief, of discouraging the separate investigation of either one of them.

The basic belief of Natural Theology was: the existence of a benevolent God who created the Universe and the natural laws which regulate the Universe. God's effect on the day-to-day operation of the universe was through His laws, and not through intervention (miracles, invisible hand of Jupiter). Knowledge of God and His design was to be had through investigating nature. Moreover, it followed that human happiness was promoted by following God's laws,[9]   failure to do so would bring punishment both in this world and the next.[10]

Another important feature of Natural Theology was the use of arguments by design for the proof of the existence of a benevolent God. This is what gives Natural Theology its claim as the conclusion of science. The most famous and influential argument by design came from Newton's *Principia*, in the General Scholium of the all important Book Three, from which we will quote at some length:

> The six primary planets are revolved about the sun in circles concentric with the sun, and with motions directed toward the same parts, and almost the same plane. Ten moons are revolved about the earth, Jupiter and Saturn, in circles concentric with them, with the same direction of motion, and nearly in the planes of the orbits of those planets; but it is not to be conceived that mere mechanical causes could give birth to so many regular motions, since the comets range over all parts of the heavens in very eccentric orbits; for by that kind of motion they pass easily through the orbs of the planets, and with great rapidity; and in their aphelions, where they move the slowest, and are detained the longest, they recede to the greatest distances from each other, and hence suffer the least disturbance from their mutual attractions. This most beautiful system of the sun, planets, and comets, could only proceed from the counsel and dominion of an intelligent and powerful Being. And if the fixed stars are the centers of other like systems, these, being formed by the like wise counsel, must be all subject to the dominion of One, especially since the light of the fixed stars is of the same nature with the light of the sun, and every system light passes into all the other systems: and lest the systems of the fixed stars should, by their gravity, fall on each other, he hath placed those systems at immense distances from one another. ... And thus much concerning God, to discourse of whom from appearances of things does, certainly belong to Natural Philosophy. (Newton 1934, pp. 543-4; 546)

We have already seen that one of the purposes of Newton's researches was to demonstrate the existence of God. What should be noted is that the success of the Newtonian Revolution in terms of winning followers and influencing the general perception of the universe was greatly supported by

---

9. An interesting point to note is that the phrase 'wealth of nations' comes from Isaiah. The passage refers to the New Jerusalem which is the promise from God of an ideal society, if only His rules are obeyed. 'The riches of the sea shall be lavished upon you and you shall possess the wealth of nations' (Isaiah 60:5).

10. See Smith's atonement passage and the analysis of its significance in TMS, appendix 2.

this aspect of his work and did not rest merely on its empirical or predictive success.

In *The Soul of Modern Economic Man*, Milton L. Myers (1983, p. 3) has shown the importance of the principle of design for the development of the social sciences, particularly a social science on the same footing as the natural sciences:

> From this belief in the overriding importance of nature they [the Enlightenment writers] derived the principle of design, an idea crucial to the reasonings of just about all of them. The principle of design is based on the belief that all causes lead to ordered effects. If the world, and all within it, operates in a precise and dependable pattern (and they believed there was abundant evidence that it did), then man acting as an individual and as a social being must be subject to this immanent and all-pervading order. Man is a product of the operations of nature, so he can be understood only in terms of the patterns of nature. ... Understanding the design in nature leads to an understanding of the design in man.

Smith's Theological Views

Smith's theological views have been frequently used as evidence of his Natural Law Outlook. T. E. Cliffe Leslie seems to have been the first to highlight this aspect of Smith's works. 'The philosophy of Adam Smith', he wrote, '... is pervaded throughout by this theory of Nature [natural laws in the social universe], in a form given to it by theology' (Leslie 1967, p. 25). In the same article Leslie writes, 'Natural theology makes the first part of Adam Smith's course of moral philosophy, and its principles pervade every other part. The law of Nature becomes with him an article of religious belief; the principles of human nature, in accordance with the nature of their Divine Author, necessarily tend to the most beneficial employments of man's faculties and resources' (Ibid. p. 27).

Evidence of Smith's Natural Theology is scattered throughout his works. As Leslie stated above, Smith lectured on Natural Theology, and as we will see in the next section of this Chapter, Natural Theology was an important part of what the Scottish Enlightenment felt was part of a natural law project, moral philosophy. Unfortunately Smith left behind no writings on Natural Theology, nor do we have any student's lecture notes. Smith's own lecture notes were destroyed at his request, religious tolerance being still an issue in Smith's day.[11]   What we know of the course comes to us from John Millar's remembrances, as relayed by Dugald Stewart: 'His course of lectures on ... [moral philosophy] was divided into four parts. The first contained Natural Theology; in which he considered the proofs of the being and attributes of God, and those principles of the human mind upon which religion is founded' (Smith 1980, p. 274). Of course, teaching a subject does not necessarily mean one agrees with the contents. However, natural theology was an important part of the Scottish tradition and nowhere in his writings does Smith ever contradict Natural Theology or its elements. In fact, it seems quite clear that he agreed with the central ideas of Natural Theology, especially that of a Divinely designed universe. Furthermore, what Smith taught in his course in moral philosophy was his system. The material covered in TMS and WN constituted two of the four sections of the course, with Smith's projected book on natural jurisprudence being a third, and Natural Theology being a fourth. The reason that Smith never seems to have intended to write a major work on Natural Theology is a question open to speculation. Smith could have felt it unnecessary, that he had nothing to add to the subject. Or, religious freedom being limited at the time, Smith might not have wanted to embark on such a sensitive area.

The most prominent case stating the importance of Smith's theological beliefs comes from Wilhelm Hasbach, who points to the 'purpose' of nature which frequently appears in Smith's writings as evidence of Divine Providence. Hasbach writes: 'Man produces and saves, in order to acquire wealth for himself, but without his knowledge or will he indirectly advances the material condition of the whole society. He is a tool in God's hand. To clarify Smith's meaning, I remind the reader of the intention of nature, of the cunning of reason, which plays so prominent a role in German philosophy most grandiosely since Hegel' (quoted in Schneider 1979, p. 51).

The concept of the Invisible Hand, which plays such an important role in Smith's system, is clearly derived from Natural Theology. Although Smith only uses the phrase three times,[12] and only twice with its usually

---

11. Foley, in *The Social Physics of Adam Smith*, notes the extent of the limited religious freedom in Smith's time, pointing out that in the year of Smith's birth, Scotland had its last excution of a witch. Smith's efforts to delay publication of Hume's *Dialogues Concerning Natural Religion* is evidence of his sensitivity to this issue. It might also reflect his disagreement with its contents. See *The Correspondence of Adam Smith* (esp. pp. 194-216) where, in a letter to William Strahan, Smith writes 'I am still uneasy about the clamour which I foresee they (the dialogues) will excite' (Smith 1977, p. 216).

12. WN, p. 456; TMS, p. 184; EPS, p. 49.

connotated meaning, it is a major element in his system. The basic idea behind the Invisible Hand is that man, acting in his own self-interest, promotes the interest of society, without knowing or intending such an outcome. Both the social order which results in TMS and the economic order in WN are the outcome of this principle.[13]

Essential to this concept is that God implanted in our nature drives and propensities which lead us to promote His ends, which - since He is a benevolent God - is the well-being of society. Macfie has noted the theological nature of the concept of the Invisible Hand, writing: '[t]he Invisible Hand is only one of the many names given in the *Moral Sentiments* to the Deity - Great Author of Nature, Engineer, Great Architect and so on' (Macfie 1967, p. 111).

The basic idea behind the Invisible Hand is one of the major themes of Natural Theology: nature is arranged so as to provide for the prosperity and happiness of mankind, as long as man followed nature's design, the natural laws. Henry W. Spiegel (1976, p. 488) has shown that this idea, as do many aspects of Natural Theology, has old theological roots:

> Those who are familiar with the history of economic ideas will be aware of the fact that Smith's Invisible Hand and the related concept of the self-regulating market and of nonpurposive social formations in general ... are secularization of thoughts that originally and earlier appeared in theological contexts, in which the unintended consequences of individual actions were attributed to divine providence.

Smith's conception of the Invisible Hand is clearly a theological one, as can be seen in an early reference to it in TMS: 'When by natural principles we are led to advance those ends, which a refined and enlightened reason would recommend to us, we are very apt to impute to that reason, as to their efficient cause, the sentiments and actions by which we advance those ends, and to imagine that to be the wisdom of man, which in reality is the wisdom of God' (Smith 1979, p. 87). Here Smith seems also to be attacking those who would take the theology out of Natural Theology.

It is with the concept of the Invisible Hand that Smith is able to attack the limitations on human actions placed by the State, whether in economics or in morality. Freedom for individuals to pursue their own self-interest, within the rules of justice, is an important element in Smith's ethics, economics and jurisprudence. Contrary to Hobbes, Smith felt that individual behavior, free of state interference, would produce not chaos but

---

13. For the role of the Invisible Hand in creating social order, see Heilbroner 1986, pp. 60-61.

order. For Smith, the world was so designed that a natural order would result from individual actions and need not be imposed by the State. Here Smith's belief in a benevolent God, natural order and natural laws is very important, since God has established natural laws which regulate individual behavior to produce social order. Such an order is essential and necessary for individual freedom. 'The effect of this faith (in a natural order) appears especially in his attitude to the individual in society, and the large balance of freedom he is prepared to give him' (Macfie 1967, p. 110). Considering Smith's skeptical opinion on the power of human reason alone to create social order, the existence of a natural order and natural laws created by a benevolent God is a necessity for Smith's system. Without it, one would have to fall back to Hobbes and the Leviathan.

Thomas Campbell (1971, p. 60) states in *Adam Smith's Science of Morals* Smith's 'belief in an all-wise Author of nature is certainly an important presupposition of his thought; it encourages him to look for systematic aspects of society'. Yet Campbell contends that Smith's theological beliefs were not the result of faith, and not an important preconception for Smith, but rather the scientific conclusion of his investigations.

> While we may admit that Smith's theology led him to expect nature to exhibit the signs of a creator, we should regard his faith as a consequence, and not a cause, of his study of nature. This is not an assertion about the source of his religious belief but about the arguments he used to support it and, more importantly, the place it holds in his system of thought: he does not deduce facts from his theology but makes theological statements on the basis of facts independently ascertained. (Ibid. p. 60)

The claim of theological conclusions drawn from observation of 'facts' is consistent with the Natural Theology prevalent in Smith's day. And this view of theology, or the role of God on earth, is a major part of the Scottish natural law tradition.

Smith, 'Nature' and Natural Theology

The orderliness of the universe and arguments from design play an important role in Smith's thinking. In his essay 'The History of the Ancient Physics,' (Smith 1980, pp. 112-114) Smith traces progress in science as the change from the conception of the universe as chaotic to that of order and coherence in nature.

> In the first ages of the world, the seeming incoherence of the

appearances of nature, so confounded mankind, that they despaired of discovering in her operations any regular system. Their ignorance, and confusion of thought, necessarily gave birth to that pusillanimous superstition, which ascribes almost every unexpected event, to the arbitrary will of some designing, though invisible beings, who produced it for some private and particular purpose. The idea of an universal mind, of a God of all, who originally formed the whole, and who governs the whole by general laws, directed to the conservation and prosperity of the whole, without regard to that of any private individual, was a notion to which they were utterly strangers. ... As soon as the Universe was regarded as a complete machine, as a coherent system, governed by general laws, and directed to general ends, viz. its own preservation and prosperity, and that of all the species that are in it; the resemblance which it evidently bore to those machines which are produced by human art, necessarily impressed those sages with a belief, that in the original formation of the world there must have employed an art resembling human art, but as much superior to it, as the world is superior to the machines which that art produces. The unity of the system, which, according to this ancient philosophy, is most perfect, suggested the idea of the unity of that principle, by whose art it was formed; and thus, as ignorance begot superstition, science gave birth to the first theism that arose among those nations who were not enlightened by divine revelation.

The natural law conception of an orderly universe, a 'complete machine' which is 'governed by general laws' and directed towards the end of human prosperity, is evident throughout Smith's writings. In TMS Smith writes, 'The happiness of mankind, as well as of all other rational creatures, seems to have been the original purpose intended by the Author of Nature, when he brought them into existence' (Smith 1979, p. 166). Recently Evensky has highlighted the importance of the design argument in Smith's works: 'The major goal of Smith's intellectual agenda was to do for moral philosophy what Newton had done for natural philosophy: to present a coherent model which discovered the Design' (Evensky 1987, p. 450). Evensky classifies Smith's system as including three parts, all related to the design: '(1) A determination of standards for individual behavior, an ethics of Design; (2) a determination of rules for interpersonal or social behavior, a system of jurisprudence consistent with the Design; and (3) an explication of the manner in which the appropriate behavior guided by appropriate rules (and institutions) will lead to the greatest wealth for the nation' (Ibid.) which was the goal of the design.

Commentators on Smith's natural law influences or in his belief in a natural order usually find confusion arising from Smith's use of the terms 'natural' and 'nature' (Bitterman 1944; Campbell 1971). Hasbach was the first to make the observation that Adam Smith misused the word 'natural'. 'Sometimes it meant in accordance with reason, sometimes in the natural course of things, sometimes corresponding to human nature, sometimes obvious, sometimes customary - and with this the task of a Smithian philology is still not exhausted' (quoted in Schneider 1979, p. 66). This confusion, which is so apparent to the twentieth-century mind, and was becoming apparent by the late nineteenth century when Hasbach was writing, did not exist for the reader in Smith's day, given the almost universal acceptance of Natural Theology. If the outcome of God's design is natural, then, since God's design was rational, what was rational was natural. And since the Author of Nature created man to fit into His design, human nature was natural and rational. And finally, since the overall design is the basic laws and principles which regulate the universe, human customs and the natural course of things will reflect the design, if man is to prosper and be happy - that is, to live in accordance with the natural laws. All of these definitions and meanings are, for Smith, equivalent to being in accordance with God's purpose.

Moral Laws as Divine Laws

The recent trend in Smithian scholarship is to argue that both Smith's ethics and his economics were scientific endeavors, within the Newtonian tradition (Campbell 1971; 1975). This is used to counter the natural law interpretation. Yet the two are complementary, not contradictory. Smith's Natural Theology gave him a belief in Divine Providence, the First Cause that ordered the universe, natural and social, to provide for the maximum happiness for mankind. Natural Theology was both a preconception and a conclusion. Natural Theology was part of the overall natural law scheme, and thus was to be viewed as fully compatible with Newtonian science. Therefore, it is to be expected that Smith's moral theory aims at being empirical and scientific. Yet, as Smith makes quite clear, the natural laws of the moral realm are God's laws.

Smith, in typical fashion, states that moral rules are derived from nature and later confirmed by man's reason. For Smith (1979, pp. 163; 165) moral rules are:

> first impressed by nature, and afterwards confirmed by reasoning and philosophy, that those important rules of morality are the commands and laws of the Deity, who will finally reward the obedient, and punish the transgressors of their duty. ... Since these, therefore, were plainly intended to be the governing principles of human nature, the rules which they prescribe are to be regarded as the commands and laws of the

Deity, promulgated by those vicegerents which he has thus set up within us.

Smith (Ibid. pp. 165-6) goes on to compare moral laws with physical laws.

All general rules are commonly denominated laws: thus the general rules which bodies observe in the communication of motion, are called the laws of motion. But those general rules which our moral faculties observe in approving or condemning whatever sentiment or action is subjected to their examination, may much more justly be dominated such. They have a much greater resemblance to what are properly called laws, those general rules which the sovereign lays down to direct the conduct of his subjects. Like them they are rules to direct the free actions of men: they are prescribed most surely by a lawful superior [God], and are attended too with the sanction of rewards and punishments. Those vicegerents of God within us, never fail to punish the violation of them, by the torments of inward shame, and self condemnation; and on the contrary, always reward obedience with tranquility of mind, with contentment, and self-satisfaction.

Adam Smith and Religion

According to Millar, as we have seen above, the second part of Smith's course on natural theology consisted of 'those principles of the human mind upon which religion is founded'. As we have seen above, Natural Theology was designed to replace organized religion, while at the same time retaining the basic moral precepts. Organized religion was rejected or de-emphasized, for it relied on revelation instead of science, and because it tended to exert too much secular power. The Enlightenment philosopher advocated freedom of religion because it increased the number of different religious sects, thus limiting the power and influence of any particular group.

Smith analyzed religion, as he did most institutions, to see how it fit into the natural order, and to see what natural principles gave rise to it. According to Smith, under certain conditions religion acts to promote the happiness and prosperity of mankind. In TMS Smith gives religion a positive role in promoting ethical behavior, thus helping promote the ends of the Author of Nature. He writes: 'religion, even in its rudest form, gave a sanction to the rules of morality, long before the age of artificial reasoning and philosophy. That the terrors of religion should thus enforce the natural sense of duty, was of too much importance to the happiness of mankind, for nature to leave it dependant upon the slowness and uncertainty of philosophical researches' (Smith 1979, p. 164).

Again we see how nature takes care to bring about the Divine plan. For Smith religion is beneficial as long as there are many sects so that no one obtains a monopoly and thus upsets social tranquillity. David Levy has made the point that religion acts on individual preferences so as to harmonize the individual's behavior with the general order of society. This is an important institutional role and is a further element in the natural laws that guide individual behavior toward social order and not Hobbesian chaos. As Levy (1978, p. 674) has noted: 'Under competitive conditions in the religion industry, the ethical imperative acted upon by a sufficient number of individuals to produce social peace.'

Based on the above analysis, we can see that Natural Theology was a very important part of Smith's system. Stein (1982, p. 679) has asserted that 'Smith placed all his ideas within the framework ... of natural theology. He believed that the scheme by which societies developed ... was part of the plan of an all-wise Author of Nature, whose "invisible hand" had shaped the design. ... It was God who lays down the general course which a society should normally take and, if the members allow it to take that course, the consequences will be beneficial to that society.' Natural Theology is an important preconception for Smith in that it gives him the view of a universe which is designed with its laws written in nature. Thus Smith searches for the natural laws of the design and equally important, he searches in the workings of nature, the efficient causes, for knowledge of the natural laws (final causes). Natural Theology not only supports the Newtonian method, it is the link between Newton and the 'scientific' method he developed and the natural law philosophers' investigations into the natural laws of social phenomena. Furthermore, Natural Theology gives a strong ethical connotation to the so-called 'natural laws' and creates biases against any human activity which would run counter to them.

3. The Influence of the Natural Law Philosophers on Adam Smith

One of the strongest connections between Adam Smith and natural law is the influence that the natural law philosophers, especially Hugo Grotius and

Samuel Pufendorf had on him.[14] This influence has been twofold: first, many of the topics Smith analyzes were first analyzed by the natural law philosophers; and second, Smith's overall outlook as to what constitutes moral philosophy and how one should analyze moral philosophy was originally shaped by this tradition. Here we limit our attention to the two dominant Protestant natural law philosophers mentioned above. We will see how influences, topics and outlook, all play an important role in Smith's development as a thinker. We will not examine similarities in the natural law philosopher's discussions of particular economic ideas (price, value, monopoly etc.), but will instead concentrate on the overall flavor of Smith's work.[15]

The Protestant natural law tradition, as exemplified by Grotius and Pufendorf, was an extension and continuation of certain strains in Scholasticism. The Scholastics, particularly Aquinas, made the distinction between positive law and natural law, with natural law as the earthly manifestation of Divine law, revealed through nature and reason, and positive law that which is created by humans. What the Protestant natural law theorists retained from the Scholastics was a belief in a natural order created by a benevolent God. This belief comprised these tenets: that knowledge of the natural order and God could be gained through the discovery of the natural laws; that these natural laws were the expression of God's will; that they governed the social as well as the physical universe; that happiness came from following the natural laws (for the Scholastics this happiness was Heaven, for the Protestant natural law philosophers it was material prosperity and Heaven); and finally, that the discovery of the natural laws which regulated the social universe would lead to a universal

---

14. Other natural law influences would include many Greek philosophers, especially the Stoics and John Locke. On the natural law influences of the Stoics, D. P. Raphael has noted : 'In the case of WN all the references to a kind of natural law in economics - the 'natural price', the system of 'natural liberty', the working of the 'invisible hand' that makes self-interested behavior contribute to the general good - show the permanent influence on Adam Smith of Stoic philosophy with its belief in cosmic harmony' (Raphael 1979, p. 87).

15. There are many examples of Grotius and Pufendorf having discussed ideas and topics later analyzed by Smith. One interesting example is the paradox of value, or what is commonly known as the diamond-water paradox. Both Grotius and Pufendorf analyzed the paradox between use-value and exchange-value, with Pufendorf using diamonds and water as his example to illustrate the paradox (Smith 1976, p. 45, footnote 31). Yet it is in the overall approach that the influence of the Natural Law Outlook has had its lasting impact. As Veblen has written: 'The characteristic spiritual attitude or point of view of a given generation or group of economists is shown not so much in their detail work as in their higher synthesis - the terms of their definitive formulations - the grounds of their final valuations of the facts handled for purpose of theory' (Veblen 1899-1900, p. 86).

social science. We will see, following Schumpeter (1954a, p. 141), that the Scottish school of moral philosophy was an outgrowth of the natural law tradition, and thus a continuation of the aim of scholasticism: 'the old universal social science of the scholastic doctors and of the philosophers of natural law survived in the new form [Scottish moral philosophy].'

Grotius and Pufendorf sought to establish the existence of universal principles of natural law binding on all men, without regard to time or place. As Peter Stein (1979, p. 625) writes, 'These principles were axiomatic; they had the same certainty and universality as mathematical propositions.' We shall see that elements of this approach can be found in Smith's work.

Grotius and Smith

Grotius developed his natural law philosophy in an attempt to establish a standard of international conduct and law. Grotius was eager to fill the international order vacuum created by the decline in the influence and power of the Papacy (Bonar 1893, p. 78; Lowe 1988, pp. 19-23). Since Grotius was going beyond the laws of a single nation, he attempted to develop principles which bore on international as well as on inter-individual and state-citizen relations.

Grotius defined natural law as follows:

> The law of nature is a dictate of right reason which points out that an act, according as it is or is not in conformity with rational nature, has in it a quality of moral baseness or moral necessity; and that in consequence, such an act is either forbidden or enjoined by the author of nature, God. (quoted in Edwards 1981, p. 63)

Important in this definition is that the law of nature is 'a dictate of right reason' which is 'in conformity with rational nature'; is based on some moral standard; and is ultimately created and defined by God. Grotius was quite clear that nature is synonymous with God: 'When I say nature, I mean God, for He is the Author of Nature' (Ibid. p. 62). Thus God's laws are nature's laws and manifest themselves through nature.

Grotius felt that the natural laws worked through a social instinct. God is the final cause of the law, human nature is the efficient cause. 'For the very nature of man ... is the mother of the laws of nature' (Ibid. p. 54). Grotius (Ibid. p. 61) further elaborates: 'The law of nature ... [as it] relates to the social life of man and that which is so called in a larger sense, proceeding as it does from the essential traits implanted in man, can nevertheless be rightly attributed to God, because of His having willed that such traits exist in us.' Grotius stressed the dependence of man on the Divine Order, but even with his religious presentation, he attempts to obtain a principle of natural law, justice and social order independent of revelation, whether from the church or scripture. Following Aquinas, Grotius makes the distinction between natural law and positive law, which Grotius calls the law of nations. For Grotius, the reason for discovering the natural law is so that positive law can be made more fully to conform to it.

Many of these themes show up in Smith's work. Like Grotius, Smith was looking for universal principles based in human nature (for Smith these are natural propensities) from which natural laws were derived. Both held that man has a social instinct which makes him naturally suited for social life. The natural laws and principles of human nature are the creation of a benevolent Deity, which they both referred to as the Author of Nature. Furthermore, this Deity is a creative, not an intervening God; Grotius goes so far as to say that even God cannot violate the natural laws. And both felt that the object of philosophy was to discover the natural laws so that man can better obey them. For Grotius this refers to the creation of positive laws, whereas for Smith obedience to the natural laws led to the dynamics of a society of perfect liberty.

Similarities do not by themselves show influence, but it is clear from other sources that Grotius played a role in Smith's intellectual development. William Scott has shown that Smith had read Grotius at an early age: 'Grotius was a tradition in the Moral Philosophy Class [taught by Hutcheson] and in its library there were a number of duplicate copies of his chief works. Amongst these there is one, on the end paper of which the signature of Adam Smith is to be found. This is a fact of no little significance, for it shows that before he was seventeen he had some acquaintance with the conception of Natural Law' (Scott 1965, p. 34).[16] As we shall see Smith's education gave him much more than 'an acquaintance' with natural law ideas.

Smith acknowledges Grotius's importance in the development of natural law in *The Theory of Moral Sentiments*: 'Grotius seems to have been the first who attempted to give the world any thing like a system of those principles which ought to run through, and be the foundation of the laws of

---

16. In Bonar's catalogue of Smith's personal library one finds that Smith owned Grotius's major works, as well as those of the other important natural law philosophers: Pufendorf; Cumberland; Vattel; Locke; and of course those of the Scottish tradition: Carmichael and Hutcheson (Bonar 1966).

all nations [the law of nature]: and his treatise of the laws of war and peace, with all its imperfections, is perhaps at this day the most complete work that has yet been given upon this subject' (Smith 1979, p. 342). For Smith, this is high praise indeed. Following this comment on Grotius, Smith tells us that it is his intention 'in another discourse endeavor to give an account of the general principles of law and government', implicitly giving approval to the importance of discovering the law of nature as the foundation of natural jurisprudence. If Smith was consistent with his other works, the general principles of law and government would have been derived from human nature, this being where the Deity placed the forces which produced the natural laws.

We can only speculate as to how Smith's natural jurisprudence would have turned out, although we get a hint from the lecture notes of his students.   Here we see that Smith, following Grotius, makes the fundamental distinction between laws of nature and laws of nations (natural law and positive law).   Smith refers to the first part of his *Lectures on Jurisprudence* as the Laws of Nature and the second part as 'the Laws of Nations'. 'Having considered the laws of nature as we proposed, as they regard Justice, Police, Revenue, and Arms, we shall proceed to the last part of our plan, which is to consider the Law of Nations, or the claims which one nation may have upon another' (Smith 1978, p. 544). This is also evident in Smith's definition of jurisprudence: 'Jurisprudence is that science which inquires into the general principles which ought to be the foundations of the laws of all nations' (Ibid. p. 347). Furthermore, in TMS Smith tells us, 'Every system of positive law may be regarded as a more or less imperfect attempt towards a system of natural jurisprudence' (Smith 1979, p. 340). Smith also argues that the law of nature, as applied to man, is universal.

> It is not probable or to be believed without good foundation that the laws of nature vary so much in other countries. We see that the laws of nature with respect to gravity, impulse, etc. are the same in all parts of the globe; the laws of generation in other animalls are also the same in all countries, and it is not at all probable that with regard to that of man there should be so wide a difference in the eastern and the northern parts.

It is also interesting to note that the material which later is published in the WN is covered in the Laws of Nature section. We should also note that the content of those lectures differs in many significant ways from the natural law tradition, but before we examine this we must first look at the other great natural law theorist who influenced Smith, Samuel Pufendorf.

Pufendorf and the Scottish Natural Law Tradition

The connection between Pufendorf and Adam Smith is less direct than that of Grotius but more comprehensive. It is through Pufendorf that the natural law tradition comes to Scotland, and it is his great work which provides the fertile ground for the roots of the Scottish school of moral philosophy to take hold. In fact, we would be justified, following Stein, in referring to the intellectual line from Pufendorf to Smith as the Scottish natural law tradition. Although this tradition is significantly different from the continental tradition, it was still a natural law tradition.

Pufendorf, like Grotius, was of the opinion that the natural laws were divine edicts although, more than Grotius, he separates himself from organized religion. Stein (1982, p. 667) has observed that 'Pufendorf held that by the fact of creating man as a social and rational animal, God prescribed a natural law for him, which in general terms bore a striking resemblance to the Gospel injunctions to love God and one's neighbor as oneself.' Pufendorf also adds that man has a duty, not only to God and one's fellow man, but to himself, a point which is of great importance to the Scottish tradition.[17]

Pufendorf's ideas came to Scotland via Gerschom Carmichael, who incidentally also taught Newtonian physics at Glasgow University.[18] Carmichael's translation of Pufendorf's great work *De Officio Hominis et Civis Cecundum Legem Naturalem*, published in 1718, included extensive notes and commentaries. These commentaries were as significant as - many felt more significant than - Pufendorf's book. In fact the Scottish school starts with these notes. Carmichael agreed with Pufendorf's contention that 'the study of moral philosophy was nothing but the study of natural law' (Ibid. p. 669). Carmichael's translation and notes formed the basis of what he taught as moral philosophy at Glasgow, basing his course on it, which in turn was the foundation of Hutcheson's course, which in turn became the foundation of Smith's. Carmichael's notes on Pufendorf are significant because they go beyond Pufendorf, building, criticizing and extending the scope and content of Pufendorf's analysis. Carmichael merged Pufendorf's natural law ideas with later developments in the natural law tradition, especially the ideas of Leibniz, Cumberland and Locke. The combination of these natural law traditions forms the Scottish natural law tradition.

---

17. For the importance of prudence in Smith, see TMS, part 6.

18. Here we again see the interconnection between Newtonianism, Natural Theology and natural law philosophy.

The influence of Leibniz is significant for it introduces the importance of Natural Theology to the Scottish natural law tradition. Carmichael was greatly influenced by Leibniz's critique of Pufendorf,[19] which pointed out the necessity of linking knowledge of the laws of nature to Natural Theology, or as he suggested, combining 'the best principles of universal jurisprudence...with wise theology' (Leibniz 1972, p. 72). Carmichael had been already moving in this direction (Moore and Silverthrone 1983, p. 77) and in his preface to his edition of Pufendorf, he tells his readers that he had 'taken particular care that the obligations imposed by the law of nature be deduced from the existence, the perfection and the providence of the deity: so that the manifest bond between moral knowledge and natural theology might be clearly exhibited' (Carmichael quoted in Moore and Silverthrone, p. 77). And in his *Synopsis Theologia Naturalis*, Carmichael reinforces this position stating 'that a genuine philosophy of morals must be built upon natural theology as its foundation' (Ibid. p. 78).

Carmichael argues that 'man's ability to live with others in society depends on natural feelings of sympathy for others, which men could never have invented for themselves and which must have been implanted in them by the supreme being' (Stein 1982, p. 669). This idea of 'natural feelings of sympathy' becomes an essential ingredient in Scottish Moral Philosophy (Hutcheson's moral sense, Smith's sympathy principle). This is particularly true for Smith, who starts TMS with the statement: 'How selfish so ever man may be supposed, there are evidently some principles in his nature, which interest him in the fortune of others' (Smith 1979, p. 9). He then develops the principle in human nature - the sympathy principle - showing how it is necessary for human survival and life in society. The final cause, the source of the principle, is never in doubt, it is nature and the Author of Nature: 'It is thus that man, who can subsist only in society, was fitted by nature to that situation for which he was made' (Ibid. p. 85).

Leibniz's influence can also be seen in the association of efficient cause with the 'external manifestations of human conduct' and the final cause with Providence.[20] The concern with efficient causes prompts many to conclude that the Scottish school was not concerned with, or rejected

---

19. See G. W. Leibniz, 'Opinion on the Principles of Pufendorf' (1706), in *The Political Writings of Leibniz*, translated and edited by Patrick Riley (1972).

20. For more on Leibniz's influence on the development of economic thought, see Werner Stark's *The Ideal Foundations of Economic Thought* (1943), pp. 26-50.

completely, final causes.[21]   With the notable exception of Hume, this is
not so. As we have already seen, Adam Smith clearly tells us that the final
cause is the Author of Nature. Yet for the Scottish tradition, it is because
knowledge of God is so severely limited and is gained through study of
nature (efficient causes) that investigations necessarily are limited to
efficient causes.

Richard Cumberland's influence on Scottish moral philosophy in general,
and on Adam Smith in particular, has not been widely acknowledged.
Cumberland's major work, *A Treatise on the Laws of Nature* was one of the
earliest systematic attacks on Hobbes's contention that man is not naturally
suited for society, thus requiring a strong central government to keep peace
and order.   Cumberland argues that 'the self-interested actions of the
individual were not, essentially, destructive but constructive' (Myers 1983,
p. 38).   To demonstrate this, Cumberland links prudence with social
welfare. 'I suppose', Cumberland writes, 'everyone seeks his own Good,
and that to act in pursuit thereof, adds to the perfection of his Nature. ...
[P]rudent care of our Happiness cannot be separated from the pursuit of the
Happiness of others' (Ibid. p. 44). Thus Cumberland argues that as part of
the Design, self-interested actions promote public welfare.

Jacob Viner (1972, p. 68) states that both the 'sentimental' school and the
'selfish' school can be traced back to Cumberland's work:

> Two main lines of development of ethical doctrine stemmed directly or
> indirectly from Cumberland's argument, although each of them also had
> much earlier sources. One of these lines stressed the role in social
> welfare of man's instinctive capacity for disinterested benevolence, and
> came to be called the 'sentimental' school. The other stressed the
> incidental harmony between behavior engaged in from calculated self-
> interest and the public good, and acquired the label of the 'selfish'
> school, where 'selfish' meant, however, merely calculated self-interest.

Locke's influence on Carmichael introduces the concept of labor as the
moral basis of private property rights, a position we find repeated in Smith:
'The property which every man has in his own labour, as it is the original
foundation of all other property, so it is the most sacred and inviolable'
(Smith 1976, p. 138).   The labor theory of value has its origins in Locke:
''tis Labour indeed that puts the difference of value on every thing' (Locke
1960, p. 338).   In fact, both the objective and subjective traditions in value
theory have their roots in Locke, and both are connected to Locke's theory

---

21. See Bitterman (1944). The importance of efficient and final cause in Smith is discussed in
the next chapter.

of the origin and natural right to private property. The subjective theory follows from Locke's individualist psychology, the objective theory from his social philosophy (Stark 1976).[22]

Smith's value theory is partly functional, in that he is looking for an invariant measure of value to use in his analysis of growth and accumulation. However, it is also part of his overall moral philosophy, as all value theories necessarily are. It is perfectly consistent with Smith's Natural Law Outlook that the moral basis of property would stem from the same source as the functional measure of the value of property. Under the design the moral and natural are united, a point Smith frequently stresses. Thus the natural value of a commodity is determined by the same principle as the moral justification of the commodity. It would have been a major inconsistency if they did contradict each other.

An important aspect of Carmichael's notes, as W. L. Taylor points out, is 'the attempt to ground human laws in the observation and analysis of the observed characteristics of human nature' (Taylor 1965, p. 26). Carmichael integrates Natural Theology with the natural law tradition, as well as bringing in Newtonian methodology. He adopts the 'experimental' method of drawing inferences from observation, which we have seen is an important part of the Newtonian method. The importance of observation for the Scottish natural law tradition comes from their unique blend of Newton, Natural Theology and natural law. Natural Theology first suggests the idea that knowledge of God and the design comes from God's creation - the universe. Newton's theory formalizes this approach, and his success gives this method 'scientific' credence. The Scots then used this method to build on the theories of Grotius and Pufendorf. The empiricism of Smith comes from this combination of influences.

Of equal importance is the change of emphasis Carmichael gives to the topics and subject areas under the realm of natural law. With Pufendorf, and also with Grotius, economics and ethics are of minor, if not incidental, concern. Carmichael changes this. 'Of the notes and commentary affixed by Carmichael to his translation, about two-thirds deals with economics and one third deals with ethics' (Taylor 1955, p. 253), the areas where the Scottish school makes its most significant contributions. Stein (1982, p. 672) summarizes Carmichael's influence as follows: 'The topics which

22. Stark writes: 'In Locke's thought value as a subjective, and value as an objective category demand each other and form a whole, exactly as his theory of individual knowledge and his doctrine of social life' (Stark 1976, p. 12). Karen Vaughn (1980) and Edward Harpham (1984) both contend that Locke had only a subjective theory of value, yet for a single theory of value in Locke one must ignore much important textual evidence.

Carmichael brought into prominence, the link between ethics and natural theology, the identification of benevolence as the prime virtue, ... the emphasis of rights rather then duties, ... the basing of property rights on labour rather then consent, - all ... became established features of eighteenth century Scottish moral philosophy.'

Most importantly, Carmichael establishes the boundaries of the realm of natural law, setting the standard for Hutcheson and Smith to follow. Hutcheson based his course on moral philosophy on Carmichael's notes and course, as well as his two major works: *Short Introduction to Moral Philosophy* and *A System of Moral Philosophy* (Taylor 1965, p. 6). Taylor shows how Hutcheson's works parallel Carmichael's lectures and how Smith's works parallel Hutcheson's (Ibid. pp. 20-25). Smith's TMS was based on Hutcheson's Book I while the WN parallels Book II. Smith's *Lectures on Jurisprudence* followed part of Book II and Book III.

The Difference Between Smith and Natural Law Tradition

The most significant difference between Adam Smith and the tradition started by Grotius and Pufendorf is in the field of jurisprudence, where they made their most important contributions. Smith, in both substance and method, made a break with this tradition in his jurisprudence. The change in approach seems to be the result of the influence of Montesquieu's *Spirit of the Laws*. Montesquieu's approach is historical and partly evolutionary. He felt that the laws of a nation are affected by many factors, including means of subsistence (economic factors), climate, custom and culture. As Carl Friedrich (1963, p. 105) has noted: 'Montesquieu turns away from the tradition of natural law, which attempted to give a general answer to [the question what constitutes a just law] ... and declares that every community must solve this task in response to its particular spirit; the historical, sociological, political and economic conditions. [...] Montesquieu ... clearly has the intention of explaining law and the laws within the context of a particular cultural system.' Following Montesquieu, Smith's *Lectures on Jurisprudence*, as well as WN and to a lesser extent TMS, are filled with historical analysis. As Stein notes, 'although Smith dealt with the same topics which were regarded by Carmichael and Hutcheson as part of the Law of Nature, and in the same order, he dealt with them historically' (Stein 1982, p. 676).

The contradictions between the Natural Law Outlook and a historical analysis become apparent whenever the historical analysis becomes sufficiently developed, exposing the relativity of social formations and human behavior and morality, a point which we will return to in Chapter

5. The next chapter examines how this contradiction is played out in Smith's works. At the end of TMS Smith states that he intended to write a treatise on natural jurisprudence or more specifically 'the general principles of law and government [what is included in Hutcheson's Book III], and of the different revolutions they have undergone in the different ages and periods of society' (Smith 1979, p. 342). The latter half of this sentence clearly shows the influence of Montesquieu, as do the *Lectures on Jurisprudence*, but the first part shows the influence of the natural law tradition.[23]   The approach of all Smith's works that he intended for publication (TMS, WN, and EPS) follow the first part of the quote, placing the source of the general principles in human nature, which is the most distinctive characteristic of the Scottish natural law tradition. Could it have been the impossibility of resolving this conflict between natural law and Montesquieu's historical method, as much as Smith's ill health, that prevented Smith from 'execut[ing] this great work to [his] own satisfaction?' (Ibid. p. 3).

4. Adam Smith's Natural Law Outlook

At this stage of the analysis it is clear that Smith was greatly influenced by natural law theories and concepts. Our task now is to see the three elements of the Natural Law Outlook which are present in Smith's work and how his theories were influenced by this outlook.

We have seen that the Natural Law Outlook came to Smith from three sources: Newtonianism; Natural Theology; and the Scottish natural law tradition. Each helped shape Smith's Natural Law Outlook and each contributed to the composition and outlook of Smith's work. The idea of the principle of design played a key role in the development of Smith's system, as it did in the development of our three influences on Smith. Implicit in the idea of the principle of design, when it is applied to social phenomena, is the acceptance of social physics. One of the most significant results of the principle of design was the idea of a single blueprint or design, which regulated both the physical and social universe. Newton's success in discovering the laws of the physical universe made him the logical source for those looking to discover the laws of society. Smith's

---

23. In *The Spirit of the Laws* Montesquieu uses the word revolutions in referring to the change and development of laws. See Chapters 21, 27, 28 and 31.

system is based on the idea of a social physics because of Newton's influence. However, we must not downplay the role of Natural Theology, for it is this that suggests the idea that the social and physical universes are similarly ordered. The use of Newton's method and model as a model to emulate clearly demonstrates Smith's belief in a social physics.[24] This is also apparent in Smith's claim that the Newtonian method is the best approach 'in every science whether of Morals or Natural Philosophy' (Smith 1983, p. 146).

Smith's naturalism is apparent in many aspects of his work. Smith's explanations are all based on human nature or on social institutions, with his social institutions being the creation of the inherent forces of human nature. We will shortly see the importance of social institutions and social forces in influencing human behavior. However, human nature itself, to the Scottish Enlightenment and Smith was presumed to be universal and naturally determined. Human nature was the same at all times and at all places. Smith refers to these universal traits in human nature as natural propensities, upon which all his theories were built. His economic theory is based on the propensities to truck, barter and exchange and to better one's condition. His ethics are based on 'some principle in ... [human] nature, which interest him in the fortune of others, and render their happiness necessary to him' (Smith 1979, p. 9); whence comes the sympathy principle.

Smith's philosophical essays also explain scientific inquiry by means of natural propensities, both in the motivation to search for explanations, and in the choice of explanation accepted. Here Smith gives a theory of scientific inquiry based on human nature, the sentiments of Wonder, Surprise and Admiration.[25] It is because these sentiments are disturbed and aroused that scientific inquiry is undertaken and the superior theory is one which best settles these sentiments.

> Philosophy, by representing the invisible chains which bind together all these disjointed objects, endeavours to introduce order into this chaos of

---

24. In TMS Smith writes: 'Human society, when we contemplate it in a certain abstract and philosophical light, appears like a great, an immense machine, whose regular and harmonious movements produce a thousand agreeable effects' (p. 316).

25. Yet Smith's materialistic explanations frequently show the influence of Montesquieu and the concern for social conditions. Thus, although the search for philosophical explanations is based in human nature, as are the criteria of evaluating competing theories, all this takes place under the requirement of certain conditions in the social environment. 'When law has established order and security, and subsistence ceases to be precarious, the curiosity of mankind is increased' (Smith 1980, p. 50).

jarring and discordant appearances, to allay this tumult of the imagination, and to restore it, when it surveys the great revolutions of the universe, to that tone of tranquillity and composure, which is both most agreeable in itself, and most suitable to its nature. (Smith 1980, pp. 45-6)

Even the formation of languages is derived from what James Becker (1961) has termed the propensity to classify. 'Mankind' Smith asserts, 'are naturally disposed to give to one object the name of any other, which nearly resembles it, and thus to denominate a multitude, by what originally was intended to express an individual' (Smith 1983, p. 204). Smith's genius, in this example as in numerous others, can be seen in his analysis of efficient causes, which in his analysis of the development of language centers on the displacement of concepts, although at a very elementary level.

We saw in Chapter 2 that an important aspect of naturalism is the use of 'state of nature' explanations; explanations which abstract from society and social forces. Although Smith follows Hume in his criticism of Locke's and Hobbes's use of the 'state of nature',[26] he nevertheless relies heavily on them. The most prominent use of such explanations by Smith is in his economics, where we frequently find that his analysis of a fundamental topic begins with a discussion of the early and rude state of society.[27] However, 'state of nature' explanations are found in most of Smith's works. His 'Considerations Concerning the First Formation of Languages' starts with such a situation:

Two savages, who had never been taught to speak, but had been bred up remote from the societies of man, would naturally begin to form that language by which they would endeavor to make their mutual wants intelligible to each other. (Ibid. p. 203, see also p. 9)

Such 'state of nature' explanations were the starting point for Smith's conjectural history. On conjectural history Dugald Stewart wrote:

In this want of direct evidence, we are under a necessity of supplying the place of fact by conjecture; and when we are unable to ascertain how men have actually conducted themselves upon particular occasions, of considering in what manner they are likely to have proceeded, from the

---

26. In L J (Smith 1978, p. 398) Smith tells us of Hobbes, that there is 'no purpose to treat of the laws which would take place in a state of nature, ... as there is no such state existing'.

27. For an example see the start of the discussion on value (Smith 1976, p. 65).

principles of their nature, and the circumstances of their external situation. ... In examining the history of mankind, as well as in examining the phenomena of the material world when we cannot trace the process by which an event *has been* produced, it is often of importance to be able to show how it *may have been* produced by natural causes ... from known principles of human nature. (Smith, 1980, p. 293)

Conjectural history arises out of the naturalism aspect of the Natural Law Outlook.

The final element in the Natural Law Outlook is the derivation of a natural moral theory, the demonstration that the laws of nature should be followed and that the results of the workings of the laws of nature are superior to the outcome that would result from interference. In Smith we have already seen that he felt that the laws and rules which were the result of his ethical theories were God's laws and rules. And we see continually in Smith the claim that the laws of nature, and natural principles and propensities are so designed to promote human happiness and prosperity - the intention of the design. Smith's defense of the society of natural liberty and laissez-faire stem from moral as much as from economic efficiency grounds.[28]

Smith's Theory of Natural Value

The impact of the Natural Law Outlook on Smith can best be seen by examining in detail one of his most important theories - his theory of value. In examining this theory we find not only the traces of the natural law influences which we analyzed above, but also we find the three essential elements of any natural law concept: social physics, naturalism and natural moral theory. We also can see in Smith's theory of value how in a significant way he moves away from the Natural Law Outlook, yet it is in such a way that Smith does not feel that it is a break with it. This non-natural law counter tendency is the subject of Chapter 4.

---

28. Smith writes: 'The property which every man has in his own labor "is" most sacred and inviolable. The patrimony of a poor man lies in the strength and dexterity of his hands; and to hinder him from employing this strength and dexterity in what manner he thinks proper without injury to his neighbor, is a plain violation of his most sacred property' (Smith 1976, p. 138). To which Myers adds 'These restraints block the way to free markets and Smith abhors them because they strike at the very foundations of his moral conception of man. ... It is a manifest violation of the laws of nature. Thus Smith's argument for free markets is not only a technical one, showing how such markets act to allocate economic resources most efficiently in a material sense, but also a moral one showing that outside interferences in such markets one, virtually, assaults on man's soul' (Myers 1983, pp. 118-19).

The purpose of Adam Smith's theory of value, as with all theories of value, is not only to arrive at the general principles which regulate prices, but to go beneath the surface phenomena of market prices to the dominant and persistent factors which in the long run, through their determination of prices, regulate society and provide for social order. This long-run price is the good's value, the expression of forces which are partially hidden from everyday casual observation but which nevertheless are the regulating forces of the market. For Smith this is the natural price, and we will see that it is the result of natural laws.

Smith's economics begins with the division of labor and all his subsequent theories flow directly or indirectly from it. Smith starts WN by stating: 'The greatest improvement in the productive powers of labour, and the greater part of the skill, dexterity, and judgement with which it is any where directed, or applied, seem to have been the effects of the division of labour' (Smith 1976, p. 13). He then proceeds to analyze what factors brought about the phenomena of the division of labor. Of its origins Smith (Ibid. p. 25) is quite clear.

> This division of labour, from which so many advantages are derived, is not originally the effect of any human wisdom, which foresees and intends the general opulence to which it gives occasion. It is the necessary, though very slow and gradual consequence of a certain propensity in human nature which has in view no such extensive utility; the propensity to truck, barter, and exchange one thing for another.

Smith leaves open the question of whether this 'propensity of human nature': is an 'original principle in human nature' or a derivative of reason and speech, what in L J he refers to as the principle to persuade 'which so much prevails in human nature' (Smith 1978, p. 493, see also p. 352).[29] From the division of labor we get prosperity, human diversity and an exchange economy, all of which promote the happiness and prosperity of mankind. Here we see the principle of design. Man is created by the Author of Nature so that he acts in a manner which promotes the well-being of mankind, the intention of the design. He acts in such a manner because certain traits are implanted in human nature by the Author of Nature. The inherent naturalism in Smith is evident in his tracing the origins of the

---

29. This, in turn, Smith suggests in TMS might be based on the natural instinct of persuasion. 'The desire of being believed, the desire of persuading, of leading and directing other people, seems to be one of the strongest of all our natural desires. It is, perhaps, the instinct upon which is founded the faculty of speech, the characteristical faculty of human nature' (Smith 1979, p. 336).

phenomena under discussion to nature.

Smith then proceeds to explore how this natural tendency exhibits itself. Initially, it accounts for the diversity of the particular members of society. Human nature is a constant, yet observation informs us of great diversity. This is an effect of the division of labor, and it creates an exchange economy, '[e]very man thus lives by exchanging, ... and the society itself grows to be what is properly a commercial society' (Smith 1976, p. 37). The act of exchange is a natural act, derived from human nature, and a society based on exchange is the natural outcome of the working of this natural propensity; it is a natural order. Smith then sets out to derive the natural laws of this natural order - the rules that regulate exchange.

Smith begins his exposition of the natural laws which regulate exchange with a 'state of nature' explanation of exchange in pre-society.

> In that early and rude state of society which precedes both the accumulation of stock and the appropriation of land, the proportion between the quantities of labour necessary for acquiring different objects seems to be the only circumstance which can afford any rule for exchanging them one for another. If among a nation of hunters, for example, it usually costs twice the labour to kill a beaver which it does to kill a deer, one beaver should naturally exchange for or be worth two deer. It is natural that what is usually the produce of two days or two hours labour, should be worth double of what is usually the produce of one day's or one hour's labour. (Ibid. p. 65)

As a society develops, land and capital, as well as labor enter into the calculation of exchange, yet Smith often tells us that '[l]abour ... is the real measure of the exchangeable value of all commodities' (Ibid. p. 47) and 'Labour alone, ... never varying in its own value, is alone the ultimate and real standard by which the value of all commodities can at all times and places be estimates and compares. It is their real price' (Ibid. p. 51).

Smith then makes the distinction of natural and market price.

> When the price of any commodity is neither more or less than what is sufficient to pay the rent of the land, the wages of the labour, and the profits of the stock employed in raising, preparing, and bringing it to market, according to their natural rates, the commodity is then sold for what may be called its natural price ... The commodity is then sold precisely for what it is worth. (Ibid. p. 72)

> The actual price at which any commodity is commonly sold is called its market price. ... The market price of every particular commodity is regulated by the proportion between the quantity which is actually brought to market, and the demand of those who are willing to pay the

natural price of the commodity. (Ibid. p. 73)

When there is a divergence between market prices and natural prices competition will bring them into line. Competition is the manifestation of another natural propensity, the desire to better one's condition. Workers, landlords and capitalists, acting in their own self-interest will naturally seek the greatest return for their respective contributions. If supply is such that it does not satisfy the effectual demand, the price of the commodity will rise. This price increase becomes the incentive for some economic actors to shift their efforts into the production of the commodity in question. This will increase its supply, and thus lower its price towards the natural price.

> The natural price, therefore, is, as it were, the central price, to which the prices of all commodities are continually gravitating. Different accidents may sometimes keep them suspended a good deal above it, and sometimes force them down somewhat below it. But whatever may be the obstacles which hinder them from settling in this center of repose and continuance, they are constantly tending towards it.

> The whole quantity of industry annually employed in order to bring any commodity to market, naturally suits itself in this manner to the effectual demand. (Ibid. p. 75)

The natural law elements and influences are clear. Prices, or more correctly exchange values, are social phenomena, yet they are treated as being regulated and determined by laws and forces which are similar to those of the physical sciences. Smith even adopts Newton's gravity; market prices gravitate towards natural prices. This is clearly a model of social physics. The naturalism is apparent in that all action is based on nature. Humans react mechanically to the stimulus of differential gain according to their natural drives and propensities. Human institutions, we are told, only interfere with the natural forces. The end result is that commodities are sold for what they are worth, their value. This is the natural moral theory aspect, when the natural laws act freely, they lead to the just outcome.[30] Such a free play of market forces is for Smith the society of perfect liberty, and it is as much a moral state as it is the natural order. Smith's value theory was an extension of the value discussion of the natural law

---

30. For the relation between natural prices and the 'Just Price', see Lowe's 'The Normative Roots of Economic Value' (Lowe 1967).

philosophers and earlier economists, particularly Cantillon.[31] Their search was for the intrinsic value of a commodity, as well as the just price.[32]

Smith's theory of economic development also runs in terms of natural propensities and the natural course of things.[33] Progress and prosperity come not through human intervention but through the absence of it and in many cases in spite of it. Smith writes:

> Man is generally considered by statesman and projectors as the materials of a sort of political mechanics. Projectors disturb nature in the course of her operations in human affairs; and it requires no more than to let her alone, and give her fair play in the pursuit of her ends, that she may establish her own designs. (Smith 1980, p. 322)

and

> Little else is requisite to carry a state to the highest degree of opulence from the lowest barbarism, but peace, easy taxes, and a tolerable administration of justice; all the rest being brought about by the natural course of things. All governments which thwart this natural course, which force things into another channel, or which endeavor to arrest the progress of society at a particular point, are unnatural. (Ibid.)

Smith's moral philosophy was an extension of the Scottish natural law tradition; a combination of Newtonianism, Natural Theology and the natural law philosophy of Grotius and Pufendorf. Nowhere does Smith give the indication that he rejects this tradition. As we have seen above, he frequently states the opposite. Yet, in one important respect, Smith breaks with the Natural Law Outlook of his times, as he implicitly develops an analysis of society as a process. However, for Smith the process was the

---

31. For the influence of the natural law philosophers on Smith's value theory, see Taylor (1965), part two, Chapter 2. Smith in the lectures is much closer to the natural law tradition, while in WN he is closer to Cantillon.

32. Smith's value theory is partly evolutionary in that the factors which determine value are dependent on the particular stage society is in. Thus as land is appropriated and capital accumulated, they, along with labor, become part of the determination of the natural price. This point is discussed in Chapter 4.

33. Smith's analysis of the natural course of economic development shows both his strengths and weaknesses. In Book III of WN, he starts off by stating the 'natural course of things', that is the natural laws which regulate economic development, and then proceeds with a historical analysis of economic development which, he admits, violates the 'natural course of things' (Smith 1976, p. 380). This tension between Smith's natural law and historical aspects of his works is discussed in the next chapter.

working out of the principle of design. But it is in his analysis of the process where Smith makes his most important contribution to our understanding of society. It is to this aspect of Smith's work that we turn our attention in Chapter 4.

4. Adam Smith and Society as a Process

In Chapter 3 we have endeavored to show the relationship between Adam Smith's theories and his belief in the natural order and natural laws in the social universe. This chapter will attempt to demonstrate how implicit in Smith's method is a non-natural law approach. Specifically, it will be argued that there is a dichotomy in Smith's works, that Smith has two research programs: a search for natural laws and the natural order and a historical and institutional investigation of existing social phenomena - each of which give a distinct vision of society. The second research program - historical/institutional - has implicit the view of society as a process, a view which essentially rejects the Natural Law Outlook. Yet Smith's natural law conceptions and preconceptions prevented him from fully developing a system based exclusively on the conception of society as a process. Like all rich theories, Smith's system lends itself to many different interpretations. The source of these diverging explanations of Smith are twofold: first, each reader of Smith brings along their own preconceptions and beliefs and thus interprets Smith in the light of their particular ideologies or purposes. The only way to try to control this source of divergent interpretations is to attempt to ascertain what Smith's theories meant to him, and separate Smith's system from what we might borrow or learn from aspects of his work.

Second, Smith's aim, the discovery of the natural laws of the social universe, necessarily contradicts his method: the use of history and institutions.[1] This leads to differing and conflicting interpretations, depending on which aspect of Smith's work one is emphasizing. It will be argued that freed of its natural law concepts and elements, Smith's system is consistent with the view of society as a process in social thought referred to in Chapter 2, a view which breaks from the attempt to construct a science of society modeled on the natural sciences.

---

1. The contradiction exists only if we reject the idea of the principle of design and allow for free will.

1. The Natural Law/Historical Dichotomy in Adam Smith

The existence of a dual nature in Smith's work is not a recent observation. The most famous example is 'Das Adam Smith Problem' of the late nineteenth and early twentieth centuries. Here the dichotomy was between Smith's two great works, *The Wealth of Nations* and *The Theory of Moral Sentiments*, specifically, between the importance of sympathy in the latter book and of self-interest in the former.

A second dichotomy can be seen in Smith's research program and in his exposition and method of investigation of this program. Smith's research program was the search for natural laws, while his method of discovering these laws included the use of history and institutional observations. This dichotomy was the result of Smith's belief in the providential order of the social universe and the influence of Natural Theology on the Scottish school of moral philosophy.

The duality in Smith's researches was first noted by T. E. Cliffe Leslie in 'The Political Economy of Adam Smith' where he points out that in Smith's time there were two approaches to analyzing social phenomena. Leslie (Leslie 1969, pp. 23-4) writes:

> Two essentially opposite systems of reasoning respecting the fundamental laws of human society were before the world at that epoch, which may be respectively designated as the theory of a Code of Nature, and the inductive system of Montesquieu - the former speculating a priori about 'Nature', and seeking to develop from a particular hypothesis the 'Natural' order of things; the latter investigating in history and the phenomena of the actual world the different states of society and their antecedents or causes - or, in short, the real, as contrasted with an ideal, order of things.

Leslie continues by observing that 'the peculiarity of Adam Smith's philosophy is, that it combines these two opposite methods, and hence is that we have two systems of political economy claiming descent from him' (Ibid.).

This point has been more fully developed by Thorstein Veblen in 'The Preconceptions of Economic Science' (Veblen 1899-1900). Veblen notes two seemingly contradictory preconceptions in Smith: 'the matter of fact point of view or preconception, which yields a discussion of causal sequence and correlations; and ... the animistic point of view or preconception, which yields a discussion of teleological sequences and correlations' (Veblen 1919, p. 100). The matter of fact point of view gave Smith a concern for material facts and historical analysis, while the animistic preconception searches for natural laws which are the creation of a Divine Providence. We have seen how Natural Theology and natural law theories and concepts have influenced Smith, the chief effect being this animistic point of view. Yet we have also seen that these two influences, in their Scottish manifestations, led to an interest in history, observation and what might be loosely called empiricism.

The historical/institutional element in Smith's thought, or what Veblen calls the matter of fact view, has its origins partly in the Natural Theology/natural law tradition of the Scottish Enlightenment and partly in the influence of Hume and Montesquieu. Hume's questioning and rejection of many of the accepted beliefs which were derived from 'the rational method' used by Locke - not the least of which was Hume's attack on social contract theory for its lack of historical validity - help to prepare the way for the historical point of view. However, it is Montesquieu who more fully breaks with animistic explanations and reliance on natural law.[2] The natural order had to be a universal order, independent of historical circumstances. Montesquieu felt that laws and social institutions were based on relative, and not absolute, factors, such as the material conditions and other existing social institutions which previously or currently existed.

In his *Account of the Life and Writings of Adam Smith, LL.D.*, Dugald Stewart (Smith 1980, p. 295) tells us: 'In Mr. Smith's writings, whatever be the nature of his subject, he seldom missed an opportunity of indulging his curiosity, in tracing from the principles of human nature, or from the circumstances of society, the origin of the opinions and the institutions which he describes.' In this statement we see the two influences on Smith: the Natural Law Outlook trying to explain a phenomenon 'from the principles of human nature', that is, from the characteristics of man implanted by Divine Providence to facilitate the harmonious working of the design, and the historical/institutional approach inspired by Montesquieu, which was concerned with 'the circumstances of society'.

For Smith, and for the Scottish Enlightenment in general (Hume possibly excepted), there was no contradiction between these two approaches, as we saw in Chapter 3. Under Natural Theology and the scientific approach of Newton, one discovered natural laws by investigating their earthly

---

2. That Montesquieu held the Natural Law Outlook is evident from reading the first chapter of *The Spirit of the Laws*. Yet his historical approach, as well as his use of the comparative method lead to a non-natural law analysis.

manifestations. History and social institutions were the data for the moral philosopher, just as observation and experiment were for the natural philosopher.[3] The Scottish Enlightenment made a distinction between final and efficient causality. This is clearly stated by Stewart in his *The Philosophy of the Active and Moral Powers of Man*, where he argues that philosophy must be concerned with both efficient and final causes, but should take great care to keep them separate and not confuse them. Stewart (1829, pp. 318-9) writes:

> When the general laws of our constitution are attentively examined, they will be found to have for their object the happiness and improvement both of the individual and of society. This is their final cause, or the end for which we may presume they were destined by our Maker. But in such cases it seldom happens that, while man is obeying the active impulses of his nature, he has any idea of the ultimate ends he is promoting, ... These active impulses may therefore in one sense be considered as the efficient causes of his conduct. ... I do not know of any author who has been more aware of this common error [confusing final and efficient causes] than Mr. Smith, who in his Theory of Moral Sentiments, always treats separately of the final causes of the different principles he considers, and of the mechanism (as he calls it) by which nature accomplishes the effect.

Stewart then goes on to demonstrate this point with a long quotation from TMS (part of which we have previously quoted):

> In every part of the universe we observe means adjusted with the nicest artifice to the ends which they are intended to produce; and in the mechanism of a plant, or animal body, admire how every thing is contrived for advancing the two great purposes of nature, the support of the individual, and the propagation of the species. But in these, and in all such objects, we still distinguish the efficient from the final cause of their several motions and organizations. The digestion of the food, the circulation of the blood, and the secretion of the several juices which are drawn from it, are operations all of them necessary for the great purposes of animal life. Yet we never endeavor to account for them from those purposes as from their efficient causes, nor imagine that the blood circulates, or that the food digests of its own accord, and with a view or intention to the purposes of circulation or digestion. The wheels of the watch are all admirably adjusted to the end for which it was made, the pointing of the hour. All their various motions conspire in the nicest manner to produce this effect. If they were endowed with a desire and

---

3. In the next chapter the status of historical investigation and its role in the Scottish Enlightenment is examined.

intention to produce it, they could not do it better. Yet we never ascribe any such desire or intention to them, but to the watch-maker, and we know that they are put into motion by a spring, which intends the effect it produces as little as they do. But though, in accounting for the operations of bodies, we never fail to distinguish in this manner the efficient from the final cause, in accounting for those of the mind we are very apt to confound these two different things with one another. When by natural principle we are led to advance those ends, which a refined and enlightened reason would recommend to us, we are very apt to impute to that reason, as to their efficient cause, the sentiments and actions by which we advance those ends, and to imagine that to be the wisdom of man, which in reality is the wisdom of God. Upon a superficial view, this cause seems sufficient to produce the effects which are ascribed to it; and the system of human nature seems to be more simple and agreeable when all its different operations are in this manner deduced from a single principle. (Smith 1979, p. 87)

This passage is used by Stewart not only to demonstrate Smith's separation of efficient and final causes, but to emphasize the importance of final causes to Smith.

For the Scottish Enlightenment the search for efficient and final causes reinforced each other, for it was through the knowledge of efficient causes that we come to understand final causes, and it is through our understanding of final causes that we come to appreciate the benevolent effects of efficient causes.[4]

2. Society as a Process in Smith

As demonstrated in Chapter 2, the view that society is a process combines elements of mechanism and organicism, of society as a multiplicity and as a unity. The influence of the natural law tradition on Smith, the search for natural laws and the emphasis on the individual, lend a mechanical and atomistic flavor to much of Smith's theories. However, the influence of Montesquieu and empiricism (observation) led Smith to develop organic types of theories and analysis. This concern for the individual, social institutions and society in general, gives Smith's work the overall flavor of

---

4. Stewart writes: 'In many cases the consideration of final causes has led to the discovery of some general law of nature, and in almost every case the discovery of a general law points out to us clearly some wise and beneficial purpose to which it is subservient' (Stewart 1829, p. 320).

a view of society as a process.

Stewart characterizes Smith's method as trying to explain social phenomena in terms of 'the principles of human nature' or in terms of 'the circumstances of society'. It is clear that the former dominates Smith's work. Following in the eighteenth-century reaction to Hobbes, Smith's TMS and WN are attempts to explain how, starting with individuals, we can arrive at social order without a leviathan. Smith's object is to elucidate how individual action leads to an orderly society; how individual behavior is regulated by internal and natural principles, independent of, and without, rule-making and enforcing institutions, such as organized religion or government. Similarly, WN is a theoretical explication of how individual behavior leads to order in the economic realm and to the promotion of society's material well-being. Even in his philosophical essays, Smith derives philosophical inquiry from human nature, the principles of which are original to the individual. Yet, when looked at closely, we see that in all of Smith's writings, there is the ever-present influence of historical society. This is the second type of explanation which Stewart mentions. This is seen at two levels. At the surface, we see Smith's concern for society and social institutions in his handling of history and social change and progress. Thus the bulk of WN is concerned with analyzing these phenomena, much like Montesquieu's *The Spirit of the Laws*. Yet, at a more significant level, society plays an active role in determining behavior and is present even in the theoretical aspects of his works.

An example of how social conditions influence Smith's theories can be seen in his treatment of the question of value. In Chapter 3 it was stated that Smith's theory of natural value was clearly intended to be a natural law theory encompassing all the elements of the Natural Law Outlook. To a certain extent this is unavoidable for a theory of value, since the purpose of value theory is to expose and explain the forces which bring about economic order, and if one is looking for universal forces and a universally correct theory of value, then one will end up with a natural law theory. Yet, as we so often see in Smith, his approach to discovering the final causes (natural laws) is through investigating the efficient causes. It is in this aspect of Smith's investigations of the value question where we see implicit the society as a process.

In keeping with the Natural Law Outlook, Smith starts his discussion on value with a 'state of nature' explanation, the 'early and rude state of society' (Smith 1976, p. 65). Here we see the natural relations which lead to a pure labor theory of value. Jeffrey T. Young has recently argued that Smith's analysis of the early and rude state fits in very well with Smith's theory of the impartial spectator developed in TMS. In such a primitive society, it would seem reasonable and just that labor be the sole criterion for determining relative exchange rates.   Young contends that the 'impartial-spectator process inform both the origin of the natural price based on labor in a hunting society and the ascription of normative significance to the natural price: first, as a kind of just price which satisfies the negative virtue of communitive justice, and second, as an efficient price which promotes the optimal allocation of resources' (Young 1986, p. 377). Young's analysis shows both the strength and weakness of Smith's approach to social phenomena. It is to be remembered that the impartial-spectator is the efficient cause device by which the intent of the Author of Nature brings about social order. Bringing such an essential element of Smith's system explicitly into his economics gives us new insights (although it should be remembered that in WN Smith does not refer to this mechanism). The impartial-spectator works as a process, and interaction among individuals and between individuals and social institutions, to which we will return for a more detailed analysis in the next section of this chapter. Its use in Smith's value theory would lead us to expect Smith's theory of value to change and evolve while society changes and evolves. And this is precisely what happens.

After the discussion of natural value in the 'state of nature', Smith proceeds to allow for the accumulation of stock and the ownership of land as private property. Under this regime, the natural price becomes that which pays the three factors of production at their natural rates; 'what is sufficient to pay the rent of the land, the wages of the labour, and the profits of the stock employed in raising, preparing, and bringing it to market, according to their natural rates' (Smith 1979, p. 72).   This explanation has never pleased economic theorists, especially those who are looking for a theory of long-run general equilibrium prices for it is indeterminate - what determines natural wages, rents and profits. Yet, when looked at through the insight of the impartial-spectator, the natural price again becomes the just price which is arrived at through a process of social mediation, which compensates those whom society has deemed to have a legitimate claim on social output at rates which society deems just. In fact, when Smith goes about the task of explaining the determinants of wages, rents and profits, (WN, Book I, Chapters 8-11) it is mostly historical and institutional factors which determine wages, rents and profits. In this light, Smith's cost of production theory of natural value is very much a society as a process explanation, and it is this aspect of the theory where the strength of Smith's approach is seen.

The weakness, both in Smith's analysis and in Young's interpretation, comes when one attempts to extend the analysis too far. For Smith, the cost of production theory is the efficient cause; however, there should be no doubt that labor is the true source and measure of value (its final cause). Young's analysis argues that Smith can with justice use his theory as an objective basis by which normative conclusions can be reached. Certainly this is Smith's intent, but the objective basis holds up only as long as the whole system of natural laws and the natural order is accepted as fact. Without the teleological aspect of Smith's system - efficient causes as design to provide for the final causes - we have to consider the legitimacy of the social and historical institutions at work. This point will be explored at the end of this chapter.

Smith's society as a process approach is seen even more clearly in Smith's moral theory and the socialization process implicit in TMS and WN. At one level, as we have seen in Chapter 3, Smith's moral theory is a natural law explanation of the moral rules by which Divine Providence intended humans to live, so as to promote human happiness and well-being. This aspect of Smith's ethics is concerned with final causes. However, Smith was interested also in efficient causes - the mechanism by which the Author of Nature obtains the desired results. These mechanisms are in many cases social forces and institutions.

In TMS and 'Of the External Senses' we are given natural principles common to all humans, which provide the final cause (since these natural principles originate from the Author of Nature). Yet the intended outcome, moral rules and behavior, only comes about through interaction with society. The sympathy principle makes us predisposed to develop into moral individuals, but this only happens through social mediation. Here Smith breaks with Hutcheson's concept of the moral sense which is innate and thus does not develop from social interaction. Born with this natural propensity to please one's brethren, we first act so as to get favorable responses from our parents, then our school friends and educators, and finally from our fellow adults. Their reactions and perceptions of our behavior have been similarly formed by their own interaction with society. Thus we have both the formation and perpetuation of social norms and mores. As Morrow has noted, sympathy is used by Smith as a 'principle of communication by means of which the sentiments of one individual influence and are influenced by the sentiments of his fellow-men' (Morrow 1969, p. 29). Our actions thus become influenced, and our sense of right and wrong becomes determined by the judgments and actions of other individuals. The resulting codes of behavior, our moral sentiments 'are the result of living in society; we know ourselves to be virtuous or vicious, not from any inner source of moral insight, but from experience gained of the approbation and disapprobation of our fellow-men' (Ibid. p. 31).[5] We know the correctness of our behavior and actions by observing those around us. Moral rules 'develop only through the slow and imperfect process of individual judgment, based on sympathy, but guided by social education and socially established rules of behavior' (Macfie 1967, p. 91). Thus, at least at this general level, Smith's moral theory has a lot in common with the social process approach. The central concern and mechanism is the interaction between individuals and society, and the resulting social institution - moral rules - thus developing out of this interaction.

It must, however, be pointed out that even with its implicit society as a process approach, it is a natural law theory built upon natural law concepts.[6] This is so, in terms of its final cause, or teleological aspect, and in terms of Smith's ultimate standard of morality, which is separated from society's reactions. We see this in Smith's distinction between praise and blame, and praiseworthiness and blameworthiness.

> Praise and blame express what actually are; praise-worthiness and blame-worthiness, what naturally ought to be the sentiments of other people with regard to our character and conduct. The love of praise is the desire of obtaining the favorable sentiments of our brethren. The love of praise-worthiness is the desire of rendering ourselves the proper objects of those sentiments. (Smith 1979, p. 126)

We should strive to be worthy of praise, independent of our actually receiving it. And this standard of morality goes beyond society and social forces. Further on in TMS, Smith writes:

> But though man has, in this manner, been rendered the immediate judge of mankind, he has been rendered so only in the first instance; and an appeal lies from his sentence to a much higher tribunal, to the tribunal of their own conscious, to that of the supposed impartial and well-informed spectator, to that of the man within the beast, the great judge and arbiter of their conduct. ... In such cases, this demigod within the breast appears, like the demigods of the poets, though partly of

---

5. The formation of moral rules and moral behavior is the general subject of TMS. Of particular importance for the role of social interaction see Part I, especially Chapter 4 and Part III, Chapter 4.

6. It should be remembered that the subtitle to TMS was 'An Essay towards an Analysis of the Principles by which Men Naturally Judge Concerning the Conduct and Character, First of Their Neighbors and Afterwards of Themselves'. As Mini has noted '"Naturally" is the key word in the subtitle: it suggests that human motivations are rooted in innate, not acquired, traits' (Mini 1974, p. 76).

immortal, yet partly too of mortal extraction. Where his judgments are
steadily and firmly directed by the sense of praise-worthiness and blameworthiness, he seems to act suitably to his divine extraction: But when
he suffers himself to be astonished and confounded by the judgments of
ignorant and weak man, he discovers his connexion with mortality, and
appears to act suitably, rather to the human, than to the divine, part of
his origin. (Ibid. pp. 130-31)

Here Smith is allowing for the possibility that the moral rules which
develop through social interaction may only be approximations of the moral
rules of the design. Praise-worthiness is analogous to natural prices while
actual praise is analogous to market prices. For Smith the actual moral
rules are to be judged by their conformity with the moral rules of the
design.

Macfie's idea of the influence and importance of society in the
development of moral rules and judgments and ultimately moral behavior
in TMS has been extended by Robert Heilbroner to Smith's economics.
Heilbroner (1982) connects TMS and WN by arguing that TMS lays the
foundation, the building blocks, for WN; specifically, the primary element
in Smith's economics is the individual economic actor who is the end result
of the socialization process in TMS.

Traditional interpretations of Smith's economics stress the primary role of
individual self-interest, based solely on human nature, in promoting
society's well-being. A strong theme in Smith's economics, in fact in his
whole system, is his individualism and distrust for 'intervening'
government. This is an approach which runs throughout Smith's career,
and is no better demonstrated than in one of Smith's earliest writings, from
which we have already quoted: 'Man ... is generally considered by
statesmen and projectors as the materials of a sort of political mechanics.
Projectors disturb nature in the course of her operations in human affairs;
and it requires no more than to let her alone, and give her fair play in the
pursuit of her own designs' (Smith 1980, p. 322). This view comes out
strongest in Smith's call for laissez-faire policies toward the economy and
his critique of mercantilism. And it is this individualism that forms the
basis of what is today mainstream economic thought. Yet what Heilbroner
shows us is that this standard interpretation of Smith gives us an incorrect
view of Smith's view of the individual. For the behavior patterns we see
in WN are largely the result of the socialization process which takes place
in TMS. Heilbroner shows how 'primal human nature' is transformed into
'the prudent individual' who is the economic actor who inhibits WN. To
demonstrate this he gives two examples of economic behavior which are
crucial to Smith's economic system and which are treated as 'natural' in

WN, but which are the result of the socialization process of TMS: capital accumulation, and social order and the class structure (what Smith calls the distinction of ranks).

Without doubt, capital accumulation is the driving force of Smith's economics. Smith tells us in WN that it comes from the desire to better our condition, a natural instinct which 'though generally calm and dispassionate, comes with us from the womb, and never leaves us till we go into the grave' (Smith 1976, p. 341). Smith is quite clear that it is his economic condition which man is trying to better. In the next sentence Smith tells us: 'In the whole interval which separates those two moments, there is scarce perhaps a single instant in which any man is so perfectly and completely satisfied with his situation, as to be without any wish of alteration or improvement, of any kind. An augmentation of fortune is the means by which the greater part of men propose and wish to better their condition' (Ibid.).

This behavior pattern (bettering our condition) is derived from 'two quite different objectives, both of which we owe to the exposure to society' (Heilbroner 1982, p. 432). The first, derived from the sympathy principle, is the desire to be thought well of by our contemporaries. This leads to a motivation which is not too dissimilar from Veblen's conspicuous consumption - that is, in both cases economic activity (accumulating wealth in this case) is determined by one's concern with social judgments.

According to Heilbroner's analysis, the Invisible Hand is the second force which plays a crucial role in WN and which is the result of societal forces and interaction in TMS. Heilbroner writes: 'As TMS makes abundantly clear, the individual who accumulates wealth pursues an end which, were he to view it objectively and with philosophic detachment, would not be worth the effort. It is only because of the social pressure for distinction and through the veiled workings of the Invisible Hand that men "without knowing it, without intending it," advance the interest of society, and afford means to the multiplication of the species' (Ibid.). Thus, TMS creates not only moral man, but acquisitive man.

The maintenance of social order, and specifically a particular order assumed in WN, is also the result of the socialization process of TMS. The acquiescence of the lower classes is founded on the propensity to sympathize with those who are well off, 'our sympathy with our superiors being greater than that with our equals or inferiors: we admire their happy situation, enter into it with pleasure, and endeavor to promote it' (Smith 1978, p. 401). This 'order-bestowing principle of subordination' helps to quench the desire of the lower class to attack the property rights of the upper classes, and leads to the creation of Government. As Heilbroner tells us: 'The deeply rooted and profoundly important "principle of authority," then, rests in part on primal human passions, in part on the working of the Invisible Hand, and in part on the social tendency to "make parade of our riches, and conceal our poverty" that arises from the differential social esteem in which each is held. *In this way the social fact of inequality, potentially the source of social disruption and unrest, becomes itself the reinforcing agency of cohesion and order*' (Ibid. p. 434). Heilbroner sums up the relationship between TMS and WN: 'TMS covers the socio-psychological process of the socialization of the individual, WN explores the socio-economic consequences brought about by socialized man through the institutions appropriate to this stage of development' (Ibid. p. 434).

When we look at how Smith's system works, we see that his view of society is that of a process, that institutions and behavior patterns develop from the interaction of individuals and society, that both individual actions and social institutions are important in understanding social phenomena. Yet Smith does not go all the way. Ultimately he must base his explanations in terms of nature and natural laws, the design. Thus Smith's natural propensities, such as the desire to better one's own condition, although their manifestations are influenced by society, always originate in nature, and are the same under all conditions. Efficient causes are linked up to final causes.

3. Natural Law Limitations on Smith's Society as a Process Approach

Smith's moral sentiments clearly are the sentiments of the natural order, for although they are developing through a process, they are developing towards a predetermined end. The moral rules which are the end product of Smith's socialization process are also the laws of God and are part of His design. Here Smith has linked efficient and final causes. The process of socialization is a creation and tool of the Author of Nature; a predetermined process. Smith, along with the Scottish Enlightenment, assumes human nature to be a constant, and since the laws of nature are contained in the make-up of humans, the laws of nature are also a constant. As Jacob Viner has observed: 'I have found not even a casual reference in *The Theory of Moral Sentiments* to the moral sentiments being influenced by changes in the physical or political environment or of their being different in different countries or at different stages of history' (Viner 1972, p. 84).

In Smith's economics we do see the tension between his concern for efficient and final causes, this being particularly evident in his theory of value. As we already have seen Smith's theory of value adjusts to changes in circumstances, yet he continually reaffirms the contention that labor is the true source and measure of value. Most historians of economic thought have pointed to the inconsistencies in Smith's theory of value as a glaring weakness, yet they see the weakness in Smith's failed attempt at developing a logically consistent universally correct theory of value. The inconsistencies in Smith's theory of value are the necessary result of attempting to discover the invariant natural laws (final causes) of a social system or phenomena by investigating its history and social setting (efficient causes). The influence of natural law and Natural Theology on Smith prevented him from seeing the conflict between his method and his research program.

Smith's natural law preconceptions also ultimately tie him down to a static theory, for although Smith's system is dynamic in its efficient causes, in its working toward the design, it is predestined toward a natural order (the design) and once this is reached - the society of perfect liberty in his economics, the establishment of rules of morality in his ethics - we have an essentially static system. The dynamics of actual events are judged by their relation to their natural positions (market prices are evaluated in relation to natural prices). Society and social relations are conceived of in terms of the natural order. Even the decay of society, which Smith projects as a negative outcome of the division of labor, can be seen in the classical view of societies growing, maturing and dying and making way for new societies.[7] This is most apparent in Smith's analysis of individual behavior. For Smith the dual determinants of individual behavior are self-interest and moral rules which, through the influence of the Invisible Hand, promote society's interest. Smith feels that these two forces will balance each other, so as to produce harmony and not disorder. Although Smith tells us that the admiration of wealth is 'the great and most universal cause of the corruption of our moral sentiments' (Smith 1979, p. 61), (it causes us to admire wealth instead of virtue)[8] his analysis does not look at the question of whether self-interest as a motive will influence the moral sentiments in any way. As society becomes more market oriented, with an

---

7. This is a cyclical view of history, not the evolutionary view which was to replace it, a topic we will return to in the next chapter.

8. This point was one of the many revisions Smith made for the 6th edition of TMS. It is also implicitly a process concept with the sentiments being influenced by environmental factors and thus evolving.

increasing influence of the profit motive in all aspects of society, will the moral sentiments produce the same moral rules along with the corresponding obedience of such rules? Such reliance on final causes prevents him from asking such questions, and gives him a method which partially hinders such an investigation. Had Smith been free of his natural law preconceptions he could have developed further his efficient causes, allowing the passions and moral sentiments, the natural propensities and natural order, to have been the result of social processes, thus establishing a method and outlook which could have dealt with evolutionary questions.

The limitations placed on Smith by his Natural Law Outlook become evident when we compare his theories with similar theories which are free of natural law influences. To demonstrate the inherent weakness of social explanation rooted in the search for natural laws, we will compare Smith's treatment of acquiescence with that of Thorstein Veblen.

Smith's theory of the distinction of ranks and social order rests on the sympathy principle, particularly the tendency to look favorably towards the good fortune of the affluent. Smith (Ibid. pp. 52-3) writes:

> Upon this disposition of mankind, to go along with all the passions of the rich and powerful, is founded the distinction of ranks, and the order of society. Our obsequiousness to our superiors more frequently arises from our admiration for the advantages of their situation, than from any private expectations of benefit from their goodwill. ... We are eager to assist them in completing a system of happiness that approaches so near to perfection; and we desire to serve them for their own sake, ... Nature would teach us to submit to them for their own sake, to tremble and bow down before their exalted station, to regard their smile as a reward sufficient to compensate any services, and to dread their displeasure, ... The strongest motives, the most furious passions, fear, hatred, and resentment, are scarce sufficient to balance this natural disposition to respect them.

Clearly, Smith's theory of acquiescence, even when we remind ourselves of the social forces inherent in the operation of the sympathy principle, is a natural law explanation which seems also, as are most natural law explanations, to be a defense of the status quo. Smith realizes the importance of acquiescence to the social order for the existence of a peaceful state relies on the submission of the inhabitants to the norms of conduct and social structure. Yet Smith takes the given social structure (a class society) as part of the natural order, not one of many possible social formations.

Acquiescence plays a similarly important role in Veblen's *The Theory of the Leisure Class*, both in its function and its effect. The success of the leisure class, which Smith would call the higher ranks, depends on its ability to obtain the acquiescence of the lower classes. Similar to Smith, Veblen contends that the existence of the leisure class, and the social order necessary to perpetuate its existence, depends on its ability to control the lower classes. Furthermore, this control is rooted in its control of the cultural and social norms. The leisure class needs the 'sympathy' of the lower classes, to use Smith's word and meaning. Up to this point Smith and Veblen are in agreement. The cleavage between the two positions becomes apparent when one turns to the question of the source of the sympathetic response. For Smith, as we have seen, it is part of human nature, placed there by the Author of Nature as part of the design. Furthermore, its net effect is the promotion of mankind's well-being. Contrarily, for Veblen the sympathetic attitude of the lower classes towards the upper classes arises from social forces and not from nature. Veblen writes: 'all canons of reputability and decency, and all standards of consumption, are traced back by insensible gradations to the usages and habits of thought of the highest social and pecuniary class - the wealthy leisure class. It is for this class to determine, in general outline, what scheme of life the community shall accept as decent or honorific; and it is their office by precept and example to set forth this scheme of social solution in its highest, ideal form' (Veblen 1931, p. 104).

Like Smith, Veblen placed a high emphasis on emulation: 'With the exception of the instinct of self-preservation, the propensity for emulation is probably the strongest and most alert and persistent of the economic motives proper' (Ibid. p. 110). However, the form of emulation depends on cultural and social factors, manifest in different activities in different societies. Smith's search for the natural order of the design leads to a teleological treatment, nature guiding behavior to particular patterns. In Veblen both the mechanisms of control and the activities of a particular society lend themselves to a great deal more variety.

Veblen's treatment also allows us to see class societies as exploitative, with social relationships based to a large extent on power. What exists in Smith is partly the result of natural forces, and what is natural is what is in agreement with the design. For Veblen, what exists is the result of social forces, and these social forces are largely the result of the vested interests of a particular class. A particular social formation is the creation of humans not nature, and the structure of the particular social formation is greatly affected by the relative power of individuals and social groups. Veblen's approach of society as a process is more general than Smith's, since it allows for many types of social formations, and it allows us to see relations of dominance and exploitation.

Smith's natural law conceptions and his concern for the final causes of the design limit his analysis. In his consideration of efficient causes, of the mechanisms of social forces, Smith adopts the view of society as a process. However, when he considers final causes, he must abandon this view for a Natural Law Outlook. All this tells us is that Smith was a product of his time, for the belief in the natural order was almost universal in the eighteenth century. Smith's contributions, not only to economics but to social science in general, come from his analysis of social processes, and it is here that we look to Smith for inspiration and build from his foundations. Unfortunately, Smith's lasting impact is in the natural law aspects of his economics, clearly seen in his influence on Ricardo and more important, on neoclassical economics. A more realistic and useful economic theory would start with Smith's historical and institutional analysis, method and outlook. This implies a view of society as a process, taking into account the change and development of social institutions and habits. This is the legacy of Smith which needs to be carried on.

5. History, J. S. Mill and the Science of Society

The Enlightenment's objective was the creation of a moral philosophy on a par with natural philosophy: to create a science of society. As we have seen in the two previous chapters, this effort for Adam Smith entailed two research projects: a historical investigation into the origin, development and workings of a market society and the search for the laws of nature as they pertain to economic behavior. In this chapter we will look at the relationship of these two projects in greater detail, particularly the uneasy position of history in the attempt to develop a scientific economics.

The attempt to construct a moral philosophy on a par with natural philosophy is significant not as an endeavor to make moral philosophy a more rigorous discipline, but in the use of natural philosophy as a model to emulate and imitate. The justification for this endeavor was the belief that moral philosophy was part of the same system as natural philosophy and thus should have the same rigor. Natural philosophy was adopted as the model for moral philosophy to follow, as a source for concepts to be displaced (metaphors and analogies) and as a guiding heuristic. The adoption of the Natural Law Outlook was synonymous with being scientific. The path of the development of moral philosophy, what is now called the social sciences, was greatly influenced by being modeled after natural philosophy. Its structure (mechanical theories); its overall preconceptions (principle of design); its final terms (nature as the final cause) and the demarcation between dominant and persistent forces to be studied and transient and temporary forces to be assumed away (treatment of history and society) all tell of this influence.

1. History and Social Thought in the Enlightenment

The place of history in the Enlightenment illustrates the inherent contradictions of that great age. History was the basis of many of the intellectual advances of this period, the impetus of many of their scholarly activities and .curiosities, and in the end, unbeknownst to them or future generations, that which shows the impossibility of the Enlightenment's goal of a science of society.

Interest in history in the eighteenth century extended far beyond the intelligentsia. One historian has noted:

> It would be no exaggeration to say that the vogue of historical books between 1750 and the outbreak of the French Revolution was as great as the vogue of political literature in the age of Shakespeare or of the novel in the age of Scott. Everyone read it and talked about it. (Black quoted in Bryson 1968, p. 78)

In the same vein, probably the most famous historian of the age, Edward Gibbon, reports that 'History is the most popular species of writing' (Ibid.). For the philosophers of the age, interest in history was more than a passing fancy, it was an integral part of their quest for a science of society and mankind. In the Enlightenment, man and society truly begin to break with the controlling influence of organized religion and the hold of tradition. Although the process has its origins in the Renaissance and becomes fully developed only with the coming of the industrial revolution, it is in the Enlightenment that this independence is perceived. The double removal of the Church and tradition as the foundation of the social order and authority created a great intellectual gap in the comprehension of man and society. Questions of the foundation of the social order, morality and authority; the legitimacy of laws, institutions and states; the basis of knowledge and perception; all of which were easily dealt with in the medieval system by appeals to authority and tradition, now required explanation. These questions are the primary concern of the Enlightenment, and the quest was to answer them with reason and science and not with appeals to authority (revelation). Their answers not only greatly affected our perception of man and society but helped shape man and society themselves. As has been commonly asserted, nature replaced God as the foundation of explanations of the universe, natural and social, and science (reason) replaced religion (revelation) as the path to our understanding of the universe.

The attempt at a science of society was based on the preconception, common to most epochs yet paramount for the Enlightenment, of a constant and universal human nature. Collingwood notes (Collingwood 1946, p. 82):

> Just as the ancient historians conceived the Roman character, for

example, as a thing that had never really come into existence but had always existed and had always been the same, so the eighteenth-century historians, who recognized that all true history is the history of mankind, assumed that human nature had existed ever since the creation of the world exactly as it existed among themselves. Human nature was conceived substantially as something static and permanent, an unvarying substratum underlying the course of historical change and all human activities. History never repeated itself but human nature remained eternally unaltered.

This preconception was necessary in order to give moral philosophy the same universality in time and place attributed to natural philosophy. Science was the discovery of the laws of nature and these laws must be invariant. An examination of society and history, however, displayed variety, not uniformity and universality, as the common characteristic. A glance at one of the most influential works of the Enlightenment, *The Spirit of the Laws* (1949), illustrates this point. Montesquieu starts with the assertion of the existence of laws of nature in the social universe as a premise that cannot be questioned, yet his research exposed the diversity in mankind, not uniformity, and instead greatly weakened this initial premise. Gladys Bryson (1968, pp. 83-4) has shown that the assumption of a constant human nature provided the possibility of a science of society:

> What could make a coherent system, acceptable to the philosophic mind, from all of the facts of history, all of the epochs, all of the personages? What principle or principles of explanation could cover such a vast collection of facts? The answer, for the philosophers, was in terms of the basic facts of human nature, which were thought to be ultimate in that they were everywhere and in all ages the same.

Given the claim of a universal human nature, history takes on a new meaning. Typical of this trend in historical research was David Hume (1902, p. 83) who declared:

> Mankind are so much the same, in all times and places, that history informs us of nothing new or strange in this particular. Its chief use is only to discover the constant and universal principles of human nature, by showing men in all varieties of circumstances and situations, and furnishing us with materials from which we may form our observations and become acquainted with the regular springs of human action and behaviour.

History was to provide the data for a scientific moral philosophy, assuming the role observation and experimentation had in the natural sciences.

Following Hume's pronouncements, history was investigated to show the uniformity of human nature, and the direction, or progress, of the development of the human race. History offered the possibility of developing universals from the particulars, for it is universals, and not particulars, that science is interested in. Again we will quote Bryson's (1945, p. 79) classic study of the Scottish Enlightenment for a penetrating summation of this insight:

> Though ethics was the section of philosophy which they hoped would be greatly illuminated by the appeal to history - Bolingbroke's phrase, 'history is philosophy teaching by examples,' comes to mind - ethical considerations were not the only philosophical ones at work by a good deal. History, besides showing the outcomes of good and bad choices, would show those principles of repetition and uniformity, those sequences of behavior, which philosophical, i.e., scientific, requirements demanded. ... Science, though it starts with particulars, does not rest in them, but searches for repetitive factors and processes.

This view led to the development of what the Enlightenment Philosophers referred to as universal history. One of the earliest and clearest statements of the purpose of universal history comes from Anne Robert Jacques Turgot's essay 'On Universal History' (1973, p. 64):

> Universal History encompasses a consideration of the successive advances of the human race, and the elaboration of the causes which have contributed to it; the early beginnings of mankind; the formation and intermingling of nations; the origin of governments and their revolutions; the progress of languages, of natural philosophy, of morals, of manners, of the arts and sciences; the revolutions which have brought about the succession of empire to empire, of nation to nation, and of religion to religion; the human race always remaining the same during these upheavals, like the water during storms, and always proceeding towards its perfection. To unveil the influence of general and necessary causes, that of particular causes and the free actions of great men, and the relation of all this to the very constitution of man; to reveal the springs and mechanisms of moral causes through their effects - that is what History is in the eyes of a philosopher.

Kant's defense of this outlook, entitled 'Idea of a Universal History from a Cosmopolitan Point of View' is a dogmatic statement of the Enlightenment's position. Starting with the assertion of the existence of 'universal natural laws' of human actions and a 'determined plan of nature', Kant asserts that such an approach to history and the study of mankind is necessary because, among other reasons, 'if we turn away from that fundamental principle (natural laws directing universal history), we have then before us a nature moving without purpose, and no longer conformable to law; and the cheerless gloom of chance takes the place of the guiding light of reason' (Gardiner 1959, pp. 23-4).

Enlightenment history had two outstanding characteristics: the use of the comparative method of historical analysis and the use of 'conjectural' (sometimes known as 'rational' or 'philosophical') history. In fact, in this case the former presupposes the latter. The comparative method is 'the recognition of similarities between the practices and beliefs of contemporary primitive or barbaric peoples and those recorded in the past history of civilization' (Burrow 1966, p. 11). The comparative method was developed as an important tool of universal history, for it allowed an empirical study of the past through the observation of present primitive societies. The most developed version of universal history was the stage theory of history, found first in Turgot, but refined and developed in the Scottish Enlightenment. This theory of history is one of the most significant ideas to come out of the Enlightenment. In essence, it states that historical development follows a certain path for all peoples (because of the universality of human nature), and that the diversity of human behavior and social institutions we observe, both historically and in the present, are the result of peoples being at different stages of development. Thus, one can study earlier stages of our history by examining contemporary primitive peoples. The comparative method gave us the discipline of anthropology and through Smith's stages of economic development (hunting and gathering, pastoral, agricultural, and commercial)[1] Marx's historical materialism. Most importantly, however, it is this conception of history, of progress and development that provides the impetus and framework for the development of the concept of evolution, perhaps the single most important intellectual development of the nineteenth century.

With the comparative method, the science of history switched its attention from chronological sequence to human progress. The overall preconception is that of a natural order of development and clearly this is presupposed by the Enlightenment Philosophers and was not merely the conclusion of their historical investigations. This can be seen in the use of conjectural history to support this preconception whenever the facts seem to contradict the theory or in its use whenever there are no historical investigations to be

---

1. See Meek (1971)

drawn upon.[2] Though history plays an important role in Smith's system and all of his works have a great 'historical sense', it is clear that for the most part Smith used history to illustrate his ideas, not as the data upon which to develop them. As Bryson notes: 'for the most part these historical accounts, accurate and informative though they may be, are used by Smith not as data from which to draw generalizations, but as examples of a theory already advanced. What he is interested to trace, primarily, is the natural progress of opulence, ... the ways in which a particular society has proceeded according to the natural order of things, ... [As John M. Clark has noted on Smith's use of history] "The germs of a genetic treatment are there, but they are tributary and subordinate to the system of natural liberty"' (Bryson 1968, p. 86). When the data contradicted his theory, Smith reverts to either conjectural history or gets muddled down in contradictions and inconsistencies (theory of value).

The Possibility of Scientific History

The reliance on history as the source of data for the construction of a scientific moral philosophy rested on the possibility of a scientific history. In Adam Smith's time, the state of historical knowledge was such that one could, with confidence, feel that conjectural history and the use of the comparative method could serve as the basis of a scientific (universal) history. Universal history[3] is the quintessential Enlightenment idea, one that has lasted up to the present. Yet the attempt to ground a science of society in history was from the beginning problematic. Skepticism as to the use value of historical knowledge, stemming from Descartes's criticism of history as an intellectual discipline, eventually gains widespread adherence, particularly among positivists.

Descartes felt that history was not only not scientific, he did not regard it as a branch of knowledge. The reasons for Descartes's objections to history were twofold: history dealt with particulars while science dealt exclusively with universals; and our knowledge of particulars comes from observations, the reliability of which Descartes questioned. Following this line of reasoning, a scientific history would have to abstract from particulars and concentrate on the universals. To a certain extent, this is the direction to which conjectural history leads. Yet for the Scottish

2. In Chapter 4 the uneasy relationship between Smith's historical analysis and his Natural Law Outlook, with particular reference to conjectural history, is discussed.

3. Robert Solomon has so aptly named universal history the 'transcendental pretense'.

Enlightenment, in principle if not always in practice, it is in history where we should hope to find the universals. The contradiction between the Cartesian conception of science and the *raison d'être* of history should be apparent to all. History without particulars is mere speculation, metaphysics at its worst. Whether history is, or can be made, scientific is an issue which was debated throughout the nineteenth century and well into the twentieth.[4] Attempts to move history, and the social sciences (including economics), to the natural science model of theory construction and evaluation necessitate the emptying of the historical content of the theories; while attempts to construct history and the social sciences on the foundation of historical knowledge require the abandonment of the natural science model. Clearly the two research programs are not complementary and cannot coexist for long in the same field.

Changes in Historiography

Ironically, the efforts of the Enlightenment Philosophers produced many effects that were not their intention. As already noted, the comparative method led to the discipline of anthropology and the stage theory lead to the idea of evolution. The rise of the field of anthropology in the nineteenth century greatly increased the knowledge of the various contemporary civilizations. Furthermore, there was a growing dissatisfaction as to the 'existing standards of historiography' (Burrow 1966, p. 66). A new history was developing, a bourgeois history. This consisted, as John W. Burrow notes in his penetrating study of the nineteenth century, *Evolution and Society*, of a 'middle-class revolt against the treatment of history as a chronicle of the deeds of an aristocratic and military caste, and a demand instead for history which shall concern itself with the man in the street, his opinions, conditions of life and the factors which have made for his happiness and unhappiness' (Ibid. p. 67).

The Enlightenment conception of a universal human nature reached its apex in the rational economic man in classical economic theory and in Bentham's utilitarian philosophy and psychology. The Natural Law Outlook continued in the neoclassical economics that was to develop out of these schools. Yet the new history, particularly as developed on the European continent, greatly questioned the central idea of a universal human nature and the growth in historical knowledge supported the

---

4. See the collection of essays edited by Gardiner entitled *Theories of History*, especially the contributions of Popper, Hempel, White, Nagal, Dray. For the argument that historical knowledge is of a different sort than that of the natural sciences see Collingwood (1946).

abandonment of this view of human nature. Furthermore, as the century progressed, this new historical perspective played an important role in the emergence of the new cosmology of evolution, leading to a change in the conception of nature and the conception of society. John Stuart Mill came to intellectual maturity in this transition period. Mill endeavors to carry forward the Enlightenment goal of a science of society modeled after the physical sciences, yet he is aware of the many difficulties encountered in previous attempts. It is to Mill's desire to hold on to the natural law view of social science while emphasizing historical and social analysis that we now turn.

2. History and the Science of Society in John Stuart Mill

It is an understatement to declare that John Stuart Mill was a product of his environment. Such is true of all, yet few have had an environment so consciously created with so singular a purpose. Mill's later emphasis on the importance of education in character formation most assuredly came from reflecting upon his own upbringing. The details of Mill's life are well known and need not be repeated here, yet it is important to note that the single most fundamental aspect of Mill's remarkable education is that he was trained to be a Utilitarian. Furthermore, all of Mill's major works were greatly influenced by this doctrine, either by his rejection and criticism of it or his efforts at rehabilitating it. One central aspect of Utilitarianism is the search for a science of society and that such a science is part of natural philosophy, and thus should be modeled after the physical sciences. Mill never abandons this facet of Utilitarianism. He divides the natural sciences into the physical sciences and the moral or psychological sciences, arguing that the moral sciences cannot be anything put part of the natural science. Before we examine Mill's views we must take a brief look at Utilitarianism, particularly as a natural law system.

The Natural Law Influence of Utilitarianism

The importance of the utility concept, and Utilitarianism, for economic theory, should not be underestimated. To this day, both the content and the structure of economic theory exposes the influence of Utilitarianism, which, in the form that it enters economic theory, is clearly a natural law system. That is to say that Utilitarianism includes all three elements that we noted Chapter 2, and is another source of natural law ideas and concepts that have dominated economic theory.

Utilitarianism is a natural law system in two respects: it contains all three elements of natural law theories (social physics, naturalism and natural moral theory), and it is an extension of the eighteenth-century natural law tradition.   Our analysis of Utilitarianism will be confined to Jeremy Bentham, who had such a great influence on Mill, and later economists, especially Jevons.

Bentham was greatly influenced by Locke and Newton. As Werner Stark has noted, 'Bentham's doctrine was in all its parts a synthesis of rationalism and empiricism' (Stark 1946, p. 587). From Locke, Bentham received the associationist psychology and the propensity for individual, as opposed to social, explanation. In Newton, he found a role model for scientific investigation. As Mitchell stated, Bentham, like many others, hoped to become 'the Newton of the Moral World' (Mitchell 1950, p. 180). With his development and application of the felicific calculus, Bentham was convinced that he had discovered the single unifying principle, analogous to Newton's gravity, which held together social phenomena.

Bentham rejected many aspects of the natural law/natural rights doctrines prevalent in the late eighteenth century. In particular, he rejected the concept of the social contract (for reasons similar to those of Hume and Smith) and he opposed the concept of natural rights derived from the state of nature, independent of society. What Bentham does not reject is the idea that the social universe is regulated by laws and principles comparable to the laws and principles of the physical universe. This is the heart of the Natural Law Outlook, and it is here, as Schumpeter has observed, 'that the Utilitarians were the historical successors of the seventeenth century philosophers of natural law' (Schumpeter 1954a, p. 132).

The evolution from natural law to Utilitarianism's influence in economic theory has been most clearly stated by Gunnar Myrdal (1954, p. 14):

> The first basis upon which a system of economic theory was constructed was the philosophy of natural law. The substitution later, of utilitarian philosophy for the philosophy of natural law did not occur suddenly and did not cause a revolution. It was a gradual process of extending and reinforcing the old basis. This, at least, is the interpretation suggested by the evolution of economic theory. First, the logical distance between the ultimate normative premises and the practical political conclusions is increased by the assertion of additional steps. Second, attention is focused on these additional steps - these are the utilitarian elements

> which are added - while the ultimate premises - which are still the
> aprioristic notions of natural law - are kept in the shadow. Bentham
> inveighed against the circular reasoning in all arguments based on natural
> law, to the effect that something is 'right' merely because it is 'natural',
> or sometimes even more simply because it is 'right'. But the result of
> his own endeavours was ... only to increase the diameter of the logical
> circle.

That Utilitarianism was a natural law system becomes evident when we
examine its structure and content.

The first paragraph of Bentham's most famous work, *An Introduction to
the Principles of Morals and Legislation* (1982, p. 11) clearly shows his
natural law orientation:

> Nature has placed mankind under the governance of two sovereign
> masters, pain and pleasure. It is for them alone to point out what we
> ought to do, as well as to determine what we shall do. On the one hand
> the standard of right and wrong, on the other the chain of causes and
> effects, are fastened to their throne. They govern us in all we do, in all
> we say, in all we think: every effort we can make to throw off our
> subjection, will serve but to demonstrate and confirm it. In words a man
> may pretend to abjure their empire: but in reality he will remain subject
> to it all the while. The principle of utility recognizes this subjection, and
> assumes it for the foundation of that system, the object of which is to
> rear the fabric of felicity by the hands of reason and of law. Systems
> which attempt to question it, deal in sounds instead of sense, in caprice
> instead of reason, in darkness instead of light.

From this famous quotation we can see in Bentham the three basic
elements of a natural law theory. First, there is the idea of a social
physics; that there are universal laws that regulate all human behavior:
'govern us in all we do, in all we say, in all we think'. Second, Bentham
shows his naturalistic inclinations by stating that these laws are grounded
in nature: 'Nature has placed mankind ...'. Third, Bentham attempts to
derive a moral theory from natural principles: 'It is for them alone to point
out what we ought to do ...   the standards of right and wrong ... are
fastened to their throne.'

Bentham is following the Enlightenment project of searching for the
natural laws of the social universe, that is, trying to duplicate Newton's
success by displacing his model and concepts on to moral philosophy. The
Utilitarians attempted, just as the eighteenth-century natural law
philosophers before them, to create a universal social science, to explain all
social phenomena by as few principles as possible, with these principles
grounded in nature. For Bentham there is one unifying principle to social

phenomena, the felicific calculus.[5]

The influence of Newton on Bentham extends to Bentham's treatment of pleasure (utility) as a physical force:

> The magnitude of a pleasure is composed of its intensity and its duration: to obtain it, supposing its intensity represented by a certain number of degrees, you multiply that number by the number expressive of the moments or atoms of time contained in its duration. Suppose two pleasures at the same degree of intensity - give to the second twice the duration of the first, the second is twice as great as the first. ...

> The quantity or degree of well-being experienced during any given length of time varies directly as the magnitude (i.e., the intensity multiplied by the duration) of the sum of the pleasures, and inversely at the magnitude of the sum the pains experienced during that same length of time. (Bentham quoted in Stark 1946, p. 598)

Bentham even suggests it is possible 'to apply arithmetical calculations of the elements of happiness' (Ibid.). The duration and intensity of pain and pleasure are clearly meant to be analogous with Newton's mass and distance. Bentham is trying to construct a natural law system, while criticizing the natural law philosophers for the very same thing. The only difference is that Bentham's final cause is nature, whereas divine providence is the final cause for the natural law philosophers, a difference in faith not in substance. Schumpeter (1954a, p. 132) summed up the natural law aspect of Utilitarianism best when he wrote:[6]

> The essential point to grasp is that utilitarianism was nothing but another natural-law system. This holds not only in the sense that the utilitarians were the historical successors of the seventeenth-century philosophers of natural law; ... but it holds also in the more significant sense, that in approach, in methodology, and in the nature of its results utilitarianism actually was another, the last natural law system. The program of

---

5. In his classic study on Utilitarianism, Elie Halevy (1972, p. 6) states that '[W]hat is known as utilitarianism ... can be defined as nothing but an attempt to apply the principles of Newton to the affairs of politics and morals.' Bentham's search for universal laws and his methodological individualism, led him to adopt the natural law philosophers' belief in a universal human nature. As Myrdal has noted, the Utilitarians believed 'in the universal and uniformity of human nature. They had taken over this belief from the eighteenth century philosophers of natural law and had never really abandoned it, although they denied it officially' (Myrdal 1954, pp. 26). Without this assumption, a Newtonian (i.e., mechanical) type social science, which for the time period meant being scientific, would not have been possible.

6. See also Schumpeter (1954b), pp. 22-23.

deriving, by light of reason, 'laws' about man in society from a very stable and highly simplified human nature fits the utilitarians not less than the (natural law) philosophers or the scholastics.

Mill's Rejection of Bentham

Bentham was the single most important intellectual influence on Mill. His education was singularly Utilitarian. The intellectual breakdown which prompted Mill's separation with the Utilitarians was most likely induced by the toll working on Bentham's *Rationale of Judicial Evidence* took on his young mind. Moreover, Mill's career can be seen as an attempt at correcting the inadequacies of Bentham's Utilitarianism while continuing Bentham's quest for a science of society analogous to the physical sciences.

Mill's mental crisis is an important event for our analysis for it causes him to evaluate all he had learned, that is, Utilitarianism. The one-sidedness of Mill's education, particularly the overemphasis of his intellectual development and the neglect of his emotional development, led him to question the usefulness of his life; could he be happy as a Utilitarian propagandist and social reformer? The twenty-year-old Mill felt he could not. The examination of the beliefs he had learned, coupled with exposure to continental thought, led him to reject Bentham's system as too narrow. Specifically, Mill repudiated their lack of what we have referred to as a 'historical sense' and their narrow conception of human nature. Patrick Gardiner (1959, p. 83) has noted: 'The Utilitarian interpretation of social phenomena was, in fact, one which was wholly unhistorical in approach, and it was Mill's growing awareness of the significance of historical studies, through his friendship with Carlyle and his reading of historians Guizet and Michelet, that helped to bring about a radical shift in his attitude towards the methodological questions raised by the investigation of society and politics.'

Mill's criticism of Bentham's view of human nature centered on the 'unusually slender stock of premises' (Mill 1962, p. 97). Mill writes: 'Man is conceived by Bentham as a being susceptible of pleasure and pains, and governed in all his conduct partly by the different modifications of self-interest, and the passions commonly classed as selfish, partly by sympathies, or occasionally antipathies, towards other beings. And here Bentham's conception of human nature stops' (Ibid. p. 99). What is left out?

Nothing is more curious than the absence of recognition in any of his writings of the existence of conscience. ... Nor is it only the moral part of man's nature, in the strict sense of the term - the desire of perfection, or the feeling of an approving or of an accusing conscience - that he overlooks; he but faintly recognises, as a fact in human nature, the pursuit of any other ideal end for its own sake. The sense of honour, and personal dignity - that feeling of personal exaltation and degradation which acts independently of other people's opinion, or even in defiance of it; the love of beauty, the passion of the artist; the love of order, of congruity, of consistency in all things, and conformity to their end; the love of power, not in the limited form of power over other human beings, but abstract power, the power of making our volitions effectual; the love of action, the thirst for movement and activity, a principle scarcely of less influence in human life than its opposite, the love of ease: - None of these powerful constituents of human nature are thought worthy of a place among the 'Springs of Action'; ... Man, that most complex being, is a very simple one in his eyes. (Ibid. pp. 100-101)

This limited view of human nature increasingly became evident with the growth in historical studies and exposure to different cultures. Mill states that had Bentham and his father had a wider exposure to different cultures, they clearly would have seen the limitations of their analysis; they were both intelligent and practical men. The increase in historical knowledge, coupled with the accelerating pace of social change in England brought about by the industrial revolution, led to a general questioning of Utilitarianism as a philosophy and basis of politics. Burrow (1966, pp. 65-6) has observed that at the time of Mill's transition: 'The constants in the utilitarian system were turning into variables; and the natural result was a new interest in the other factors in the social situation, history and society.'

Mill on the Method of Social Inquiry

Mill's determination to construct a science of society led him to first investigate what should be the proper methods to be employed in such an enterprise. Mill accepted the view that moral philosophy was part of natural philosophy making, as noted above, a distinction between physical science and moral science. In his essay 'Nature' Mill rejects the use of nature as a standard of right or wrong, because, among other reasons, nature is morally neutral, producing both beneficial and harmful effects. 'The scheme of nature', Mill writes, 'regarded in its whole extent cannot have had, for its sole or even principle object, the good of human or other sentiment beings. What good it brings to them is mostly the result of their own exertions' (Mill 1958, p. 44). Mill, however, upholds the view that human behavior is within the realm of nature. In the first chapter of Book 6 of A System of Logic (Mill 1874, p. 581) entitled 'On the Logic of the Moral Sciences' Mill confronts this issue:

> At the threshold of this inquiry we are met by an objection, which, if not removed, would be fatal to the attempt to treat human conduct as a subject of science. Are the actions of human beings, like all other natural events, subject to invariable laws? Does that constancy of causation, which is the foundation of every scientific theory of successive phenomena, really obtain among them? This is often denied; and for the sake of systematic completeness, if not from any very urgent practical necessity, the question should receive a deliberate answer in this place.

In answering this objection, Mill makes the distinction between exact and inexact sciences. Exact sciences, for which Mill uses astronomy as an example, are highly developed sciences in which all or almost all of the relevant information is available for the discovery of the laws of nature and for the explanation and prediction of phenomena that is within the realm of the particular science. The moral sciences, those which are concerned with human behavior, have not developed to the point of exact sciences. Lacking the necessary information, they are thus inexact sciences. The difference is in degree, not in substance. 'The science of human nature is of this description [inexact science]. It falls far short of the standard of exactness now realized in Astronomy; but there is no reason that it should not be as much a science as Tidology is, or as Astronomy was when its calculations had only mastered the main phenomena, but not the perturbations' (Ibid. p. 588).

Mill's pronouncements on methodology are extensive, yet over a hundred years after his death there is still a dispute as to what method Mill felt appropriate to the study of society. The crux of the disagreement centers on whether Mill advocated the deductive or the inductive method. Followers of the deductive method frequently place Mill as one of their intellectual progenitors (the primary exception to this trend is Popper), while those who advocate the importance of induction cite Mill's frequent use of induction and his defense of induction as the basis of all science.[7] As with many of the contradictions in the social sciences, the confusion stems from the uneasy relationship between historical and social analysis and the attempt to construct a science of society modeled after the natural sciences.

Mill's Natural Law Outlook can be seen in his adherence to the law of

---

7. Alan Ryan's *John Stuart Mill* (1970), especially Chapters 2-4, provides an excellent overview of this debate and a solution which should have ended all disputes, yet seems to have not. See also Hollander (1985) for an account of this dispute with regards to Mill's economics.

universal causation.[8] This view holds that all phenomena, including social phenomena, are determined (caused) by that which exists at the same time and that which has previously existed. This is a deterministic view of the universe. What the law of universal causation leaves out is the possibility of self-movement, of free will in the fullest sense of the phrase, as we see in Mill's science of Ethology, at least in the short run. Mill's methodology differentiates between levels of explanation. The highest level is that of a natural law and at this level deduction is the proper method to be employed. Yet such exact sciences are rare, in Mill's day as in our own. Thus these sciences must rely on generalization derived from induction, what Mill called empirical or statistical laws. Such efforts cannot be the basis of an exact science yet they are useful in suggesting and in verifying natural laws. Mill calls this combined use of deduction and induction 'inverse deduction'.[9]

As has been stated above, Mill objected to the lack of historical context in Bentham's system, yet he agreed with Bentham's goal of a science of society modeled after the natural sciences. History had shown the inadequacies of Utilitarianism, yet could it, through induction, be the basis of moral philosophy? To this, Mill answered no. Mill's reasoning is centered on the reliability of historical observation and the logical problems of induction - the movement from particulars to universals. Commenting on Sedgwick's claim that in the study of man, history is analogous to experiment in the study of nature, Mill writes (Mill 1868, Vol. 1, pp. 138-9):

> The evidence of history, instead of being analogous to that of experiment, leaves the philosophy of society in exactly the state in which physical science was before the method of experiment was introduced. The professor should reflect, that we cannot make experiments in history. ... There is not a fact in history which is not susceptible of as many different explanations as there are possible theories of human affairs. Not only is history not the source of political philosophy, but the profoundest political philosophy is requisite to explain history: without it, all in history, which is worth understanding, remains mysterious. ... History is not the foundation, but the verification, of the social science: it corroborates, and often suggests, political truths, but it cannot prove them. The proof of them is drawn from the laws of human nature, ... [T]he usefulness of history depends upon its being kept in second place.

---

8. See *A System of Logic*, Book 3, especially chapter 5.

9. It should be noted that Mill's induction is always from particulars to particulars and not from particulars to universals, the standard view of induction.

Mill's analysis of history and historical knowledge is best seen in his essays on the historians who influenced him, particularly Michelet. In 'Michelet's History of France' (Ibid., Vol. 2) Mill describes the three stages of historical inquiry. The first stage analyzes the past from the viewpoint of the present, placing the historian's thoughts, feelings and motives into the peoples of the past. This is certainly inadequate, for it distorts the meaning of past events.[10] In the second stage of historical analysis, the attempt is made to understand the past as it was then comprehended, 'to realize a true and living picture of the past time, clothed in its circumstances and peculiarities' (Ibid. p. 205). The third stage amounts to a philosophy of history, and allows the possibility of a science of history.

> [T]he highest stage of historical investigation, in which the aim is not simply to compose histories, but to construct a science of history. In this view, the whole of the events which have befallen the human race, and the states through which it has passed, are regarded as a series of phenomena, produced by causes, and susceptible of explanation. ...
>
> To find on what principles, derived from the nature of man and the laws of the outward world, each state of society and of the human mind produced that which came after it; and whether there can be traced any order of production sufficiently definite to show what future states of society may be expected to emanate from the circumstances which exist at present, - is the aim of historical philosophy in its third stage. (Ibid. p. 207)

As for the possibility of developing such a history solely from deduction, based on the laws of nature and the laws of human nature, Mill (1874, p. 633) was doubtful.

> But, while it is an imperative rule never to introduce any generalization from history into the social science unless sufficient grounds can be pointed out for it in human nature, I do not think any one will contend that it would have been possible, setting out from the principles of human nature and from the general circumstances of the position of our species, to determine *a priori* the order in which human development must take place, and to predict, consequently, the general facts of history up to the present.

According to Mill, history at best can 'afford empirical laws of society'

---

10. This is, for the most part, essentially the historical method of the Scottish Enlightenment, particularly their use of conjectural history.

(Ibid. p. 634); it is in the laws of human nature and the deduction from them that we can construct a science of society.

Mill places much emphasis on the laws of human nature. 'All phenomena of society', Mill (Ibid. p. 607) writes, 'are phenomena of human nature, generated by the action of outward circumstances upon masses of human beings; and if, therefore, the phenomena of human thought, feeling, and action are subject to fixed laws, the phenomena of society can not but confirm to fixed laws.' Even more forceful is Mill's statement (Ibid. p. 608):

> The laws of the phenomena of society are, and can be, nothing but the laws of the actions and passions of human beings united together in the social state. Men, however, in a state of society are still men; their actions and passions are obedient to the laws of individual human nature. Men are not, when brought together, converted into another kind of substance, ... Human beings in society have no properties but those which are derived from, and may be resolved into, the laws of the nature of individual man.

The limited view of human nature held by Bentham was replaced by Mill with the science of Ethology - the science of character formation. It is here where we find the most quintessentially Millian approach and theory, an attempt to mix a prioristic natural law theory and the results of history. Mill objected to Bentham's narrow picture of mankind not because it was completely wrong, but because it assumed that human nature was universal and a constant. Yet history demonstrated to Mill the 'extraordinary pliability of human nature'. Mill's response to this contradiction was to separate the pure science of human nature - Ethology - from the actually observed human nature. Mill states (Ibid. p. 599): 'mankind have not one universal character, but there exist universal laws of the Formation of Character'. Ethology studies these laws. Mill calls Ethology 'the Exact Science of Human Nature' (Ibid. p. 602) which is based on real laws. It is also a deductive science, not based on empirical generalization, but deduced from introspection. Yet Mill (Ibid. p. 605) brings induction into the picture by stating that:

> It is hardly necessary again to repeat that, as in every other deductive science, verification *a posteriori* must proceed *pari passu* with deduction *a priori*. The inference given by theory as to the type of character which would be formed by any given circumstance must be tested by specific experience of those circumstances whenever obtainable; and the conclusions of the science as a whole must undergo a perpetual verification and correction from the general remarks afforded by

common experience respecting human nature in our own age, and by
history respecting times gone by. The conclusions of theory can not be
trusted, unless confirmed by observation; nor those of observation,
unless they can be affiliated to theory, by deducing them from the laws
of human nature, and from a close analysis of the circumstances of the
particular situation.

Here we see the method of inverse deduction clearly spelled out.

Human behavior is perceived as being determined by natural laws and
given circumstances, as with any other object or being within the realm of
nature. The main problem with developing an exact science which could
predict human behavior, according to Mill, is the inability of obtaining all
the relevant information. If we want to predict the actions of a single
human we must know completely their history and the state of their mind.
This information, particularly regarding our knowledge of the mind, is far
from available. One of John Maynard Keynes's great insights is that this
type of information cannot be known, for our present state of mind is the
result not only of our past, but also of our expectations about the future,
which is not only unknown, but is unknowable.

The pliability of human nature stems from the changing circumstances,
which act as a changing friction to the social physics of Ethology. The
major difference between Mill's conception of this human science and the
physical sciences is that in the long run humans can adjust and change their
character, both individually and for society as a whole. Mill cites
education, in the broadest sense of the word, as playing the key role in the
shaping of individual character. The implicit weakness in Mill's theory of
socialization, is that he does not adequately examine the role of social
institutions in the process of character formation and he leaves out almost
completely human free will. He states that in the long run individuals can
change their character, thus leading to a change in the factors which
determine their behavior, yet the behavior is still completely determined by
laws and circumstances; one of the circumstances, character, has merely
changed. Yet if humans have the free will to shape their character over the
long run then they must have the free will to make choices in the short run
which reflect the same free will. Mill is avoiding the dangerous possibility
of self-movement; dangerous in that it conflicts with his natural law
preconception of the law of universal causation. This preconception causes
Mill to not fully appreciate the fullness of the human subject, particularly
the fact that societies are human creations and not creations of nature. Such
an insight would certainly lead Mill to reject the use of the physical
sciences as the model to emulate for the construction of the social sciences.

Mill felt that, given all relevant data, human action would be as predictable as phenomena in the physical sciences; the problem is that all relevant data is not available. Mill agrees with Bentham that human actions are deterministic according to the laws of nature and that if this is true of the individual it is also true of society. Mill had rejected Bentham's conception of human nature, not his conception of society and the science of society. From the study of history Mill learns of the 'extraordinary pliability of human nature' (Mill 1924, p. 125) and of the diversity of societies. How can this be reconciled with the view of natural laws of society and human nature. This very contention was at the heart of Mill's objections to Utilitarianism, and also at the decreasing ability of classical political economy to adequately describe and interpret the economy of the nineteenth century (Lowe 1965, p. 194). Mill's solution to this dilemma was to separate theory into levels of analysis. Mill felt that although societies and human nature were in the realm of nature and thus subject, via the law of universal causation, to natural laws, these laws worked in conjunction with other factors, particularly the given circumstances and context of the phenomena. These factors are treated as analogous to friction in the laws of motion. The laws of motion are natural laws. Yet, in order to fully understand and predict the actual movements of objects one had to account for the other factors, such as friction, which influence the actual movement of bodies. Mill gives these other factors much more leeway in the moral sciences, for although at any given moment human activity is determined by fixed laws, over time humans, through education, can develop and change their character, leading to a change in what determines human behavior. 'The circumstances in which mankind are placed', Mill (Ibid. p. 632) states, 'operating according to their own laws and to the laws of human nature, form the characters of human beings; but the human beings, in their turn, mould and shape the circumstances for themselves and for those who come after them. From this reciprocal action there must necessarily result either a cycle or a progress.' Mill (Ibid. pp. 632-3) goes on to state: 'The progressiveness of the human race is the foundation on which a method of philosophizing in the social sciences has been of late years erected, ... This method, which is now generally adopted by the most advanced thinkers on the Continent, consists in attempting, by a study and analysis of the general facts of history, to discover the laws of progress: which law, once ascertained ... enable us to predict future events.' By progressiveness, Mill means cumulative change; he states that we cannot impute any providential design in this process.

Here Mill is coming very close to the view of society as a process discussed in Chapter 2 and applied to Adam Smith in Chapter 4. Mill is emulating Smith's mixture of individual analysis and historical and institutional analysis (socialization, or what Mill refers to as character formation). Mill has improved on Smith because he allows for a variety of character formation and institutional arrangements. Mill writes in his *Autobiography*: 'all questions of political institutions are relative, and that different stages of human progress not only will have, but ought to have different institutions' (1924, p. 114). Mill's chapter on 'Competition and Customs' in the *Principles of Political Economy* is another example of his recognition of relativity of social institutions. Yet, as with Smith, Mill's account is ultimately unsatisfactory, although highly suggestive, and for the same reasons. Mill holds fast to the idea that all explanations must be in terms of the laws of human nature, and must be explained in terms of individual actions, a view which is consistent with methodological individualism. Mill is constrained to such a social theory by his following of the physical sciences as his model, a point noted by Alan Ryan (1970, p. 149):

> Mill, it is clear, wants to see a sociology which can mirror for social life the achievements of Newtonian mechanics; ... In the search for laws of social behavior, differences between social phenomena and those studied by mechanics became apparent, and this leads Mill to modify the deductive simplicity of physics, in favor of an approach which he, following Comte, calls the method of inverse deduction. ... The claim that there can be a science of society similar in its methodological structure to physics, rests on Mill's assumptions that the laws governing the behavior of people in social interaction can be inferred mechanically from the laws governing individual people in isolation from society.

Constrained to a view of a deterministic and atomistic universe ruled by natural laws, Mill bases his social thought on universals. The analysis of particulars in social phenomena, which highlighted the relativistic nature of human activity and society, could not be allowed to interfere with the search for a science of society modeled after the natural sciences. Mill clearly knew of the dangers of a prioristic theorizing, yet he could not see that his own social thought was based on a set of preconceptions, the Natural Law Outlook, which could only be held a priori. Mill senses the problem of his approach, stemming from the failure of Bentham in his efforts, and divides social thought into a pure theory, which is deductive and which is at the level of natural laws, and an applied theory, which deals with actual social phenomena. This latter analysis is very important for Mill, for he always saw himself as a social reformer. Furthermore, as an empiricist, he felt that all knowledge must be based, at least at some level, on observation. Yet, in the final analysis, history is relegated to the verification of theories and for suggesting, by the construction of empirical laws, possible natural laws, but in the science of society, it must always take second place.

Mill's Political Economy

In Mill's political economy, the tension between the search for natural laws and the analysis of social and historical context is much greater than in any other aspect of Mill's thought. The reason for this is simple. It is in Mill's political economy where much of the social reform that he advocated is put forth. Thus Mill's economics required substantial historical and social analysis. To support Mill's reforms, however, Mill needed a theory which had the highest credentials as a science, both for his own satisfaction as a scholar and for the success of the advocated reforms.

The tension manifests itself in the famous dichotomy between production and distribution. Mill accepts, with little important modifications, the economics of Ricardo as it applies to production.[11] On production, Mill writes (Mill 1987, pp. 199-200): 'The laws and conditions of the production of wealth partake of the character of physical truths. There is nothing optional or arbitrary in them. Whatever mankind produces, must be produced in the modes, and under the conditions, imposed by the constitution of external things, and by the inherent properties of their own bodily and mental structure. ... We cannot alter the ultimate properties either of matter or mind, but can only employ those properties more or less successfully, to bring about the events in which we are interested.' Mill's analysis of this aspect of economics is fully supported by his views on methodology, which were first worked out in his essay 'On the Definition of Political Economy; and on the Method of Investigation proper to it' (Mill 1974). In the essay on methodology Mill argues that political economy is an abstract and a prioristic science like geometry.Mill (Ibid. p. 146) states very strongly the a prioristic nature of political economy:

> But we go further than to affirm that the method *a priori* is a legitimate mode of philosophical investigation in the moral sciences; we contend that it is the only mode. We affirm that the method *a posterior*, or that of specific experience, is altogether inefficacious in those sciences, as a means of arriving at any considerable body of valuable truth; though it admits of being usefully applied in aid of the method *a priori*, and even

---

11. Ricardo's economic theory is almost a caricature of a prioristic natural law theorizing. Ricardo's only saving grace is that his model of society is based on assumptions which basically held at Ricardo's time.

forms an indispensable supplement to it.

Mill is even more forceful in the *Logic*, arguing that since political economy considers only that part of human nature which is concerned with wealth, and since that part of human nature is ruled by a single law of human nature then political economy is clearly a science on a par with other deductive sciences. Thus, in his analysis of production, Mill adopts not only the method of Bentham, but also the narrow conception of human nature. Mill, however, is very much aware of the limitations of political economy as a deductive science. He states that anyone who would attempt to apply the results of theory to any real economic issue without first fitting it to the particular circumstances in which we find the economic phenomena, 'places himself in the wrong' (Ibid. p. 145)[12].

However, Mill states, in the realm of the distribution of society's product, the laws of nature no longer hold, being replaced by the laws and customs of mankind:

> It [adherence to natural laws] is not so with the Distribution of wealth. That is a matter of human institutions solely. ... [I]n the social state, in every state except total solitude, any disposal whatever of them can only take place by the consent of society, or rather of those who dispose of its active force. ... The distribution of wealth, therefore, depends on the laws and customs of society. The rules by which it is determined are what the opinions and feelings of the ruling portion of the community make them, and are very different in different ages and countries; and might be still more different, if mankind so chose. (Mill 1987, p. 200)

Mill's reforms came under this aspect of economics, and it is here that Mill relies on historical and social analysis.

The neoclassical economists who followed Mill took great exception to Mill's separation of production and distribution into different spheres. Certainly both production and distribution must be part of the same system. Although the neoclassical critics of Mill have touched upon an important truth, they have done so only accidentally, for they felt that both production and distribution were within the realm of nature, determined by natural laws. In fact, the marginal productivity theory of income distribution was designed to show just that. Mill's error was in placing production under the determination of natural laws, when in actuality nature plays the same role in both production and distribution - minimal. Just as the physical production of commodities is to an extent limited by the laws of nature, that

---

12. We see in the next chapter that this is exactly what Walras suggests economists do.

is one has to follow physical laws in the use of physical inputs etc., so too distribution. The resources of society must be distributed in a manner so that the physical requirements of society, and of the individuals in a society, are met. If these basic necessities are not fulfilled then the society will not be a viable entity. Yet these minimum requirements place very few constraints on the manner in which a particular society produces and distributes output, especially on developed capitalist societies. Most societies, particularly the one Mill was writing about, and even more so for our own, produce much more then the minimum necessary for social reproduction. All the interesting questions for a modern capitalistic economy revolve around the creation and disposal of the surplus. The existence of poverty and hunger in contemporary advanced capitalistic societies, particularly the United States of America, is a social embarrassment, caused by how they distribute their output, not because of any insufficiency in output. Similarly, all aspects of the production of goods and services, beyond the minimum physical laws, are humanly created and determined, and in no way the result of natural laws. Consider the production of steel. To a certain extent the choice of inputs to use to produce a particular type of steel is influenced by nature. One could not substitute butter for coal, coke or iron ore. Yet, the most significant factor in how steel is produced at any given time is the state of technology, and technology is a human creation. Furthermore, the assignment of costs, of what particular inputs will be renumerated, and at what rates, is socially determined. In the case of steel production, one of the costs, pollution, is not borne by the participants, but by society. Clearly man, not nature, is the active and important factor.

It is often suggested that technology is merely the discovery and application of the laws of nature, thus nature is still the dominant force, but such a view can only be advanced if one has excluded history and social institutions from one's conception of human activity. The most important development in the nineteenth century which is attributed to technology is the rise of the factory system. However an historical analysis would show that the factory system sprang from the desire of employers to control the employees and not because of economies of scale due to technology. The type of technology that is developed in any particular society reflects what that society values and needs, or more correctly, following Mill, by 'the opinions and feelings of the ruling portion of the community' (Ibid.). Had Mill applied an historical and social analysis to the questions of production, especially to the factory system and the social division of labor, he might have come across this point. Yet such an act would have meant the abandonment of the search for a science of society on a par with the natural sciences, a step Mill's natural law preconceptions prevent him from taking.

Mill's analysis of money offers another illustration of the limitations the Natural Law Outlook placed on Mill's analysis. In the *Principles of Political Economy* (1987, p. 488) Mill states: 'There cannot, in short, be intrinsically a more insignificant thing, in the economy of society, than money; except in the character of a contrivance for sparing time and labour. It is a machine for doing quickly and commodiously, what would be done, though less quickly and commodiously, without it: and like many other kinds of machinery, it exerts a distinct and independent influence of its own only when it gets out of order.' It is often remarked that Mill is one of the outstanding representations of the quantity theory of money school on these matters and this is certainly true. And as with all other quantity theorists, past and present, such a view is only possible if one, like Mill, excludes the historical and social aspects of the development of money; one could hold such a theory (currently under the guise of monetarism) if one is completely ignorant of history or if one's conception of monetary history is conjectural history or what is now referred to as rational reconstruction. But as Wesley Mitchell, one of the few outstanding historians on money, states, such a view is counter to the facts. Mitchell (1967, p. 579), commenting on the above passage of Mill, writes:

> If one takes a long historical perspective it would be hard to make a statement which is more demonstrably false than that people who make very little use of money did, less quickly and commodiously, what people are enabled to do when they have developed full-fledged pecuniary institutions. It is possible to go a good deal further than this and to hold that the use of money has been a far-reaching influence in shaping the development of culture at large and economic activities as an inherent part of culture. Also the use of money has come to exercise a profound disciplinary influence over men's thoughts in all sorts of direct and subtle and indirect ways. The use of money affects men's habits of thought. The very calculating frame of mind, which is one of the essential characteristics of the psychology that Bentham developed and which Mill accepted [as applied to economics], is in large measure a quality that men have learned in the use of money.

Mill's delegation of history to second place prevents him from connecting his insights into the processes of character formation, his science of Ethology, with the type of behavior observed in a market setting. Had he done this, he would have seen that the rational economic man, which he accepts from Bentham as an accurate description of man in his economic activities, is the result of market society, not the cause. Furthermore, he could have joined his conception of the pliability of human nature and the relativity and pliability of human institutions with his analysis of production, seeing it, as Marx did, as a social activity, and thus equally open to, and in need of, reform. Moreover, his analysis of power, which in the political realm was in many ways ahead of its time, could have been infused into his economic analysis, thus seeing production as the social division of labor, and not the application of the laws of nature.

Like Smith, Mill's historical analysis and consideration of social institutions give his theories and explanations a great richness, frequently yielding important insights. Yet the attempt to construct a science of society, with the natural sciences as the model, ultimately prevents an adequate explanation of man's economic activities.

6. Natural Law and the Marginal Utility Revolution

In the 1870s the marginal utility revolution started a process whereby the scope and content of political economy would become drastically altered. The eventual change is highlighted by the transformation of the name of the discipline from political economy to economics. The eradication of the adjective 'political' reflects the elimination of context from the analysis. Just as the change in terminology was gradual, so to was the decline in historical and social context, yet the trend to construct an economic theory separate from the context of economic phenomena is clear.

The question as to whether the marginal utility revolution represents a break with classical political economy does not produce universal agreement amongst historians of economic thought. A good number of historians of economic thought view the emergence of marginalism as part of a continual process of scientific development in which no real break with the classical economists occurs (Blaug 1978). The argument of this chapter is that the marginal utility revolution contained elements of both abrupt change and continuity. From this perspective, we can see that in regard to method, scope and content, the marginalists have little in common with classical thought. Nonetheless, a concern for long-run equilibrium prices; support of laissez-faire policies; the desire to be scientific (emulate the natural sciences); and the treatment of economic forces, laws, and economic man as elements of nature are common to both classical and neoclassical economics. This chapter, it is hoped, will clarify the origins of these differences and similarities, by arguing that the marginal utility revolution was a continuation of the classicals' search for natural laws in the social universe (i.e., economic phenomena controlled by natural laws), while at the same time abandoning the classicals' concern for historical and social context. The classical economists felt that the laws of economic society could be understood only in their historical and cultural context, which is why the scope and method of classical economics is partly historical and institutional. This aspect of classical analysis was abandoned by the marginalists, thus creating a new and distinct economics.

That there are essential differences between classical and neoclassical economics is hard not to recognize.   Practically all the important marginalists, with the notable exception of Alfred Marshall, viewed their work as a distinct break with the classical school and went to great lengths to stress this point. The marginalists contended that they had developed a scientific economics. Yet it is in their very concern for the development of a 'scientific' economics and 'scientific' methods of analysis that we see their continuity with the classical economists! The marginalists accept completely the classical view of the existence of natural laws in the economic realm of human existence and, again following the classical economists, they accept without reservation or scrutiny the idea that the social universe is ordered in a manner similar to the physical universe. The marginal utility revolution is thus a continuation of the Natural Law Outlook embodied in classical theory.

1. On Preconceptions

The marginalists accepted the Natural Law Outlook uncritically and without any serious analysis of the validity of this view.   It was thus a preconception. Preconceptions are 'convictions that shape the general trend of a man's thinking without being themselves submitted to critical scrutiny' (Mitchell 1950, p. 203). They are accepted uncritically as the building blocks with which scientists start their theoretical investigations. They are frequently the accepted common sense of a given historical time, but can also include personal prejudices and 'wishes dressed up as convictions' (Ibid.). Preconceptions cannot be analyzed by those who hold them, for once we examine them they cease to be preconceptions and become instead postulates and assumptions. Wesley Mitchell has written that:

> Preconceptions are ... intriguing ... [because they] are parts of us. They grow up in our minds. We are but dimly aware of the role they play in shaping our conclusions about the matters on which we focus attention .... [E]ven in our most rigorous work we are influenced by them. (Ibid.)

Since preconceptions are accepted uncritically, they frequently define what we accept as the foundation of our knowledge, our epistemology.

As a science develops and matures it usually begins to investigate its preconceptions, stripping them away layer by layer, providing a clearer understanding of the foundations and logic of the discipline. In economics, this process was taken up in the late nineteenth century by members of the British Historical school (Leslie 1967 [1888]) and in America by Thorstein Veblen (1899; 1900). However, with a handful of exceptions, the profession has not been receptive to such investigations. In fact, Jevons and Menger attacked both the validity and the usefulness of such an analysis.[1] Before we get more deeply into the problem of the natural law preconceptions of the marginalists, it is important to first examine the dual nature of classical theory so that we can highlight both the continuity and divergence between classical and neoclassical economics.

Most critical assessments of the marginal utility revolution emphasize technique over substance. This is accomplished by focusing on the importance of the marginal principle while de-emphasizing the role of utility. This has been best stated by T. W. Hutchison's often quoted comment: 'What was important in marginal utility was the adjective rather than the noun' (Hutchison 1953, p. 16). This approach to the history of economic thought reached its apex in Schumpeter's *History of Economic Analysis* where he argues that one can analyze the history of economics as the successive development and refinement of techniques independent of the content of the theories.[2]

The importance of the utility concept and its most consistent application, Utilitarianism, for the marginal utility revolution, as well as for modern neoclassical economics, should not be underestimated. This is particularly evident when we consider that marginal utility theory is primarily a value theory and the function of value theory is to depict the underlying ordering properties of the economy. The marginalists claim that value is determined by utility is an implicit acceptance of some form of Utilitarianism, usually the Utilitarian model of human actions.[3] The previous chapter argued that Utilitarianism is a natural law system, including all three elements which we noted in Chapter 2, and is another source of natural law ideas and concepts which the marginal utility revolution adopts.

---

1. See Jevons (1965) for his comments on Leslie. As for Menger, the main point of his *Investigations* is to argue the uselessness of historical research for the development of pure theory.

2. This is ironic considering Schumpeter's analysis of the importance of visions. Schumpeter does note that the early marginalists did have basically the same vision as Smith and Mill, but he was referring to their conception of competition and the economic process, not to their preconceptions. (Schumpeter 1954a, p. 892)

3. For the importance of the term 'utility,' see Veblen (1909), Downey (1910) and Stark (1947). For the mainstream interpretation, see Rosentein-Rodan (1960).

2. The Natural Law Preconceptions of Jevons, Menger and Walras

In examining the preconceptions of William Stanley Jevons, Carl Menger and Léon Walras we find that, regardless of their many differences, they all held the view that the social universe in general and economic phenomena in particular were regulated by natural laws. It was also their opinion that the method of investigation for the social sciences should be similar to that of the physical sciences. In this section we look at each of the three original marginalists to examine the extent of their natural law preconceptions.

W. Stanley Jevons

Jevons's natural law preconceptions are evident in many aspects of his work, but are most transparent in his adherence to Utilitarianism. Jevons's debt to Utilitarianism was considerable; in the preface to the second edition of *The Theory of Political Economy* (1879, p. vii) he wrote: 'In this work I have attempted to treat Economy as a Calculus of Pleasure and Pain.' Bentham's influence is felt throughout the *Theory*; pleasure and pain are for Jevons, 'undoubtedly the ultimate objects of the Calculus of Economics' (Ibid. p. 40). Jevons treats men as hedonistic creatures because he believes this is how we find them in nature (Ibid. p. 41). In fact, Jevons criticized John Stuart Mill for his abandonment of Bentham's conception of human nature, objecting specifically to Mill's claim that human nature was 'extraordinarily pliable'. Jevons rejects Mill's view of human nature in no uncertain terms: '[N]o phrase could better express the misapprehensions of human nature which, it is hoped, will cease forever. ... Human nature is one of the last things which can be called 'pliable'. Granite rocks can be more easily moulded than the poor savages that hide among them' (Jevons 1890, p. 290). Elsewhere he writes 'that there are natural laws even of human nature which ... [men] cannot break' and 'it is indispensable that in every thing we do we should obey the natural laws under which we are placed' (Jevons 1981, pp. 51; 39).

Jevons, like the other marginalists, thought that value was dependent upon utility. 'Repeated reflection and inquiry have led me to the somewhat novel opinion, that value depends entirely upon utility' and in order for us to 'arrive at a satisfactory theory of exchange' we must 'trace out carefully the natural laws of the variation of utility' (Jevons 1879, pp. 1-2). These natural laws reveal that the utility of a good is a function of 'the quantity of [the] commodity in our possession', that is, its scarcity which is, in turn, a condition of nature. Thus value is determined by two natural forces: man's hedonistic nature (from which the law of diminishing marginal utility comes) and scarcity.

Jevons's natural law preconceptions are also manifest in his claim that economics is a physio-mathematical science, and therefore should adopt the same method of analysis.

> The Theory of Economy ... presents a close analogy to the science of Statical Mechanics, and the Laws of Exchange are found to resemble the Laws of Equilibrium of a lever as determined by the principle of virtual velocities. The nature of Wealth and Value is explained by the consideration of indefinitely small amounts of pleasure and pain, just as the Theory of Statics is made to rest upon the equality of indefinitely small amounts of energy. (1879, p. vii)

For Jevons, economics is a mathematical science because it deals with quantities (Ibid. p. 4) and he writes, 'there can be no doubt that pleasure, pain, labour, utility, value, wealth, money, capital, &c. are all notions admitting of quantity' (Ibid. pp. 10-11). To demonstrate the applicability of mathematical reasoning for the moral sciences, Jevons uses Bentham's Utilitarianism, thus giving approval of Bentham's attempt at 'moral Newtonianism'. The object of his scientific investigations were 'the natural laws of Economics' (Ibid. p. 12), and 'the tracing out of the mechanics of self-interest and utility' (Ibid. p. xviii). While explicating his equation of exchange, he added, 'the equations employed do not differ in general character from those which are really treated in many branches of physical science' (Ibid. p. 110).

In his *The Principles of Economics* (1965, p. 198) Jevons states that economic theory 'consists of those general laws which are so simple in nature, and so deeply grounded in the constitution of man and the outer world, that they remain the same throughout all those ages which are within our consideration'. Thus the laws of economics are universal truths, applicable under any institutional setting.

Jevons (1879, pp. 19-20) believed that natural laws could best be understood intuitively:

> The science of Economics, ... is in some degree peculiar, owing to the fact, pointed out by J. S. Mill and Cairnes, that its ultimate laws are known to us immediately by intuition, ... That every person will

choose the greater apparent good; that human wants are more or less quickly satiated; that prolonged labour becomes more and more painful, are a few of the simple inductions on which we can proceed to reason deductively with great confidence. From these axioms we can deduce the laws of supply and demand.

Jevons felt that eventually statistical analysis would develop to the point where his theories could be empirically verified, but for the development of these theories, observation and history are irrelevant; knowledge of natural laws is inborn.

In his Introduction to Cossa's *Guide to Political Economy* (1880, p. ix), Jevons does admit to some value for historical investigations, writing:

> One valuable result which will probably be derived from the reading of Professor Cossa's work is the conviction that the historical method must play a large part in economic science. Without for a moment admitting, with some extreme advocates of that method, [Leslie as an example] that there is no such thing as an abstract science of Economics, the student will readily become convinced that in such matters as land tenure, agriculture, the organization of industry, taxation, &c., theory must be applied with very large allowances for physical and historical circumstances.

Yet Jevons would not let historical investigations interfere with the development of theory. The minor role Jevons assigned to historical factors and historical investigations in economics can be seen in his *Money and the Mechanism of Exchange*, a typical example of Jevons's applied work. In the preface Jevons states: 'In preparing this volume, I have attempted to write a descriptive essay on the past and present monetary systems of the world, the materials employed to make money, the regulations under which the coins are struck and issued, the natural laws which govern their circulations' (1882, p. v). Jevons then proceeds to give a history of money where the broad themes are dominated by conjectural history with particulars used to add substance. Yet an investigation that is concerned with the actual history of money would develop the theories from the particulars, instead of attempting to fit the particulars into the preconceived history. Jevons writes: 'The earliest form of exchange must have consisted in giving what was not wanted directly for that which was wanted' (Ibid. p. 3). Why? Because Jevons's theory of exchange, which is built on individualistic and hedonistic foundations, dictates that such a history must have happened.[4] In Jevons's mind this theory is a law of nature. Jevons

---

4. Social anthropology (Mauss 1967) has since demonstrated that this is contrary to the actual history of exchange.

then proceeds to analyze the difficulties of barter and the development of money from these inefficiencies and difficulties. The historical record shows that money was developed long before exchange and market forces played an important role in the solution to the economic problem, that money was typically first used in ceremonial exchange and that barter exchange economies are myths. The rest of Jevons's analysis suffers from this shallow conjectural history, treating money at all times and in all places as having the same essence, the same functions, as it does today. Jevons's attempt to discover the 'natural principles which govern the use and circulation of coins' (Ibid. p. 67) necessitates his avoidance of the actual history of money.

Carl Menger

Menger's natural law preconceptions can be seen in three aspects of his work: the desire to investigate the 'essences' of economic phenomena; the classification of economics as a 'theoretical science' in which the object is to search for 'exact laws'; and the establishment of his theoretical system on primary elements which are naturally determined.

Menger was a social ontologist, believing that a 'general plan of reality exists. All social phenomena [are] conceived in relation to this master plan. This structure of reality serves both as a logical starting point and as a criterion of validity' (Kauder 1957, p. 417). According to Menger, actual economic phenomena do not give us information about the overall design of the social universe. For this we need to comprehend 'essences' - 'the reality underlying phenomena' (Ibid. p. 413). Thus, in order to understand an economic fact we must get behind its actual existence; we 'understand [the phenomenon] when we recognized the reason for its existence and for its characteristic quality (the reason for its being and for its being as it is)' (Menger 1985, p. 43).

Menger's objective is to try and understand essences in order to arrive at 'exact laws'. This is the purpose of his economics. In *Investigations into the Method of the Social Sciences* (1985), Menger makes the distinction between theoretical sciences and historical-empirical sciences. The latter study corporeal entities, actual concrete phenomena as they appear in history and in reality. Theoretical science explores essences and exact laws, and is the ultimate aim of science. Much of the debate between Menger and the historical school revolves around Menger's contention that only a theoretical investigation into essences, separated from actual phenomena, can arrive at exact laws:

> Exact research reduces real phenomena to their simplest elements,
> thought of as strictly typical, and attempts to determine their strictly
> typical relationships, their 'laws of nature' ... The development of *real*
> phenomena, accordingly, exerts no influence on the way in which exact
> research undertakes to solve the theoretical problem. (Ibid. p. 112)

Menger's 'exact laws' are, as Kauder has described them, 'the
Aristotelian forms which actualize the potential, i.e., they provide laws and
concepts valid for all times and places' (Kauder 1957, p. 415). In his
Investigations, Menger frequently points out that what he calls 'exact laws'
are commonly known as 'laws of nature', and that his 'exact method'
(theoretical science) is analogous to the physical sciences' investigations into
natural phenomena: the 'analogy of social phenomena and natural
organisms' (Menger 1985, p. 131). Specifically, Menger argues that law,
language, the origins of markets, the origins of communities and states, and
his most famous example, the origins and development of money, are the
result of a 'natural process' (Ibid. p. 130).

Menger reduced economics to its most basic elements - needs, satisfaction
and goods - upon which he built his analysis:

> The most original factors of human economy are the needs, the goods
> offered directly to humans by nature (both the consumption goods and
> the means of production concerned), and the desire for the most complete
> satisfaction of needs possible. ... All these factors are ultimately given
> by the particular situation, independent of human choice. The starting
> point and goal of all economy ... are ultimately given to the economic
> human, strictly determined in respect to their nature and their measure.
> (Ibid. p. 63)

Towards the end of the *Investigations* Menger (Ibid. p. 218) summarizes his
whole approach:

> The exact orientation of theoretical research ... examines the phenomena
> of *abstract economic reality*, phenomena which are strictly determined,
> ... [and] arrive[s] at exact laws of economic reality. The high value of
> these laws for the theoretical understanding of the economic aspect of
> social phenomena has already been stressed by us repeatedly, as well as
> the fact that their formal nature is no different from that of the laws of
> all other exact sciences and of the exact natural sciences particularly.

Menger's *Principles of Economics* should be viewed as a theory of
essences, exact laws and naturally determined primary elements. Starting
from the basic elements of needs, goods and the desire for the most

complete satisfaction, Menger gives a genetic account of the essences of these phenomena, and shows how they are regulated by exact laws and how they are determined by nature. Menger says that you cannot deny 'the conformity to definite laws of phenomena that condition the outcome of the economic activity of men and are entirely independent of the human will' (Menger 1981, p. 48). In finding the essence of a good in its utility, Menger writes 'we have traced the differences in the value of goods back to their ultimate causes, and have also, at the same time, found the ultimate, and original measure by which the values of all goods are judged by men' (Ibid. p. 140). Needs, which according to Menger 'arise from our drives and the drives are embedded in our nature' (Ibid. p. 77), and the desire for betterment are natural forces, and these natural forces regulate actual economic phenomena (prices). Menger (Ibid. p. 192) writes:

> The prices of goods, which are symptoms of an economic equilibrium in the distribution of possessions between the economies of individuals, resemble ... waves. The force that drives them to the surface is the ultimate and general cause of all economic activity, the endeavor of men to satisfy their needs as completely as possible, to better their economic position.

Thus we can see that Menger's theory is in full conformity with the Natural Law Outlook, his basic elements being determined by natural forces, his theory being concerned with 'essences' of phenomena (which should be interpreted as the natural properties of phenomena) and his search for 'exact laws' (laws of nature) being the purpose of the theory.[5]

Marie-Esprit Léon Walras

Walras's natural law preconceptions can be seen as a mixture of Jevons's and Menger's. Like Jevons, Walras believed that economics was a

---

5. Unlike Jevons and Walras, Menger rejected the use of mathematics in economic theory. Frequently historians of economic thought (see Schumpeter 1954a, p. 826) have stated that it was his lack of training in mathematics which led him to eschew its use. According to Menger's son Karl Menger (a famous mathematician in his time) this was not the case. Although Menger strongly felt that there were natural laws which ordered economic activity, his economic actors were not rigidly chained to the pure logic of choice. Menger's subjectivism seems to be the reason he rejected mathematics. As Erich Streissler has noted, he incorporated 'practically all the ideas which make the application of the marginal calculus difficult and hazy' (1973, p. 172). Menger was interested not only in pure economics (natural laws), but also the factors which deviated particulars from their essences and he felt that this important aspect of economic analysis would get lost in a mathematical depiction of his ideas.

physio-mathematical science completely analogous to the physical sciences.[6] This being the case, the same method should be used. Like Menger, Walras was concerned with the essence of phenomena, which he called 'universals'. And in common with both Jevons and Menger, he held a Newtonian view of the universe, particularly with regards to the economic realm, and his theory's most basic elements were naturally determined.

Early in his *Elements of Pure Economics*, Walras states his reason for using the mathematical method: the 'pure theory of economics is a science which resembles the physio-mathematical sciences in every respect' (Walras 1954, p. 71). He asserts that the use of the mathematical method 'promises to convert pure economics into an exact science' (Ibid. p. 47). Walras argues that a pure science, analogous to the natural sciences, must be developed before an applied science which accounts for human factors, can be developed. Walras (Ibid. p. 71) writes:

> It must be evident to the reader ... that I do not claim that this science constitutes the whole of economics. Force and velocity are also measurable magnitudes, but the mathematical theory of force and velocity is not the whole of mechanics. Nevertheless, pure mechanics surely ought to precede applied mechanics. Similarly, given the *pure theory of economics*, it must precede *applied economics*; and this pure theory of economics is a science which resembles the physio-mathematical sciences in every respect.

Commenting on this aspect of Walras, Pokorny (1978, p. 395) has noted that: 'Walras became committed to ... [the] goal of fashioning social sciences after the model of mathematics, geometry and mechanics almost as soon as he began to be concerned with the social studies; and ... (the) basic theme of his economics (is that it) represented a "consistent application" of, and ultimately a "complete analogy" with Newton's mechanics.'

Like Jevons, Walras claims an 'analogy between the conditions of equilibrium in the exchange of two goods, and those of a lever' (Ibid. pp. 396-7). Walras (1954, p. 374) writes: 'The law of supply and demand regulates all exchanges of commodities just as the law of universal gravitation regulates the movements of all celestial bodies. Thus the system of the economic universe reveals itself, at last, in all its grandeur and

---

6. Menger, although against the use of mathematical reasoning in economic theory, still held that economics was analogous to the physical sciences.

complexity: a system at once vast and simple, which, for sheer beauty, resembles the astronomic universe.' The analogy between economics and mechanics is the subject of his last paper, 'Economique et Mécanique' (Walras 1909), in which he argues that there is a 'perfect' and 'striking' analogy between the two subjects.   Walras argues that the physio-mathematical method is appropriate in economics, just as it is in the physical sciences, because it deals with quantities and because its laws are mathematical: 'leurs rapports et leurs lois sont de nature mathématique' (Walras 1909, p. 313). Walras then goes on to show how the mathematical structure of economics is similar to that of rational mechanics and celestial mechanics, that is, their equations are exactly the same, with just the variables changed. With such formal similarities, Walras states that the analogy is obvious. Walras concludes, 'Mathematics would be the special language for discussing quantitative facts and it should go without saying that economics is a mathematical science on a par with mechanics and astronomy' (Mirowski and Cook 1990, p. 213).

The similarity between Walras's pure economics and the mathematical structure of mechanics should not surprise anyone familiar with the development of neoclassical economics. The similarity does not come from the inherent similarity of the subject matter as Walras suggests, but from the modeling of economic theory on physics by the neoclassics. As Mirowski (1984a, p. 366) has noted: '[N]eoclassical economic theory was appropriated wholesale from mid-nineteenth century physics; utility was refined so as to be identical with energy.'

Walras's pure economics is similar to Menger's theoretical economics in that both writers treat economics as if it were a physical science and they are both concerned with essences and universals, rather than historical facts. Walras (1954, p. 61) states in his *Elements*:

> A truth long ago demonstrated by the Platonic philosophy is that science does not study corporeal entities but universals of which these entities are manifestations. Corporeal entities come and go, but universals remain forever. Universals, their relations, and their laws, are the object of all scientific study.

Using a dichotomy resembling Menger's theoretical-historical distinction, Walras states that 'we may divide the facts of our universe into two categories: those which result from the play of the blind and ineluctable forces of nature and those which result from the exercise of the human will, a force that is free and cognitive' (Ibid.). Free will is one of those factors which interferes with the natural laws and thus creates the difference between particulars and essences.[7] Pure economics, according to Walras (with Menger and Jevons in full agreement), is certainly in the former category; it studies the operation of natural laws in the economic realm of social phenomena. In an article published 14 years before the *Elements*, Walras (1860, p. 200) argues that the phenomenon of value is part of natural science while the phenomenon of property was part of moral science: 'La théorie de la valeur d'échange et la théorie de la propriété diffèrent en raison du caractère respectif de leur point de vue. L'une est une science naturelle parce qu'elle est la théorie d'un fait naturel; l'autre est une science morale parce qu'elle est la théorie d'un fait moral: c'est ce qu'il faut établir.'[8]

Walras's pure economics is not only regulated by natural laws; its primary elements are also based on nature. Walras (Ibid. p. 201) writes: 'Les faits naturels se distingueront donc des faits moraux en ce que les premiers auront leur origine dans la fatalité des forces naturelles, les seconds dans la volonté libre de l'homme.'[9] This is also seen clearly in Walras's treatment of value, which for him is caused and determined by natural forces.

> Maximum effective utility, on the one hand; uniformity of price, on the other hand; ... constitute the double condition by which the universe of economic interests is automatically governed, just as the universe of astronomical movements is automatically governed by ... gravitation. ... In one case as in the other, the whole science is contained in a formula ... which serves to explain a countless multitude of particular phenomena. Furthermore ... the mechanism of free competition is a self-driven and self-regulating mechanism (Ibid. p. 305).

And he further states:

> [A]ny value in exchange, once established, partakes of the character of

---

7. In pure economics rational economic man acts according to the pure logic of choice, which is a misnomer, since one's options and choices are predetermined. Thus the common critique of neoclassical economics (Veblen 1909; and more recently Shackle 1972) has been that man is not an active force but merely a reactive agent.

8. 'The theory of exchange value and the theory of property differ by reason of the respective character of their point of view. The one is a natural science because it is a theory of natural reality; the other is a moral science because it is a theory of moral reality (acts): this is what is necessary to establish.'

9. 'Natural reality distinguishes itself from moral reality in that the first has its origins in the fatality of natural laws, the second in the free will of men.'

a natural phenomena, natural in its origins, natural in its manifestations and natural in essence. ... (For things to) have any value at all, it is because they are scarce, that is useful and limited in quantity - both conditions being natural. (Ibid. p. 69)[10]

Just as Jevons had before him, Walras proclaims the immutability of natural laws and the futility of trying to go against them: 'It is said we cannot command nature except by obeying her. This applies also to value' (Ibid.). Ingrao and Israel have pointed out, as have others, most notably Jaffe, that Walras's general equilibrium has an ethical connotation:

[A]t the point of equilibrium, all parties to the exchange maximize their own utility within the constraints of the available resources. In a state of equilibrium, each of the parties in the market obtains the maximum satisfaction of their needs according to their initial availability of goods. (Ingrao and Israel 1985, p. 15)

Here we see a clear example of the natural moral theory aspect of natural law theories; the natural outcome, that is, the result of the natural forces is also the most beneficial outcome - that which best promotes the well-being of mankind.

Walras's theory of general equilibrium is the quintessential natural law system, for it is a theory of rational price determination - 'rational' in the sense used by the natural law philosophers, who thought of the universe as being rational, because it was determined by universal (natural) laws.

Our brief review of the three originators of the marginal utility revolution clearly indicates that their efforts attempted to illuminate the natural laws of the economic realm. All three argued at length that the essence of economics (scientific economics, theoretical economics or pure economics) was essentially the same as the physical sciences, and that the laws of economics were analogous to those of the physical sciences. This demonstrates a belief in a social physics, and is consistent with the Natural Law Outlook of the principle of design in both the physical and social universes.

All three also went to great lengths to place nature as the final cause of the economic forces which bring about the natural laws. They were thus

---

10. Walras here assumes that the usefulness of a good is a product of the nature of the good, that is, the functions and services it can perform, yet clearly the usefulness of a product is socially determined, both in terms of the historical and cultural development of a given community and in their level of technological development. Later on in the *Elements* Walras brings in diminishing marginal utility, which is for marginalists a trait in human nature, and, along with scarcity, determines value.

consistent with the naturalism inherent in natural law theories. This is most evident in their theory of value which states that the value of a product is determined by two conditions of nature, scarcity and diminishing marginal utility. Yet their naturalism is evident in many other aspects of their theories, most obviously in their use of 'state of nature' explanations. All three developed their theories from the analysis of individual behavior outside and independent of any social factors; man as we find him in the 'state of nature'.

Furthermore, as we have just seen with Walras, all resisted any human institutions which would run counter to the natural laws; free competition is for them the natural order. Their theories have a strong normative aspect which is consistent with the natural moral theory aspect of the Natural Law Outlook.

3. The Natural Law Outlook of the Later Marginalists: Clark, Edgeworth and Pareto

The success of the marginal utility revolution rests not in the hands of its originators but in those of their followers and refiners. Of the three original marginalists, only Menger was successful in building up a following sufficient to be called a school. However, the Austrian school has never really attracted many followers or exerted much of an influence on the subsequent development of economic theory. It was up to Vilfredo Pareto to build the Lausanne school from the theories and methods developed by Walras. The English marginalist tradition rests more on Alfred Marshall and Francis Edgeworth than on Jevons. And in America, marginalism sprang up around the work of John Bates Clark, who, like Marshall, had independently arrived at the marginalist method and theory of value. If the marginal utility revolution was an extension of one aspect of classical theory - the search for the natural laws of the economic realm - then the Natural Law Outlook should be present in subsequent marginalists. In fact, not only do we see that their theories are structurally natural law theories - that is, they are built around the ideas of a social physics, naturalism and a natural moral theory - but frequently they openly espouse the natural law foundation of their theories. This we will see by examining aspects of the works of Clark, Edgeworth and Pareto. Marshall, who attempts to follow both the natural law and historical/institutional aspects found in classical economic theory, does not fit in with the dominant trend at the time and will be examined in an appendix (see p. 137).

The most extreme attempt by a marginalist to construct a natural law theory in economics was made by John Bates Clark. This aspect of Clark's work, which is included in all the leading marginalists', was highlighted best by Clark's student, Thorstein Veblen (1919, pp. 190-1):

> Mr. Clark's premises, and there with the aim of his inquiry, are the standard ones of the classical English school (including the Jevons-Austrian wing). This school of economics stands on the pre-evolutionary ground of normality and "natural law", which the great body of theoretical science occupied in the early nineteenth century. ... This Order of Nature, or realm of Natural Law, is not the actual run of material facts, but the facts so interpreted as to meet the needs of the taxonomist in point of taste, logical consistency and sense of justice.

In the preface to his *The Distribution of Wealth*, Clark states that '[I]t is the purpose of this work to show that the distribution of the income of society is controlled by a natural law, and that this law, if it worked without friction, would give every agent of production the amount of wealth which that agent creates' (Clark 1965, p. v). Much of this book is devoted to an analysis of the static state, which is Clark's natural order. From static conditions he develops natural laws (marginal productivity theory, diminishing marginal utility, increasing marginal costs) from nature and human nature. He then proceeds to use these laws to explain the dynamic state. This is valid, Clark tells us, because '[T]here is ... a distinct set of economic laws, the action of which is not dependent on organization. They are fundamental; and we now have to note that they are universal. They act in the economy of the most advanced state, as well as in that of the most primitive' (Ibid. p. 26). Clark, in an earlier publication, states that all economic phenomena are under one general law, the 'universal law of economic variation' - '[o]ne law governs economic life' (Clark 1894, p. 261).

More than most economists, Clark's theories center around the natural order being an expression of God's design and intent. Clark felt that '[n]inety-nine one hundredths of the work of society is done by natural law' and that 'the recognition of natural law in the organic and social world' (Everett 1982, p. 57) was the basis of all knowledge. John Henry, in a series of articles on Clark, has shown that Clark was motivated in the construction of his theories to advocate and defend free market capitalism as the only just and moral economic system; they 'were developed to support a particular a priori ethical or political position' (Henry 1983, p. 375).

Edgeworth's natural law preconceptions can be found in his enthusiastic acceptance of Bentham's Utilitarianism, both as a model of how to construct a social theory and as the correct philosophy. Edgeworth follows Bentham's suggestion that the hedonistic calculus is subject to mathematical formulation and analysis, and just as Jevons had before him, he sees this as the foundation of a scientific economics. Edgeworth writes (1967, pp. 9, 12):

> The application of mathematics to the world of soul is countenanced by the hypothesis (agreeable to the general hypothesis that every psychical phenomenon is concomitant, and in some sense the other side of a physical phenomenon), the particular hypothesis adopted in these pages, that Pleasure is the concomitant of Energy. ... 'Mécanique Sociale' may one day take her place along with 'Mécanique Celeste,' thronged each upon the double-sided height of one maximum principle, the supreme pinnacle of moral as of physical science. As the movements of each particle, constrained or loose, in a material cosmos are continually subordinated to one maximum sum-total of accumulated energy, so the movements of each soul, whether selfishly isolated or linked sympathetically, may continually be realising the maximum energy of pleasure, the Divine love of the universe.

Edgeworth's main contribution to economics is the indifference curve, from which was derived the Edgeworth box and contract curve. The indifference curve portrays autonomous human preferences based on the law of diminishing marginal utility and the desire to maximize total utility. The contract curve (and the Edgeworth box, which Edgeworth never draws but which is in all its essentials spelled out in his *Mathematical Psychics*), describes isolated exchange between two individuals guided by natural laws and independent of any social relation. It is a 'state of nature' explanation of what is essentially a social phenomenon, market participation. If natural laws are universal truths, then they have to be independent of particular social formations Thus what is required for a scientific analysis, that is the discovery of natural laws, is an explanation without society.

Pareto,[11] like Clark, wanted to develop a scientific economics, one that would be independent of particular social institutions. Pareto tells us that science is the study of uniformities, for without uniformities all is chaos. In the economic realm, the object of analysis for Pareto is human behavior and nature. Pareto states: 'Human behavior reveals uniformities which

---

11. Pareto's primary purpose was to 'apply to the social science - of which the economic sciences are merely a part - the experimental method which has given such brilliant results in the natural sciences' (Pareto quoted in Ingrao and Israel 1985, p. 27).

constitute natural laws. If these uniformities do not exist, then there would be neither social science nor political economy, and even the study of history would largely be useless' (Pareto 1966, p. 97).[12] Pareto follows Walras in constructing a theory of general equilibrium which provides for the laws of economics.   Yet, unlike Walras, Pareto is conscious of the implications of claiming to have discovered natural laws and of the philosophical baggage which is carried by the terms 'utility' and 'natural law'. Pareto substitutes ophelimity for utility and obstacles for disutility (costs, scarcity) in an attempt to develop a value-free science, one liberated from the old metaphysics. 'The principal subject of our study', Pareto (1971, p. 106) writes, 'is economic equilibrium. We will see shortly that this equilibrium results from the opposition between men's tastes and the obstacles to satisfying them.' However, Pareto makes no effort to free the theory from its natural law structure. His economics is essentially the same as Walras, a general equilibrium theory based on natural conditions and natural laws. Typical of his time, Pareto constructs his pure economics independent of social institutions in order to arrive at economic laws based on the uniformities of human behavior. *Sans* society, these uniformities must derive from nature.

In arguing for a scientific study of society, Pareto (1966, pp. 106-7) draws the familiar neoclassical analogy between mechanics and economics. Although Pareto extends the analogy of mechanical equilibrium to social equilibrium (whereas most marginalists confine the analogy to economic equilibrium), he realizes the many important differences between the two phenomena, and tells us that mechanics should have a limited use, particularly that of theory construction.

> The human intellect proceeds from the known to the unknown. Thus, where we have extensive knowledge of the equilibrium of a material system, this equilibrium can serve as an example to help us gain a conception of economic equilibrium. This latter in its turn can help us to form an idea of social equilibrium. (Ibid. p. 105)[13]

Implicit in this procedure (developing theories from physics to economics to sociology) is the natural law concept of a unifying thread running

---

12. Vincent Tarascio has noted that in 'Pareto's pure economics, economic man resembles a mechanical man. This is the point Pareto was making when he stated, "For the determination of equilibrium, the individual can be replaced just as well by curves"' (1973, p. 158).

13. Here we have an explicit recognition of the role of displaced concepts in the construction of theories. What Pareto, and economists in general, lacks is an understanding of their lasting effects.

through both the physical and the social universe (the principle of design). It is the acceptance of the idea that the social universe is regulated by similar principles as the natural, and thus the social sciences can safely adopt the form and theoretical structure of the natural sciences. Pareto is displacing the concept of equilibrium, without justifying such a displacement. Under the Natural Law Outlook, no such justification was necessary.

Pareto's economic theories were developed as a stepping stone for his overall social theory. In his sociological writings that Pareto tries to exorcise the ghost of natural law. In the *Trattato di Sociologia Generale* Pareto examines different types of natural law theories, finding that they are based on either universal consent, right reason or divine will, all of which he finds unscientific, relying on sentiments instead of analysis. Pareto (1966, p. 208) writes:

> The subjective argument by accord of sentiments seems to be as follows:
> The mind intuitively perceives that existing laws are not an arbitrary, or
> even a wholly logical, product, that there is in them a substratum which
> is not affected by will or intention but exists intrinsically. This induction
> is in agreement with the facts and should properly be formulated thus:
> There are certain activating causes of non-logical behavior from which
> men derive their laws. These activating causes - or Residues - relate to
> the conditions under which men live and change with those conditions.

Pareto seems to be moving away from the Natural Law Outlook by emphasizing that the laws 'relate to the conditions under which men live and change with those conditions', yet he is also saying that the idea that there are laws which 'exist intrinsically ... is in agreement with the facts'. And these laws are the result of activating causes that Pareto calls the 'residues'. The residues are what Pareto calls 'certain human instincts' (1966, p. 217) and in Pareto's social theory they play an important role in generating social equilibrium, which is the main concern of his theories. Nature, when she created man, endowed him with certain instincts which generate a social equilibrium. As Werner Stark has pointed out, with his residues Pareto 'has taken reality and drained out of it human freedom and historical variability and thus gained a model which is amenable to treatment in mechanistic terms' (Stark 1963, p. 136). A scientific theory of social equilibrium modeled on the natural sciences must necessarily be a natural law theory, based on a belief in social physics and grounded in naturalism. When applied to actual problems and issues, the theory's conclusions, being based on science, are thought to be above political argument. When its conclusions become the standard for right and wrong, the theory becomes a natural moral theory. We thus end up with all three aspects of the Natural Law Outlook.

4. Marginal Utility Theory as a Natural Law System

In a now famous article Mirowski (1984a) demonstrated that the marginalist revolution has its origins in nineteenth-century physics. He suggests that to a large extent the marginal revolution consisted of adopting the equations of physics, replacing physical science variables by economic ones (utility for energy), and thereafter claiming to have discovered a scientific economics. Yet the more important question is why use physics as a model for economics? It is the thesis of this chapter that the belief in the existence of natural laws in the social as well as the physical universe led to this development.

The marginalists are more consistent in their natural law beliefs in that they find little use in the study of history and institutions for the construction of economic theories. They are looking for universal truths and such truths exist independent of society, as Walras tells us, much like Plato's universals. Since physics seemed at the time to have come closest to developing a body of universal truths, it was quite natural for the marginalists to adopt it as a model to emulate. Adam Smith and the classicals (particularly Mill) as well as Marx wrestled with the question of the exact nature of society, never becoming fully satisfied with the idea that the social realm is perfectly analogous to the physical. In contrast, the marginalists accepted the Natural Law Outlook as a preconception. As Frank Knight has noted, the marginal 'utility theory should be seen as the culmination historically and logically ... of the eighteenth-century craving for a principle which would do for human conduct and society what Newton's mechanics had done for the solar system' (Knight 1931, p. 604). Yet the use of physics as a model for economics presupposes the idea of a single structure for both social and natural realms. As we have already seen, the idea of a similar structure comes from the principle of design; the natural and social universes were created and are regulated by the Author of Nature.

Most investigations into the natural law foundations of economics stress the independence of the developed theories and concepts from their philosophical origins. However, the philosophical preconceptions of theorists are important as they influence both the form and content of their theories. The marginalists are no exception. Their preconceptions permeate every aspect of their work, yet are most transparent in their theory of value, their reliance on 'state of nature' explanations, and in their concept of general equilibrium.

The concept of value is at the heart of the marginal utility revolution. The whole corps of their theories and concepts have their origins in and are variations of it. The theory of value in economic theory has been incorrectly labeled price theory. Value theory is essentially about the underlying order of the economy - that which regulates material phenomena yet goes unseen. For the marginal utility theorist, utility is the regulating force. Utility determines human motivation and action, as well as the material phenomena of prices. Specifically, marginalists' theory of value states that the value of a commodity is determined by its scarcity, which determines the amount of disutility necessary to obtain a commodity, and by the happiness we achieve in consuming the commodity, that is, the marginal utility derived from consuming the commodity. The amount of utility received in the consumption of the commodity is subject to the universal law of human nature, the law of diminishing marginal utility. The difficulty of producing the commodity is subject to the universal law of increasing costs. The value of the commodity is arrived at when the two natural laws are allowed to operate, as the forces of supply and demand, achieving equilibrium when the forces of both natural laws reach a balance. The structure of this theory was taken directly from rational mechanics and its independence from social institutions (with the exception of natural institutions: private property, perfect competition and voluntary exchange) shows its attempt at universality.[14] It is used by the marginalists to explain the question of value under all conditions and societies. It is clearly a natural law theory, showing both the social physics and naturalism aspects of natural law theories.

One development that the marginal utility school introduces into economic theory is the analysis of individual exchange. This innovation was

14. The classification of some institutions as natural and some as not natural shows the implicit normative elements in all natural law theories. The label 'natural' gives automatic approval to the justice and legitimacy of the phenomenon it is attached to. For classical and neoclassical economists a natural institution is one that arises out of the independent self-interested actions of individuals, what the neo-Austrians now refer to as the spontaneous order. Thus money, in their theories, is natural for it evolves from the autonomous actions of individuals, whereas the Federal Reserve Bank is not natural for it was created by the government. That these so-called natural institutions can only be shown to be 'natural' by conjectural history and not by the actual development of such phenomena shows the strong ideological element in natural law theories.

developed in order to arrive at a natural theory of exchange and value. The most refined of these types of theories is Edgeworth's contract curve, which we have already demonstrated as a 'state of nature' explanation. Another example of the use of 'state of nature' explanations in marginal utility economics is the reliance on Robinson Crusoe parables to explain economic activity. Robinson Crusoe is the neoclassical counterpart to the seventeenth-century noble savage, alone in the 'state of nature', independent of society, in fact living in pre-society. Such explanations are designed to demonstrate the natural laws of human nature; theories developed from them must thus be natural law theories.

The marginal utility concept of equilibrium is the natural order, which exists when human interference is eliminated and the laws of nature are allowed to run unimpeded. William Jaffe has recognized this aspect of Walras's general equilibrium, calling it a normative scheme and not a depiction of reality. This point was noted by Jaffe when he wrote that Walras's aim was 'to construct a model showing the conditions under which a capitalist system, while still governed by the ineluctable forces and constraints of the real world, might work in conformity with principles of "commutative justice" derived from natural law philosophy' (Jaffe 1977, p. 574). This is true for all behavioral equilibrium theories, which rely on unsocialized individual actions to achieve a balance of forces and thus a state of equilibrium. The determination of equilibrium, therefore, rests on the exclusion of history and institutions which interfere with the natural laws. Marginalist equilibrium economics is the quintessential social physics.

The Wrong Turn

The marginal utility revolution represented a turning point in the history of economic thought. The classicals' dual interest in natural laws and history was abandoned, with the marginalists following exclusively the natural law approach, attempting to discover a scientific economic theory independent of society. This led them, as Donald Winch has pointed out, to 'go further towards excluding historical and institutional categories from pure economics' (Winch 1973, pp. 69-70) by narrowing the boundaries of economic theory. Such an approach necessarily implies that the social and physical universe are similarly ordered, both in the structure and origin of their laws. This is the Natural Law Outlook.

At the time of the marginal utility revolution, the German Historical school also claimed to have made a break with classical political economy. From our analysis of the dichotomy in classical political economy we can see that the German Historical school was merely following one aspect of classical thought, turning in the opposite direction of the marginalists. As Shackle (1973, pp. 328-9) has observed, the marginalists were faced with a choice between 'adherence to rationality, strictly defined, as the essential principle of [their] model of the world and of [their] procedure in analyzing it, on the one hand; and on the other, the abandonment of any aspiration to see the economic aspect of human affairs as a self-contained, unified and simple whole, every feature of which would reflect one and the same natural law.' They chose the natural law approach.

The advantage that classical political economy has over the marginal utility school, in terms of explaining the economies of their respective times and of giving insights into its structure and driving forces, stems from its concern for efficient causes. The classicals' epistemology was based on the belief that final causes (the natural laws of the design) could only be understood by examining how they worked on earth: through efficient causes. Hence the concern for history and institutions. For Smith there was no contradiction in the search for natural laws and in studying history and institutions, for he saw society evolving towards its natural order. Thus the three value theories in Smith can be interpreted as applicable for different stages of a society's development. Yet, even though society was evolving, it was doing so under the influence of an overall design and towards a predetermined, or natural, end. Marginal utility economics, in terms of its pure theory, by contrast, is concerned only with universal truths and natural laws, with final, and not efficient, causes. Their analysis of efficient causes was therefore either metaphysical, such as Walras's auctioneer - or, as in Menger, those factors which hampered the pure operations of the market mechanism. Most of them do not, like the classicals, argue that an investigation into actual market behavior will help us to understand pure theory. Although many attempted to combine an analysis of actual market behavior with their pure theory, the pure theory is always insulated from being influenced by the actual market phenomena. In most cases it is the concern for final causes, grounded in nature, which prevent them from understanding observed market behavior as social and not natural phenomena. An example of this is Jevons's business cycle theory, wherein his natural law preconceptions led him to look towards nature to explain business cycles, leading to the now infamous sun spot theory (see Mirowski, 1989, Chapter 3). If you remove final causes from classical political economy, which to some degree is what Marx does, there is still much left - a body of historical and institutional analysis, useful and pertinent for its time. Marginal utility economics *sans* natural laws (final causes) is empty. Its value is tied to the legitimation function of social theories.   The reality it explains is the reality it constructs.   In the final analysis, the marginalists' theories explain only their preconceptions.

Appendix: On Marshall

Conspicuously absent from our analysis is Alfred Marshall. Marshall was not only one of the original creators of marginal analysis, but more than the others he successfully promoted and developed neoclassical economic theory. In many ways Marshall is not a typical marginalist, for he attempts to follow both avenues originated by Smith, and is also quite skeptical of the use of the physical sciences, or at least mechanics, as a role model for the developing of economic theory. However, we will see that Marshall's outlook is firmly a natural law one and that even in his call for an organic economic theory he is still under the influence of the Natural Law Outlook.

Unlike Jevons, Menger and Walras, Marshall took great pains to stress that his marginal utility theory of value was a continuance of English political economy. Marshall writes: 'My acquaintance with economics commenced with reading Mill, while I was still earning my living by teaching Mathematics at Cambridge; and translating his doctrines into differential equations as far as they would go: and, as a rule rejecting those which would not go' (Quoted by Shove 1965, pp. 432-3). 'Marshall translated as many as possible of Ricardo's reasonings into mathematics; and he endeavored to make them more general' (Ibid. p. 438). Marshall did not see his work as a synthesis of classical and neoclassical theories, but as an extension of the former. The development of the marginal principle was for Marshall an extension and generalization of Ricardo.

Marshall's classical roots are nowhere better seen than in the historical and methodological sections of his *Principles of Economics*. Following Smith and Mill, Marshall emphasized the need for both induction and deduction. Marshall writes: 'It is the business of economics ... to collect facts, to arrange and interpret them, and to draw inferences from them' (Marshall 1920, p. 24). He quotes approvingly the German Historical economist, Schmoller: 'Observation and description, definition and classification are the preparatory activities. But what we desire to reach thereby is a knowledge of the interdependence of economic phenomena. ... Induction and deduction are both needed for the scientific thought as the left and right foot are both needed for walking' (Ibid.).

Marshall thought that both aspects of classical economic theory were necessary for an understanding of the economy, the historical/institutional investigation and the 'scientific' search for natural laws. Thus Marshall not only wanted to develop classical economic theory in the light of the marginal principle and translate it into mathematics, he set out to collect the historical data to explain the evolution of the economic community. 'By the early seventies', Hutchison (1962, p. 69) has written:

> Marshall had both worked out the Mathematical framework of his theory and plunged into the historical study of economic life. A synthesis of analysis and history seems to have remained his objective, but as to how this was to be achieved, in particular as to the role of history in the scheme of his life-work, he seems to have had many hesitations, and made many shifts of emphasis, in what G. F. Shove calls 'his restless' quest after realism.

The concern for induction led Marshall to pay particular attention to the institutional and historical aspects of economic life. Although basically a methodological individualist, Marshall states that 'economists study the actions of individuals but study them in relation to social rather than individual life' (Marshall 1920, p. 21). In the description of his methodology he placed the most importance not on mathematical reasoning, but on the 'illustrat[ion] by examples that are important in real life' (quoted in Shove 1965, p. 447). If such an illustration were not possible, Marshall discarded the theory.

The dual nature of Marshall's thought has been much noted. Keynes eulogized him as a master economist and historian. Joan Robinson hints at this dual nature when she wrote: 'Marshall's analysis was half in historical time and half in equilibrium. ... His world is inhabited by businessmen, housewives, workers, trade union leaders, bankers and traders ... he was studying a recognizable economy in a particular phase of its historical development' (Robinson 1980, p. 53). Though Marshall tried to balance the two approaches, one clearly dominates. As Veblen (1919, p. 173) observed:

> Professor Marshall's work, ... is, in aim, even if not always in achievement, a theoretical handling of human activity in its economic bearing, - an inquiry into the multiform phases and ramifications of that process of valuation of the material means of life by virtue of which man is an economic agent. And still it remains an inquiry directed to the determination of the conditions of an equilibrium of activities and acquiescent normal situation. It is not in any eminent degree an inquiry into cultural or institutional development as affected by economic exigencies or by the economic interest of the man whose activities are analyzed and portrayed.

The dual nature of Marshall's work can also be seen in his use of mechanical and biological analogies. In his article, 'Distribution and Exchange' (Marshall 1898), Marshall makes the case for the use of both mechanical and biological analogies in economic theory. Mechanical analogies are useful, according to Marshall, for the early stages of the development of a theory and for problems of 'statics', but when the analysis moves to a 'higher plane', the analysts should switch to biological analogies and organic reasoning. Marshall (1898, pp. 39-43) writes:

> It has been well said that analogies may help one into the saddle, but are encumbrances on a long journey. ... There is a fairly close analogy between the earlier stages of economic reasoning and the devices of physical statics. But is there an equally serviceable analogy between the later stages of economic reasoning and the methods of physical dynamics? I think not. I think that in the later stages of economics better analogies are to be got from biology than from physics; and consequently, that economic reasoning should start on methods analogous to those of physical statics, and should gradually become more biological in tone. ...
>
> Mechanical analogies ought, therefore, not to be abandoned hastily on the ground that economic events react upon the conditions by which they were produced; so that future events cannot happen under exactly the same conditions as they did.
>
> But the catastrophes of mechanics are caused by changes in the quantity and not in the character of the forces at work: whereas in life their character changes also. 'Progress' or 'evolution' industrial and social, is not mere increase and decrease. It is organic growth, chastened and confined and occasionally reversed by decay of innumerable factors, each of which influences and is influenced by those around it; and every such mutual influence varies with the stages which the respective factors have already reached in their growth.
>
> In this vital respect all sciences of life are akin to one another, and are unlike physical sciences. And therefore in the later stages of economics, when we are approaching nearly to the conditions of life, biological analogies are to be preferred to mechanical, other things being equal.

In this lengthy quotation, we can see that Marshall feels physical analogies are helpful in the earlier stages of theory construction (a position in conformity with the other marginalists), he is thus aware of the radical aspect of displaced concepts. Marshall also seems to be aware of the conservative aspect of displaced concepts for he sees the mechanical view of the social universe hampering social inquiry when theories attempt to become less abstract and closer to the facts, or whenever time is a factor.

Like the classical economists, Marshall studied philosophy and came to the conclusion that there is an essential difference between social and physical phenomena. As we have seen above, Walras also noted the difference between phenomena that were the result of blind forces and those in which free will played a role. However, unlike Walras, Marshall felt that this difference should be reflected in theoretical, not just in applied economics.

Marshall felt that his *Principles* was an attempt to use each method of reasoning, namely mechanical and organic (biological), based on the level of analysis. In the analytical portions, Books 2, 3 and parts of 5, mechanical reasoning is employed; his price theory is the best example of this. In Books 1, 4, and other parts of 5, Marshall claims to employ organic reasoning and thus relies on organic analogies. An example of this type of analysis is Marshall's explanation of the rise and decline of a firm (Marshall 1920, p. 269):

> A business firm grows and attains great strength, and afterwards perhaps stagnates and decays; and at the turning point there is a balance or equilibrium of the forces of life and decay: ... [a] balancing of forces in the life and decay of a people, or of a method of industry or trading. And as we reach to the higher stages of our work, we shall need even more and more to think of economic forces as resembling those which make a young man grow in strength, till he reaches his prime; after which he gradually becomes stiff and inactive, till at last he sinks to make room for other and more vigorous life. But to prepare the way for this advanced study we want first to look at a simpler balancing of forces which corresponds rather to the mechanical equilibrium of a stone hanging by an elastic string.

Marshall is of the opinion that the two methods of analysis are complementary, that organic reasoning is merely a more advanced form of reasoning with mechanical reasoning a necessary stepping stone to this higher plane of analysis. Marshall (1898, p. 43) writes:

> The words 'balance' and 'equilibrium' belong originally to the older science, physics; whence they have been taken over by biology. In the earlier stages of economics, we think of demand and supply as crude forces pressing against one another, and tending towards a mechanical equilibrium; but in the later stages, the balance or equilibrium is conceived not as between crude mechanical forces, but as between the organic forces of life and decay. ... The Mecca of the economist is economic biology rather then economic dynamics.

Thus for Marshall, organic conceptions are closer to reality, but mechanical concepts are necessary in order to develop and comprehend the organic ones. Marshall's conception of organic reasoning, however, seems to be no more than a more advanced and dynamic form of mechanical reasoning. It is an evolutionary approach where the path of development is predetermined. And it is dominated by natural forces - life and decay - and not social institutions. Marshall thus is not breaking with the Natural Law Outlook, just moving economics from one natural science to another.

Most interestingly, Marshall feels that the development of economic theory has taken the path he has suggested, moving away from mechanical conceptions and towards organic ones. This is completely contrary to the thesis of this book, and thus merits a closer examination. In his *Principles*, Marshall gives an account of the development of economic theory along the lines he has suggested, highlighting an organic aspect of economic development, the pliability of human nature. Marshall claims that modern economics (the marginal utility school) emphasizes how human nature has developed and evolved, thus necessitating a corresponding change in economic theory. Marshall's case is worth quoting at length (1920, pp. 631-3):

> This change in the point of view of economics is partly due to the fact that the changes in human nature during the last fifty years have been so rapid as to force themselves on the attention; partly to the direct influence of individual writers, ... and partly to the direct influence of a similar change in some branches of natural science.
>
> At the beginning of the last century the mathematico-physical group of sciences were in the ascendant; and these sciences ... have this point in common, that this subject-matter is constant and unchanged in all countries and in all ages. ... As the century wore on, the biological group of sciences were slowly making way, and people were getting clearer ideas as to the nature of organic growth. They were learning that if the subject-matter of a science passes through different stages of development, the laws which apply to one stage will seldom apply without modification to others; the laws of the science must have a development corresponding to that of the things of which they treat.
>
> At last the speculation of biology made a great stride forwards ... as those of physics had done in earlier years; and there was a marked change in the tone of the moral and historical sciences. Economics has shared in the general movement; and is getting to pay every year a greater attention to the pliability of human nature, and to the way in which the character of man affects and is affected by the prevalent methods of the production, distribution and consumption of wealth. The first important indication of the new movement was seen in John Stuart Mill's admirable *Principles of Political Economy*.
>
> Mill's followers have continued his movement away from the position taken by the immediate followers of Ricardo; and the human as distinguished from the mechanical element is taking a more and more

prominent place in economics. ... [T]his temper is shown ... above all
in [the work] of Jevons, which has secured a permanent and notable
place in economic history by its rare combination of many various
qualities of the highest order.

Marshall's analysis could not be further from the reality of the situation.
The marginal utility school, following its singular concern for the discovery
of the natural laws of the economic universe, developed a model of
economic man based on a fixed human nature. In fact, Jevons is most
outspoken about this point. As we have seen above, he singles out this
aspect of Mill's analysis - the pliability of human nature - for attack.
Jevons's comment is worth quoting again: 'Granite rocks can be more
easily molded than the poor savages that hide among them' (Jevons 1890,
p. 290). The universality of human nature is one of the strongest and most
obvious natural law aspects of the marginal utility school.

Marshall's analytical economics is very much within the Natural Law
Outlook. Marshall changes the terminology: 'natural' becomes 'normal',
but as Hutchison (1962, p. 72) has noted: 'the extent of the significance of
this change might easily seem to be fairly small, particularly as when he
first adopted the adjective "normal" which he took to mean competitive,
though later recognizing a "normality" apart from free competition'.
Despite the limitations that Marshall ascribes to the mechanical outlook for
economics and the importance he gives to historical and institutional
analysis, Marshall's economics is still within the Natural Law Outlook.

7. 'Scientific' Economics and the Loss of Historical Sense

In many ways modern economic theory is the last embodiment of the Enlightenment's ideas and vision. The other fields and disciplines that owe their origins to this epoch, or which were radically altered by it, have since developed a more critical understanding of their subject matter and, what is more important, of their discipline. The uncritical commitment to the Enlightenment world view by the social theorist is a clear sign of the ceremonial aspect of social theory overshadowing the instrumental, yet nowhere is this commitment more evident than in neoclassical economic theory. Perversely, the other social sciences, after decades of advances, are slipping back into this simplistic vision through the influence of 'economic imperialism': the restructuring of the social sciences based on neoclassical economic theory, all in an attempt to be as 'scientific' as economics.

The purpose of this chapter is to demonstrate the path by which economics became 'scientific' and how the desire to be scientific required the emptying of historical and social context from the investigation of economic phenomena. This will be accomplished by first briefly examining the conception of science held by economists and the influence of this conception on the development of economic theory, particularly with regard to the concept of equilibrium. The influence of the Vienna Circle on the conception of science will be examined, indicating its views on historical knowledge and its role in the development of axiomatic general equilibrium theory. The net effect of this influence is not only the final loss of what Schumpeter (quoted on page 2) called an historical sense, but the total separation of economic theory from the object it hopes to explain, the economy.

1. Conception of Science in Economics

It should be quite clear from the prceding six chapters that one of the dominant themes in the development of economic theory is the attempt to construct a scientific explanation of the economy and society. In this attempt, the question of what it means to be scientific often went unexamined. Being scientific meant emulating the natural sciences. This entailed using the natural sciences not only as a model but also as a source of concepts to be displaced into economics to act as guiding heuristics. The overall preconception behind such an endeavor is the Natural Law Outlook, the idea that the social universe is subject to universal natural laws analogous to, if not the same as, those in the natural universe. Much of the motivation behind these efforts was the honest desire to provide a scientific explanation of economic phenomena, yet the political aspect of these ventures should not go unnoticed. The use of the models and metaphors of the natural sciences by economists had the net effect of placing the economy in the realm of natural phenomena and out of the sphere of the social, and thus not open to human interventions. This outcome is clearly the intention of many economists, from the mercantilists up to the present. This is not to be interpreted as a questioning of the motivation or the intellectual honesty of these theorists, for a large number thoroughly accepted the Natural Law Outlook and thus believed that their theories were unbiased, objective science. If one holds the Natural Law Outlook then it would be intellectually dishonest not to attempt to construct a science of society based on the natural sciences. The problem lies in the lack of a critical analysis of the preconceptions on which theoretical structures are based.[1]

As the last chapter demonstrated, the aim of the marginal utility revolution was to create a pure economic theory, one that is independent of history and social context. It was the marginalists' opinion that only a pure theory of economics could become truly scientific. Jevons, Walras and Menger all felt that such a pure theory was independent of society, yet each noted some role for historical research. Walras states that an investigation into the actual economy was necessary to arrive at real world concepts which could then be developed into a pure theory. To give an example: Walras's auctioneer has its origins in the operation of the Paris Bourse (Ingrao and Israel 1990, p. 103). Moreover, Menger felt that his *Investigations* (1985) was complementary to historical research and Jevons felt that some day statistical research would be able to give economic theory the type of hard data so important to the development of the natural sciences. Furthermore, all three made extensive excursions into the actual operations of the

---

1. Such a critical analysis was first fully provided by Thorstein Veblen in his essay 'The Preconceptions of Economic Science' (1919).

economy, commenting on public policy and offering economic assessments and analyses. Yet all felt that these efforts, important as they were, should be kept separate from the generation (they would most likely say the discovery) of pure economic theory: the natural laws of the economy.

The views of the early marginalists reflect the widespread attitude of that era, as should be expected. The growing acceptance of this attitude can best be seen in the histories of economic thought from the late nineteenth and early twentieth centuries. The discipline of the history of economic thought has been frequently used by economic theorists to argue their perspective. It has never been enough to develop a new theory or idea; theorists have felt compelled to find hints of their theories in their forebears[2], or to rewrite the history of economics from the perspective of the new theory. Therefore, it is not surprising that we find a move to promote the conviction of economics as a science, on a par with the natural sciences, in the historiography of economics following the marginal utility revolution. One of the first such historians of economic thought to reflect this attitude is Luigi Cossa, who stated that political economy 'first investigates the natural laws of economic phenomena' (Cossa 1880, p. 10) and that 'Political Economy is distinct from all historical and descriptive branches of economics. These branches deal with concrete facts about wealth as they have variously appeared at different times and in different places, while Political Economy as such, is confined to the abstract and unvarying play of typical and assured phenomena' (Cossa quoted in Stark forthcoming). For Cossa 'science ... is any system of general truth, applicable to any given order of facts' and economics is 'a science in the strictest sense' (Ibid.). Furthermore, Cossa argues (Ibid.):

> Though the conditions of civilization are variable in their very nature, this does not force us to ignore that the laws of the physical world, the psychical qualities of individuals, together with certain familiar tendencies in social organizations, are now, always were, and will be always the same. Accordingly those numerous economic facts which spring from them can never undergo any substantial change. Who is so bold ... as to maintain that the principles of profit and loss, of the influence of scarcity on value, and of the price of merchandise upon output have purely local and provisional value?

A slightly more extreme example of these views can be found in Joseph Rambaud's *Histoire des Doctrines Economiques* published in 1899. Rambaud writes: 'If Political Economy is a science, that is to say if it

---

2. Keynes seems to have carried this to the extreme in his appraisal of Malthus.

discovers and possesses truths ... these truths must have their place in the order divine, and ... the laws which coordinate them must be amongst the innumerable manifestations of the eternal wisdom that has created and governs the world' (1899, p. 450; quoted in Stark forthcoming) and '[i]n the economic, as in the physical and moral worlds, so long as these two latter do not change, there must exist immutable natural laws imposed upon man who knows them and conforms to them more or less perfectly' (Ibid. p. 510). In *Cours d'Economie Politique*, Charles Gide writes that political economy 'studies the spontaneous relations that arise between men living together as it might study the relations which arise between any bodies whatsoever, those necessary relations which derive from the nature of things ... Hence it tends to set itself up as a natural science' and 'When we apply the word science to any branch of human knowledge ... we mean to say that the facts with which it deals are connected by certain constant relations which have been discovered and which are called laws' (Ibid.). Similarly G. H. Bousquet, in his *Essai sur l'Evolution de la Pensée Economique* (1927) states: 'The sole and only end of [economic] theory should be the rational and consistent systemisation of concrete reality without any practical or normative tendency, after the model of the physical, chemical, or mechanical theories' and 'I judge that it is absurd to study the social sciences otherwise than the natural sciences ... The natural sciences should be the guides and models of the social sciences' (Bousquet 1927, pp. 277; 151, quoted in Stark forthcoming). More recently, William Letwin has equated 'scientific' economics with 'a mechanistic explanation of an economic process' (Letwin 1965, p. 213).

Yet it is from Joseph Schumpeter that we get the clearest statement of the conception of science held by economists and the path to which this goal of being scientific is achieved. In the *History of Economic Analysis* Schumpeter defines science as 'any kind of knowledge that has been the object of conscious efforts to improve it' (1954a, p. 7). Yet Schumpeter feels that economics should strive to be an 'exact science': an intellectual endeavor which more or less adopts methods 'similar in logical structure to those of mathematical physics' (Ibid.). Schumpeter (Ibid. p. 969) states that it is only through the concept of equilibrium that economics can become an exact science.

> [F]rom the standpoint of *any* exact science, the existence of a 'uniquely determined equilibrium (set of values)' is ... of the utmost importance, even if proof has to be purchased at the price of very restrictive assumptions; without any possibility of proving the existence of uniquely determined equilibrium ... at however high a level of abstraction, a field of phenomena is really a chaos that is not under analytic control.

2. Equilibrium and 'Scientific' Economics

No better example of the important role of displaced concepts in the construction and development of theories can be found than that of the role the concept of equilibrium has played in economic theory. Although a detailed history of the development of the concept of equilibrium in the history of economic thought is beyond the limited scope of this book, a brief examination of this concept will help to highlight the importance of displaced concepts, particularly in directing the path of development of a theory.

Economists borrowed the concept of equilibrium first from chemistry and then from mechanics and physics in an attempt to explain the economy as a natural law system. So important to the pretense to science is the concept of equilibrium that many historians of economic thought have found the concept of market equilibrium in Plato, Aristotle and St Thomas Aquinas, even though each wrote about non-market societies and economies.[3] Science discovers natural laws, which are, of course, universals, thus they could be discovered at any time. A rational reconstruction of the history of economic thought from the perspective of general equilibrium theory thus claims that when these early writers wrote about what we consider economic phenomena, and when they noted interdependencies, what they were actually observing were general equilibrium forces. For Plato, Aristotle and even St Thomas Aquinas to have discovered even a hint of market forces producing economic equilibrium would have entailed an extraordinary amount of imagination, for the economies they experienced were traditional and command, but not market oriented. Any analysis that they would have provided of a market economy would be a work of fiction. These efforts, however, highlight the roots the concept of equilibrium has in the Natural Law Outlook, for all three of these great philosophers believed that there was a natural order to the social as well as the natural universe. The philosophers' lasting influence on Western Social Thought lies in their preconceptions as to the nature of social laws, and not any insights into the operation of market forces.

It is not until the 1600s that some economic variables gain the independence from social and political control that one can find market forces operating. It is in the attempts to explain these new forces that we

---

3. See Spiegel 1975.

get the first valid use of the equilibrium concept in economics. The Mercantilists were attempting to understand and explain the behavior of the areas of their economies which had become independent, to a certain extent, from the control of tradition and politics: international trade and money.

In attempting to explain the unity of economic phenomena (in the narrow fields just mentioned) the Mercantilists adopted the concept of the circle, referring to market activity as the 'circle of commerce'. The use of the circle is an important conceptual device in their writings, as well as the use of analogies from circulation. Both come from a long tradition in Western philosophy, dating back to the Greeks, of viewing the circle as evidence of a divinely created natural order. S. Todd Lowry has noted: 'there was a Platonistic tradition perpetuated through the Renaissance and into the Enlightenment to the effect that circular configurations were evidence of a "guiding hand" requiring the intervention of the creator, since in nature things tend to move in a straight line, and the perfection of the circle requires the intervention of a rational power' (Lowry 1974, p. 430). By the time of the Enlightenment, the concept of the circle was commonly used as 'a literary symbol of nature and harmony' (Ibid. p. 431). For the Mercantilists, it provides the conceptual heuristic with which to construct their arguments and develop their theories.

The particular content of their theories is not as important for our purpose as is the method and object of their analysis. The Mercantilists' contribution to economic analysis comes in their recognition that, freed from state control, certain economic phenomena still displayed regularities and uniformities. They discovered the interdependence, as well as independence, of economic phenomena. In particular, Edward Misselden (1623; 1971) and Thomas Mun (1664; 1856) contended that the acts of buying and selling were part of one process, which they called the 'circle of commerce'. Arguing against Gerard de Malynes (1623; 1973), who advocated a return to strict state control of commerce, Misselden suggested that the laws of commerce not only should be independent of state control, but that in effect they were like the laws of nature: beyond state control.

Misselden's analysis is interesting for it foreshadows many future developments. Misselden differentiates between natural exchange and political exchange. Natural exchange is concerned with the intrinsic value of goods; and political exchange relates to 'outward valuation' and is 'in Merchants' terms called the price, ... or rate of exchange' (Misselden 1971, p. 97). Political exchange is determined in the short run by 'circumstances of time, and place, and persons' (Ibid.) and thus includes many uncertainties. Yet this does not lead to either chaos or a violation of justice, for natural exchange regulates political exchange: the intrinsic value (natural exchange) acts as the 'center, where unto all exchange have their natural propension' (Ibid.).[4] The radical nature of Misselden's analysis was aptly recognized by Joyce Appleby when she wrote: '[w]hat Misselden's arguments threatened was the accepted dividing line between the natural and the social' (Appleby 1978, p. 47). Economic phenomena were now being moved from the social aspect of life, which was undoubtedly the proper realm for the interference of the sovereign, to the natural aspect.

Withdrawing the economic sphere - or at least the act of exchange - from state control raised the question of what would provide order if the sovereign did not? And along with the concern for order come questions of justice: the public's interest in the preeminent question of a sufficient and affordable supply of subsistence goods. Misselden's genius was to point to an aspect of the universe that was orderly, that is nature, and then to place economic phenomena in this category. As Appleby (Ibid. p. 80) notes:

> Central to the efforts to analyze market relations was the conviction that there existed a determinable order. When Edward Misselden and Thomas Mun challenged Gerald de Malynes' belief that a properly run economy required the wisdom and authority of the monarch, they redirected attention from the council chamber to the activity in the market. In denying the central place to sovereignty, however, they did not suggest that individual market decisions determining the flow of coin were random or idiosyncratic. Rather they assumed a uniformity operating at all economic levels. This assumption led to the idea of economic laws and the conviction that anarchy was not the inevitable alternative to external control. It laid the scientific foundations for individual economic freedom.

The actual operations of markets in the seventeenth century did not, by themselves, suggest the idea of an equilibrium system. As Appleby states clearly: 'The actual round of economic activities in seventeenth-century England was composed of richly varied parts not all suggestive of uniformities. ... What happened in any given market was conditioned by custom, prescribed by law and shaped by events throughout the commercial sphere. ... The creation of this economic model was not, however, done in a vacuum. Adopting the scientific mode of analysis for the study of the market was a selective act, ... [owing] much to the larger intellectual currents of the period' (Ibid. p. 243).

The development of the conception of the market as an orderly system

---

4. This is strikingly similar to Adam Smith's natural value/market value distinction.

comes from the explicit adoption of the equilibrium metaphor in order to treat the market not only as an inherently orderly system, but as a natural system displaying an order analogous to that observed in the natural universe. Much of Adam Smith's fame, and standing, as the founder of modern economics, stems from his development of an economic theory that more fully resembled Newton's physics, the accepted standard for science then. Chapter 3 demonstrated how Newton influenced Smith's theories, most importantly his method. Smith's economics, as Chapter 4 explained, was partly historical and partly an equilibrium theory, both of which were part of Smith's, and Newton's, conception of the Natural Law Outlook. The natural law/historical dichotomy gives Smith the dual role of solidifying the equilibrium concept in social science while at the same time presenting an alternative. Myers has argued that equilibrium plays an unusual role in Smith, for although Smith's morals and economics contain equilibrium concepts, Smith never seems to be satisfied with them. 'Smith's treatment of economic equilibrium', Myers (1975, p. 561) writes, 'was very tentative and contingent. He did not try to present the idea in an exact and well-defined form, nor did he devote much space to it in his works.' Smith theory of value as it is first developed in Chapter 7 of the *Wealth of Nations* is clearly modeled after the concept of equilibrium as developed by Newtonian physics. Following the heuristic of the market as an equilibrium system, Smith's analysis follows, to the extent that it can, Newton's. The equilibrium aspect of Smith's theory of value is the establishing of the concept of natural value: the price 'to which the [market] prices of all commodities are continually gravitating' (Smith 1976, p. 75). Smith further bolsters the scientific credentials of his analysis by displacing not only the concept of equilibrium to the behavior of markets, but also the concept of gravity reinforcing the idea that the economy is a natural system. Starting with the displaced concept of Newtonian equilibrium to understand the market, Smith follows Newtonian analysis by depicting the equilibrium as a balance of forces which operate through the actions of the individual atoms of the market. Economic theory since Smith has followed the equilibrium heuristic further down the physics road, yet Smith is not so naive. Smith is more interested in efficient causes and processes than final causes, thus his analysis quickly shifts to historical and institutional factors. Smith's limited adoption of the concept of equilibrium reflects his natural law preconceptions, the mixture of equilibrium and history that is distinctive of the Scottish Enlightenment.

In Adam Smith's works, as has already been argued, there is a dichotomy between his research program and his method of investigation. Smith's objective was to discover the natural laws of the social universe, the existence of which he derived from the Natural Law Outlook. However, under the influence of Natural Theology and Newton, Smith's method of discovering these natural laws was to investigate their operation in the real world. Thus the bulk of the *Wealth of Nations* consists of historical and institutional analysis. The contradiction between Smith's method and research program led to the frequent conflicts between Smith's natural laws and his observations of actual events and his occasional call for interventionist policies. This is necessarily the case. Society is a human creation and not the result of natural forces and natural human propensities. Thus social phenomena are inherently different from natural phenomena in that their creation and meaning are socially bound and not the result of universal natural laws.

Walras's development of the theory of general equilibrium was an important turning point in economic theory. Along with Jevons and Menger, Walras helped to move economic theory away from the social sciences and towards the natural sciences. All three felt that for the discovery of pure theory, one should abstract from society and history, and concentrate instead on finding universal natural laws. Walras, along with Jevons and Menger, excluded social and historical factors from the development of pure theory because they fully held the Natural Law Outlook. It is under this outlook, as with Smith and the Mercantilists, that they framed their theories in terms of equilibrium. Their starting point was a vision of the economy as a natural order, the result of natural forces, with equilibrium as the state when economic phenomena were in their natural positions.

Their equilibrium view of the economy was a preconception and not a conclusion derived from an empirical investigation into the operations of market economies. This is evident in two aspects of their works. First, as was clearly demonstrated in Chapter 6, they excluded the validity of observation in forming pure theory. Second, an investigation into how actual economies operated would have shown change and evolution as the norms of market economies and not static equilibrium.

William Jaffe (1976; 1977) has written at length on the normative character of Walras's general equilibrium, stating that 'Walras's aim, even in his 'pure economics', was prescriptive or normative rather than positive or descriptive. His objective was to formulate an economic system in conformity with an ideal of social justice compatible with the inexorable exigencies of man's nature and his environment' (Jaffe 1983, p. 334). Even more forcefully, Jaffe (Ibid. p. 341) writes:

> Walras's latent purpose in contriving his general equilibrium model was

not to describe or analyze the working of the economic system as it existed, nor was it primarily to portray the purely economic relations within a network of markets under the assumption of theoretically perfect regime of free competition. It was, as Pareto perceived, rather to demonstrate the possibility of formulating axiomatically a rationally consistent economic system that would satisfy the demands of social justice without overstepping the bounds imposed by natural exigencies of the real world.

Donald Walker has strongly disagreed with Jaffe's thesis; stating that Walras was an objective scientist, searching for objective truths. Walker states that Walras made a clear distinction between positive and normative economics. According to Walker, Walras's 'pure economic theory ... establishes truth, ... which is the study of the natural laws of exchange, or the theory of social wealth' (Walker 1984, p. 453). What Jaffe only alludes to, and what Walker completely does not see, is that it is Walras's Natural Law Outlook that leads him to frame the economic universe in terms of general equilibrium. The Natural Law Outlook implicit in Walras's system is evident in his belief that economics is analogous to the natural sciences, particularly mechanics, and in his belief in the existence of universal natural laws in the economic realm of the social universe, independent of both time and institutions. Walras, along with Jevons, went to great lengths to argue that economic theory is a physio-mathematical subject, similar, if not completely analogous, to mechanics and astronomy. The adoption of mathematics as the language for economic theory was supported by the apparent similarity between economic theory and mechanics. Philip Mirowski (1989) has explained this similarity by clearly demonstrating that the marginalist revolution was merely the coping of the equations of physics and renaming the variables to give them economic meaning. But, as Mirowski (1986, p. 187) has pointed out: 'The most curious aspect of this program to make economics more rigorous and more scientific is that not one neoclassical economist in over one hundred years has seen fit to discuss the appropriateness or inappropriateness of the adoption of the mathematical metaphor of energy in a prerelativistic gravitational field in order to discuss the preferences and price formation of transactors in the marketplace'.

The Natural Law Outlook, as a preconception (vision), was hidden from the realm of inquiry, and thus went unquestioned. It should also be noted that the physics (Newtonian for the classicals, conservation principle for the neoclassicals) which economic theory has modeled itself after was developed to demonstrate and support the idea of a divinely ordered universe (Mirowski 1989, p. 103).

Guy Routh (1975) has demonstrated the political motivations and biases of the marginalists and how the particular developments of their theories were designed, as with Smith and the Mercantilists, to support their political views. The adoption of a view of the economy as an equilibrium system regulated by nature has great political value, for it propagates the idea that the economy is 'harmonious' if left to itself and that it is beyond human engineering and manipulation. Both aspects were important in fighting the rising socialist sentiments of the mid-nineteenth century. The historical and institutional analysis that interested Smith, when carried out in the nineteenth century did not yield the type of society Smith had envisioned. Such an analysis supported reform and intervention and not laissez-faire.[5] In order for economic theory to justify and legitimate the existing economic system it became essential to exclude such factors.

The development of general equilibrium theory since Walras has, at least on the surface, moved away from Walras's open belief in natural law philosophy,[6] although even Pareto, who wrote about the dangers of natural law philosophy (Pareto 1966, pp. 206-7) would occasionally let his guard slip. Yet they have not swayed from the Natural Law Outlook. For as in Walras's theory, we can see the Natural Law Outlook implicit in the development of general equilibrium theory from their insistence in emulating the natural sciences (particularly theoretical physics), in the development of their models, and in the exclusion of historical and institutional factors as playing any meaningful role.[7]

As has been argued throughout this book, the attempt to create a science of society leads to the progressive withdrawal of historical and social context from the analysis of society. The hostility towards history and social analysis by those who desire a scientific social science stems primarily from two factors. First, natural science is concerned with universals; while history is concerned with particulars, often denying the existence of universals. Second, actual history is often inconvenient for those looking for the natural laws of society, for diversity, and not

---

5. This can be seen in the work of the German and English Historical schools and even more so in Karl Marx's writings.

6. Samuelson called the teleological aspects of both nineteenth-century physics and economics the 'Pathetic Fallacy' (quoted in Mirowski 1989, p. 103), claiming that instead of demonstrating the provincial design of the universe, the models and assumptions of physics, and the emulation of them by economists, merely makes theorizing simpler.

7. Philip Mirowski (1989, Chapter 4) has shown how the recent attempts by neoclassical economists to develop an institutionalist theory, particularly game theory, have failed miserably, giving institutions no meaningful role for they have failed to see the evolutionary nature of institutions.

homogeneity, is the conclusion of historical analysis and the study of comparative systems. Thus history must either be eliminated or be reconstructed so that it fits the existing conventional wisdom. Yet if economics is to be an empirical science, like the natural sciences, it must have data and be able to explain that data; history is the storehouse of data for the social sciences. Jevons's and Walras's conception of a scientific economics had to change radically for economics to become scientific. In the twentieth century we see the elimination of history in economic theory, followed by its reconstruction. Before we get to modern thought it will be instructive, I think, for us to take a brief look at the origins of the mathematical formalism which eventually comes to typify the idea as to what is a scientific social science.

3. Mathematical Reasoning in Social Theory

The view that the economy and society had a determinable order consisting of uniformities and regularities, operating in a mechanical and atomistic fashion and promoting the welfare of society, developed not from the analysis of market interdependence by the Mercantilists, but from the speculations of the natural law philosophers.

As with the Mercantilists, the natural law philosophers did not attempt to separate the natural from the moral, the positive from the normative; they were as much advocates as analysts. The placing of nature as the final cause in their theories was an explicit recognition of the principle of design and the moral aspect of the natural order. Whereas the Mercantilists were preoccupied with the narrow question of economic order in international trade and money, the natural law philosophers' concern was with the comprehensive question of social order. The catalyst for many of the writings on social order in the seventeenth century was Thomas Hobbes.

In the *Leviathan* (1964), Hobbes established the subject which was to dominate social inquiry for the Enlightenment: whence comes social order? Of greater consequence, however, was that Hobbes also established the framework in which social inquiry was to take place. According to Hobbes, human nature was the foundation upon which social theories were to be constructed.

Hobbes formulates his theory of social order by first investigating the nature of man. Hobbes's analysis of human nature states that '[N]ature hath made men so equall, in the faculties of body, and mind' (Hobbes

1964, p. 82) with equal desires and 'equality of hope in attaining of our end' (Ibid. p. 83) that, in the state of nature, social order is not possible. Hobbes's reasoning is worth quoting at length:

> [I]f any two men desire the same thing, which nevertheless they cannot both enjoy, they become enemies; and in the way to their end, (which is principally their owne conservation, and sometimes their delectation only) endeavour to destroy, or subdue one another. And from hence it comes to passe, that where an invader hath no more to feare, than another mans single power; if one plant, sow, build, or possesse a convenient seat, others may probably be expected to come prepared with forces united, to dispossesse, and deprive him, not only of the fruit of his labour, but also of his life, or liberty. (Ibid. p. 83)

Thus the nature of man creates a 'warre of every man against every man'. Hobbes's solution is the Leviathan, an order-bestowing force (for Hobbes this should be a strong monarchy) which would establish and enforce law and order.

Hobbes's conclusion was almost universally rejected by subsequent philosophers, but all accepted the form of his argument: social order, and more generally social theory, should start with the nature of the individual (human nature). Furthermore, human nature was to be considered universal and constant, independent of social influences; that natural law and not custom, history or institutions, was the object of science.

For Hobbes, as Myers has noted, 'self-interest [was the] ... prime mover among the various motives in natural man and he emphasized its great personal and social importance ... [Which was that it was] the most destructive of human motives' (Myers 1983, p. 28). Subsequent philosophers accepted Hobbes's emphasis on self-interest (although many placed it more on a par with the other passions) yet rejected his conclusion that the nature of man made him unsociable. The legacy of Hobbes is the manner in which he analyzed man. Commenting on Hobbes's method, Myers has noted: 'he begins his study of man by stripping away the disguising and obscuring paraphernalia of social life in order to see man in his natural and essential state. Hobbes removes man from institutions and customs, hoping to see him as he really is. His method might, in a sense, be likened to the mathematical because he is subtracting elements from what makes up the totality of man's condition and nature, the remainder being the denominator common to all individuals' (Ibid. p. 30).

Myers notes that the use of the mathematical analogy is particularly applicable to Hobbes and to his lasting influence on social thought. Hobbes felt that his method of reasoning, and in fact all correct reasoning, was merely mathematics. In the *Leviathan*, Hobbes writes that 'when a man reasoneth, hee does nothing else but conceive a summe totall, from addition of parcels; or conceive a remainder, from subtraction of one summe from another' (Hobbes 1964, p. 22).

The philosophers who attacked Hobbes's conclusion did so by arguing either that man's nature was not anti-social, as did Richard Cumberland who argued that trade and self-interest led to a social equilibrium of sorts, or that man in a state of nature had natural rights, and thus formed a government to protect these rights, as was argued by John Locke.

Hobbes is reviving the Greek philosophers' naturalistic view of the social universe. Together with the Copernican revolution in the natural sciences, a new vision of the universe was brought forth. The Natural Law Outlook of the Middle Ages, in which divine revelation was the final standard as to what constituted a natural law, was replaced with a 'scientific' Natural Law Outlook. God was still the final cause, but the reliance on revelation was replaced by reason (Descartes) and/or by observation (Newton). Regardless of whether one was a Cartesian or a Newtonian, the world was now viewed as a great machine, and the role of science was to figure out the laws that regulated it. As we would expect, through the DMD thesis, the new conception of nature led to a new conception of society. The new vision was transmitted to the social sciences largely through the use of displaced concepts from the natural sciences to the social. According to the principle of design, both the social and the natural universe were regulated by natural law. Furthermore, this law was essentially mechanical in nature, so that the same method of analysis should be used.

We have seen in Chapters 4 and 5 how the attempt to construct a science of society built on historical and social analysis at first was optimistic, but in the end became problematic. It is clear that by the end of the nineteenth century the goal of a science of society, particularly of a scientific economics, was increasingly being tied to the development of a mathematical economics while decreasing the role of history and society.

Jevons and Walras saw the need for a mathematical economics, yet their justification of it was quite different from the factors that lead to the eventual dominance of mathematical formalism. Jevons argued, and Walras agreed (see Walras 1909) that economics was inherently a mathematical discipline because its objects of analysis were quantities, and to him it was self-evident that one investigated quantities with the tools, and in the

language, of mathematics.[8]   Jevons was hopeful that eventually statistical
analysis would develop to the point where economics could be as empirical
as the natural sciences. It is ironic that it is Jevons's and Walras's theory
of value that negates this very point. The quantities their theories analyzed
(utilities and disutilities) were not only unmeasurable, they were not
observable, a point only Menger of the early marginalists seems to have
understood.

By the time neoclassical economists realized the inherent problem in the
marginal utility theory of value as an empirical science, they were already
committed to the view that a scientific economics is one that emulates
theoretical physics.   To justify the pretense of being scientific meant
imitating physicists and using their concepts as the driving heuristics
(displaced concepts), yet the content of marginal utility economics did not
lend itself to being treated in a mathematical sense. A new justification for
mathematical formalism was required in order for economics to further its
search for the natural laws of the economy. We find this in the work of the
Vienna Circle, to which we now turn.

The Vienna Circle

The Vienna Circle consisted of a group of scientists, philosophers and
social scientists who met in Vienna during the 1920s to discuss issues
related to what is now called the philosophy of science. Its prominent
members included: Otto Neurath; Moritz Schlick; Friedrich Waismann;
Felix Kaufmann; Karl Menger (son of Carl Menger); Kurt Godel; Hans
Hahn; and Rudolf Carnap. The philosophers Ludwig Wittgenstein and Karl
Popper, although not members, had extensive contact with many of its
members and were instrumental in its development: Wittgenstein as an
important influence and Popper as an advocate of its world view. Their
philosophical outlook is called logical positivism.

The goal of the Vienna Circle was to provide a unified science and to
purge philosophy of all traces of metaphysics. As one of its leading
participants expressed it: 'The Vienna circle devotes itself more and more
to the task of expressing unified science (which includes sociology as well
as chemistry, biology as well as mechanics, psychology - more properly
termed "behavioristics" as well as optics) in a unified language, ...
displaying of the interconnections of the various sciences' (Otto Neurath

---

8. A point not frequently noted, but nevertheless important, is that, although the original
justification of mathematics in economics was to facilitate the analysis of quantities, mathematics
is not an empirical science.

quoted in Ingrao and Israel 1990, pp. 189-90). Scott Gordon (1991, p. 593) has recently summarized the goal of the Vienna Circle as such:

> The Vienna Circle [attempted to develop] ... a unified philosophy that would state the foundations of human knowledge. In calling their manifesto 'The Scientific Conception of the World' they did not mean that they intended to delineate the particular world-view of natural scientists, or to restrict their principles to the domain of material phenomena. Though they often seemed to have physics in mind when speaking of 'science', and matter and energy in mind when speaking of 'phenomena', they felt that they had arrived at foundational epistemic principles that apply to all properly conducted attempts to obtain knowledge, not excluding those that deal with psychological and social phenomena. Indeed, the manifesto of the Circle, issued in 1929, ended with the confident statement that 'We witness the spirit of the scientific world-conception penetrating in growing measure the forms of personal and public life, in education, upbringing, architecture, and the shaping of economic and social life according to rational principles.

Their desire to combat metaphysics was aimed at German idealism, which then dominated philosophy in Germany. The Vienna Circle attempted to develop a philosophy of science based entirely on empiricism. They attacked all non-empirical statements as metaphysics, which, for them, literally meant nonsense. They did not claim that such statements were correct or incorrect, just that they had no meaning. They were greatly influenced and encouraged by Ludwig Wittgenstein's *Tractatus Logico-philosophicus*, which presented an argument that language must be strictly representational: 'that a language of communication consists of terms that directly correspond to sensory-world entities' (Ibid.).[9] The hope here was to construct a natural language, independent of history and society. At first they were encouraged by the success they had attacking idealist philosophy, yet it soon became apparent that their critique regarding the meaningfulness of statements could be equally applicable to the natural sciences. They were thus running the risk of destroying the foundation upon which their world view was based. They accepted the results of contemporary science as depicting the natural laws, yet the scientific theories of their day, as in any other, did not rely exclusively on empirical statements and observation, and frequently were not verified or verifiable according to their verification principles.

Just as Descartes had objected to the subjective nature of observation,

---

9. Wittgenstein later abandons this view, partly, the legend goes, as the result of his discussions with Piero Sraffa.

particularly in regard to historical knowledge, the logical positivists came to realize the subjective nature of scientific investigations. 'To overcome this difficulty' writes John Passmore (1967, p. 55), 'Schlick drew a distinction between "content" and "structure." We can never be sure, he argued, that the content of our experience is identical with the content of any other person's experience ... For scientific purposes, however, this does not matter in the slightest. Science is interested only in the structure of our experience.' Increasingly, the logical positivists emphasized the structure of a theory; not its empirical content. The question of verification gradually changed to the possibility of being verified or put to a falsification test.

One last point on the logical positivists that should be mentioned. Their attack on the metaphysics of German idealism was at the same time an attack on historicism and on the ideologies and political philosophies which frequently used history and sociological analysis to support their theories, most importantly Marxism. The Vienna Circle's attack on history and social analysis is clearly as political as it was philosophical. The pinnacle of logical positivism in this regard is Karl Popper's *The Poverty of Historicism*.

4. Axiomatic General Equilibrium Theory

The importance of the Vienna Circle for our purpose is that they provided the rationale for the axiomatization of economic theory.[10] In a recent article in the *Journal of the History of Economic Thought*, Lionello F. Punzo (1991) argues that the revolutionary change in economic theory came not in the 1870s with the marginal utility theorists, but owes its origins instead to the Vienna Circle of the 1920s and 30s. It is the economic theory that developed out of the philosophical vision of the Vienna Circle which finally breaks all ties between economic theory and historical and social analysis; between economics and the object of its analysis, the economy.

Recent scholarship in the history of economic thought has brought to light the important role the Vienna Circle had on the development of economic theory, particularly modern general equilibrium. E. Roy Weintraub first demonstrated the lasting influence of this school for economics in his

---

10. The work of the Vienna Circle led to the move to create a scientific history, that is to discover the general laws of history which would be analogous to those of the natural sciences. The leader in this movement was Carl Hempel. For a very good discussion of this debate see Gordon (1991).

investigations into the development of the concept of equilibrium. Weintraub's (1985) history of the development of general equilibrium theory from 1930-1950 filled a great void in the historiography of economics and demonstrates the significance, the driving role, mathematics has played in this period. Yet Weintraub does not make the connection between the path of development of economics and the adoption of the concept of equilibrium as the guiding heuristic for the development of economic theory. Furthermore, although it is common to emphasize the importance of mathematics in the development of economic theory, the accepted conventional wisdom is that mathematics only provided new and improved tools to help theorists better develop and express their theories. Much more important is the role mathematics has had in determining the path economic theory has taken. It is in Bruna Ingrao and Giorgio Israel's work that this issue has been most successfully raised. In their 1985 article 'General Economic Equilibrium Theory: A History of Ineffectual Paradigmatic Shifts' and more recently in their book, *The Invisible Hand: Economic Equilibrium in the History of Science*, Ingrao and Israel have demonstrated how the equilibrium metaphor as a heuristic became solidified as a model. Furthermore, the factors that lead to the adoption of equilibrium as a guiding heuristic, which we have called the Natural Law Outlook, or the desire to create a science of society based on the natural sciences, are also the factors that strengthened the equilibrium heuristic into the dominant model in economics. Equilibrium's role as a heuristic is to raise interesting questions, give new insights and perspectives. Primarily, as a heuristic, its function is to provide a tool with which one can come to an understanding of the ordering properties and processes of the market economy. Thus when the classical economists used equilibrium as a heuristic, they conceived of the economy as having a structural order. From this they set out to discover the dominant and persistent forces in the market economy which created this order. The classicals then set out to investigate how actual market outcomes were influenced by this underlying order, particularly the processes by which actual outcomes might gravitate towards these long-run positions; the underlying order. The usefulness of the equilibrium concept is judged by the insights it yields on actual economic behavior and outcomes. It is a perspective from which to view the economy.

With the increased effort to be scientific in the late nineteenth century, not only did the concept of equilibrium change, but its theoretical significance was radically altered. The concept of equilibrium changed from a structural equilibrium, that is, a balance between the sectors of the economy determined by the method of production and other social and historical factors, to a behavioral equilibrium where the economy's balance is achieved through the interaction of individual psyches. The final state of equilibrium was when all psyches were satisfied that they could not improve the level of satisfaction through further economic activity, and hence all such activity ceased. With this less realistic notion of equilibrium came a shift in emphasis away from the real and towards the ideal. Developing the concept of equilibrium was now of fundamental importance. Thus, not only did the concept of equilibrium change, its role had changed. It was now a model. Attention started to shift towards understanding the properties of the model and not the structure of the economy.[11] The history of the concept of equilibrium in the twentieth century is dominated by the search for the existence, uniqueness and stability of equilibrium, with the tools and level of abstraction in economic analysis chosen based on their utility in solving these problems, and not actual economic problems.

This development in economic theorizing owes a great debt to the Vienna Circle. The similarities between the two should be obvious, for both were attempts to develop a grand unifying theory that would explain all phenomena. The most important lasting influence of the Vienna Circle is its role in the increased mathematical formalism. Through economics, logical positivism is asserting influence on modern social science long after it had been rejected as a philosophy. Jevons's and Walras's call for a mathematical economics was based on the role mathematics then played as a tool for describing physical laws, particularly in the importance of measurement. This radically changed under the influence of the Vienna Circle, as Punzo (1991, p. 4) notes: 'in the program of redesigning economics initiated in Vienna, the use of mathematics as a tool to attain, at least in principle, exact measurability and quantitative predictability of the values of economic variables yielded to the logical calculus.' Mathematics became the language of economic theory, and the logic of mathematics, and not the logic of the market, became the principal object of study. Furthermore, mathematics was adopted as the language of economics because it was seen as the language of a unified science, the Vienna Circle's vision of discovering the natural order of the physical and social universes. As Ingrao and Israel (1990, p. 182) have noted: 'Mathematics had previously been a tool for describing physical laws and had made it possible to forecast the behavior of real processes in numerical terms. Now

---

11. The change to a pure economics was slow and gradual and not universally accepted. Contemporaneous with the marginalists were the English and German historical schools, as well as the Institutionalists in America, all of whom concentrated their efforts on understanding the actual economy.

it was to take on the new role of unifying theories.'

Economic theory's full and final acceptance of mathematics as its language, and logic, culminates in Gerard Debreu's development of axiomatic general equilibrium theory. Axiomatics developed out of the Vienna Circle's shifting attention from empirical content to logical structure. The basic premise of axiomatics is that one can develop a theory from clearly defined axioms, and as long as one follows the rules of mathematical logic, the theories developed will be logically valid. Hence, if one could not develop an empirically acceptable theory, for reasons such as an inability to measure adequately the phenomena in question, one could, with equal validity, state propositions about the phenomena which were known to be true, and then develop a theory. The theory is thus developed independently from the phenomena it hopes to explain. Debreu defends the use of the axiomatic method in the introduction to his *The Theory of Value* (1959, p. x):

> Allegiance to rigor dictates the axiomatic form of the analysis where the theory, in the strict sense, is logically entirely disconnected from its interpretation. ... Such a dichotomy reveals all the assumptions and logical structure of the analysis. It also makes possible immediate extensions of that analysis without modification of the theory by simple reinterpretations of the concepts.

The theory, its axioms and theorems, are all that exist for the axiomatic method; structure and not empirical content is what matters. Ingrao and Israel (1990, p. 183) quote one of the originators of this method to illustrate this point: 'Hilbert's famous remark that in his axiomatic presentation of Euclidean geometry, the words "point", "line", and "plane" could be replaced by "chair", "table", and "glass of beer" without impairing the truth of the theory. In this way Hilbert strongly underlied the *emptying of content* carried out with regard to mathematical theories.'

The adoption of the axiomatic method thus further narrows the boundaries of economic science. The axiomatic method is more than just a 'rigorous' analysis. Use of this method for the social science implicitly assumes that social structures are analogous to those of pure logic. Implicit in this view is Galileo's idea that the universe was written in mathematics (God's language) and the principle of design. The principle of design enters the analysis in two ways. First, if the world is rationally ordered then mathematics, which is reason, operates by the same principles and thus the design could be discovered by investigating mathematics. Second, if the social universe, like the physical universe, is rationally ordered, then its laws are mathematical, and could not only be demonstrated by mathematical equations, but could be discovered by investigating the properties of these equations.

The axioms chosen by modern general equilibrium theorists were not derived from observation, but are either the same as the earlier marginalists had developed (based on their natural law preconceptions) or are chosen so that the theory will obtain the desired results.[12] Jonas Kornai (1971) has extensively demonstrated that many, if not most, of the assumptions of general equilibrium theory are empirically incorrect or meaningless. This gulf between the theory and reality was highlighted by Kornai (1971, p. 28) when he wrote:

> In reality, there are mammoth corporations and the role of government is great. GE [general equilibrium] theory assumes atomized markets and 'perfect' competition. In reality, there exist sharp conflicts of interest. GE theory sees peaceful harmony in the market. In reality there is concentration and rapid technical progress. GE theory 'disregards' increasing returns of scale, one of the most significant aspects of technical progress and one of the fundamental explanations of concentration. In reality, the information structure is highly intricate and complex. GE theory describes a system governed in an entirely reliable manner by a single signal, namely prices.

The axiomatic method further weakens the usefulness of general equilibrium theory, for as Ingrao and Israel (1985, pp. 91-2) have noted:

> [the axiomatic method] following the canons of formalism ... radically and uncompromisingly empties the theory of any empirical reference. ... Debreu's interpretation of general economic equilibrium theory makes it a self-sufficient formal structure which loses even the feature of being a 'model' at all. The concepts of the theory are no longer understood as the outcome of a process of abstracting from real phenomena, nor as the formalism of 'ideas and knowledge relating to a phenomena'. Neither do they require empirical verification to prove the validity. ... The dichotomy between mathematical structure and the interpretative content of that structure strips general economic equilibrium theory once and for all of its ambition to provide an interpretative schema to analyze the functioning of an economy of competitive markets.

John B. Davis (1989) has also noted the referentiality problem of axiomatic general equilibrium, adding the static nature of their a priori concepts. Not only are these concepts, such as commodity, consumer, producer, price, logically unconnected to any real commodity, consumer, producer and price, their static nature prevents the analysis from capturing the importance

---

12. An example of this is the convexity assumption which is used to provide stability.

of the economy as an historical process.

Schumpeter argued that the determination of the existence, stability and optimality of equilibrium was of paramount importance, regardless of the level of abstraction. The solution of these three problems is seen by economists as the two hundred year old quest for the Invisible Hand Adam Smith wrote about: 'can a decentralized economy relying only on price signals for market information be orderly?' (Hahn 1982, p. 126). Smith tried to demonstrate the order in a market economy by analyzing both the efficient and final causes that determined such an order, hence Smith's system is concerned with nature (for Smith the final cause) and society (the efficient cause). For the marginalists, being scientific meant searching only for final causes (pure theory) with efficient causes relegated to applied economics. Thus their systems only consider nature and natural forces. Modern general equilibrium theory has superseded the marginalists by abstracting from both society and nature, for they do not claim that their axioms are forces of nature, or even empirically correct. Only by leaving out both society and nature have they thus been able to prove Smith's Invisible Hand theorem. Yet this can only be done by excluding from our analysis such factors as money, expectations and production - in a word, capitalism. Furthermore, to quote again from Ingrao and Israel's (1985, p. 102) seminal work in this field:

> All the formal developments of the theory which most clearly and explicitly preaches 'the ability of a competitive system to achieve an allocation of resources that is efficient in some sense' have failed to show how the system can achieve equilibrium except 'by decree,' namely, by the direct imposition of a system of equilibrium prices compatible with the features of the economy in question, which can only be achieved in a centrally planned economy.

Prices are thus not the result of the market forces of competition. It is the great irony of modern economic theory that in order to demonstrate Adam Smith's Invisible Hand, which was developed to counter Hobbes's call for a strong central government, neoclassical economic theory necessitates a Leviathan.

General equilibrium theory, in its modern form, should be seen as the last natural law system, yet it is a very peculiar version, for although it has all three elements of a natural law system specified in Chapter 2, it has no natural foundations. With the development of the axiomatic method, economic theory is no longer based on any conceptions of natural forces, and is instead based on hypothetical assumptions that are independent of the real world.[13] However, for all practical purposes, Debreu's axioms, when they have any economic meaning, are no different from the assumptions of nature made by earlier neoclassical economists. The naturalism of modern general equilibrium theory can be seen in this reliance on nature, however hypothetical the conception may be, as a final cause and in the 'state of nature' explanation offered of social phenomena - an explanation which is independent of society.

Modern general equilibrium theory excludes history and society from having any meaningful role. Pure theory is developed free of these complicating factors and there is no necessity to change the pure theory because of changes in the institutional structure of the economy. From this economists feel free to apply their theories irrespective of the social setting. Furthermore, an increasing number of economists apply neoclassical economic theory beyond economics proper (economic imperialism), everything from the family to law and politics. This is because the pure theory is concerned with universal laws based on nature.

That modern general equilibrium is built upon the assumption of a social physics is so obvious it hardly needs any elaboration. Based upon this notion is the justification for the level of formalism in economic theory as well as the whole forecasting industry. Economic theory treats economic phenomena as merely variables that are part of larger equations, differentiated only by measures of quantity and not substance. Without the belief in social physics, questions of the existence and stability of equilibria become meaningless.

As stated above, the physics which economic theory has adopted as its model was designed to demonstrate the efficiency of nature and the benevolence of its results. Modern general equilibrium theory has a much more modest goal: to demonstrate the efficiency of the market for allocating resources among competing uses. The claim of efficiency for the market, as well as the concern for demonstrating the optimality of equilibrium outcomes demonstrates the natural moral theory implicit in modern economics. It is the overall presumption of neoclassical economic theory that equilibrium values have some special significance beyond just being one of many possible outcomes. It is this opinion which leads economists to favor market over non-market solutions, competition over cooperation, competitive over concentrated markets and to measure social well-being in terms of the market values, either real or with shadow prices.

The political effect of the equilibrium view of the economy has been best

---

13. It is worthwhile here to recall Collingwood's statement on the tendency of visions of nature to move from the tangible to the mind. Axiomatics thus can be seen as such a development.

noted by John Kenneth Galbraith when he stated that the net effect of neoclassical economic instruction was to prevent students from asking dangerous questions. Questions beyond the natural operations of the market are outside the purview of economic theory. Moralists try to interfere with the market, economists know better. When one suggests some sort of social intervention into the economy, one must either demonstrate market failures (externalities, public goods) or one must take recourse in political or sociological justifications. The presumption is always in favor of the natural operations of the market.

Modern general equilibrium theory has only the pretense of being scientific, if by scientific we mean the pursuit of knowledge about the world we inhabit. Although it adopts the form of physics, and thus looks like a scientific endeavor, neoclassical economics analyzes hypothetical economies, not any actual economy, and thus cannot be considered a science. The scientific application of the axiomatic method would include the development of empirically correct axioms, developed from an investigation into the actual operations of the economy.[14] Following this step, it would develop these assumptions to their logical conclusion. Yet modern general equilibrium theory does just the reverse, it starts with the conclusion that the economy is an equilibrium system which includes a distribution of resources and prices which provides for an optimal allocation of societies' resources in which no market participant wishes to alter their position, and then chooses the axioms which would provide such a result. This procedure is more characteristic of an ideology then a science.[15] Furthermore, modern general equilibrium theory has yet to adapt its theory to the existence of the large modern corporation, the most characteristic institution of our economy. The insistence on developing pure theory independent of actual conditions has left modern general equilibrium theory with little use for explaining an economy which has developed beyond the 'cigarette economy' of the World War Two prison camps.

In Chapter 1 we took a brief look at the process by which social theories were developed, specifically the interaction between the social and natural realms, and the role of displaced concepts. As we have seen in this chapter, the concept of equilibrium embodies much of this process. The organic view of nature held by the Physiocrats is displaced into an organic view of society. From this view, a structural equilibrium theory is

---

14. This assumes that the logic of mathematics is the logic of society, a dangerous assumption.

15. See Kornai (1971) for an analysis of the assumptions of general equilibrium theory, as well as the dubious scientific procedures it follows.

developed, where the parts are understood in relation to the whole, and where attention is on the flows within the economic organ. The development of mechanical conceptions of equilibrium, with the Newtonian Revolution, is eventually displaced into a mechanical view of society by the classical and neoclassical economists, and to the treatment of economic phenomena as the result of the balance of forces. The quest of the Enlightenment was a science of society, so it is to be expected that the natural sciences would be the field from which to harvest concepts to be displaced into the analysis of society. This explains the first two of Schon's questions on displaced concepts: where do they come from and why are some concepts chosen over others? Our concern, however, has been primarily with the third question: what is the lasting impact? The displacement of the concept of equilibrium on to economics, in fact the whole project of attempting to construct a science of society based on the natural sciences, has greatly shaped the resulting theory. Specifically, in the move towards a 'scientific' (mathematical) economic theory, it became necessary to progressively empty economic theory of all historical and social context.

It is thus in the conservative function of displaced concepts that we find the lasting effect of the search for natural laws in the economy, for as the economic theorists' attention was diverted to questions of existence, stability and optimality, they were ignoring questions of the interaction between institutions and individuals, the life process called society.

8. Beyond Natural Law Economics

In his 1988 Nobel lecture, Maurice Allais (1990, pp. 5; 6) provides a contemporary statement of the Natural Law Outlook in economics:

> [T]he prerequisite of any science is the existence of regularities which can be analyzed and forecast. This is for example the case in celestial mechanics. But it is also true of many economic phenomena. Indeed, their thorough analysis displays the existence of regularities which are just as striking as those found in the physical sciences. This is why Economics is a science and why this science rests on the same general principles and methods as the natural sciences ...
>
> I have been gradually led to a twofold conviction: human psychology remains fundamentally the same at all times and in all places; and the present is determined by the past according to invariant laws. It seems to me that, to a very large extent, the social sciences must, like the physical sciences, be based on the search for relationships and quantities *invariant in time and in space.*

Allais is expressing the perspective held by the vast majority of economists. More importantly, this position is the implicit premise upon which most of their work is based. Here we can see the crux of our argument on the loss of historical sense, for to find invariants in time is to erase history, and to find invariants in space is to erase culture. All that is left to build an economic theory on is nature, and as we have seen in the previous chapter, in axiomatic general equilibrium theory, it is a hypothetical, and not an actual nature. Allais, in the above-quoted lecture, stresses the importance of empirical evidence and empirical verifications, almost in a naive sense, as if he were unaware of the objections philosophers of science and scientists have raised about these issues. Knowledge of recent, and not-so-recent developments in these fields makes the slavish adherence to the emulation of physicists almost comical.

It should be evident that the adoption of the 'scientific' approach to economics was the result of the search for the natural laws of the economy. This search started with an explicit belief in the Natural Law Outlook, and for all practical purposes, never abandons it. The Natural Law Outlook leads to the emulation of the natural sciences by social theorists, and such emulation leads to the displacement of concepts from the natural sciences on to economics.

There are three objections to the emulation of the natural sciences by economists. First, as Philip Mirowski has so expertly and convincingly demonstrated, neoclassical economic theory is modeled after a scientific theory which has long since been replaced. And although economists have occasionally attempted to adopt the metaphors of the new physics, they have done so only at the most superficial level, using the words but not fully displacing the new concepts.[1] To have fully displaced the concepts developed by Einstein and Heisenberg, among others, would have been to abandon the neoclassical research program, for it would entail the abandonment of determinism and the acceptance of relativity and uncertainty.

More importantly, however, is the second objection, that is the abandonment by scientists and philosophers of science of the belief in a single, universally correct, scientific method. It is the emulation of such a method which has given economics the pretense of being a hard science. Yet the positivism of the Vienna Circle has been a total failure in the two areas which comprised their whole research program: 1) being able to provide guidelines of how science ought to be carried out and 2) being able to describe how science is in fact carried out. It has accordingly been abandoned by scientists and philosophers of science, only economists seem to have missed this development. Not only are economists imitating outdated physics (a critique I find weak, for it implies that they should imitate current physics), they hold as the scientific ideal a method natural scientists have since abandoned.[2] Furthermore, there is a large degree of disarray in the field of mathematics, which, in the highest forms of the Natural Law Outlook following Descartes, is thought to be God's language. According to one observer, '"the present state of mathematics is anomalous and deplorable. The light of truth no longer illuminates the road to follow. ... The loss of truth [is] ... a tragedy of the first magnitude [in which] the concept of a universally accepted, infallible body of reasoning ... is a grand illusion ... The age of Reason is gone." Any thought that mathematics has

---

1. Mirowski's (1989, pp. 378-386) biting analysis of Samuelson is enlightening as well as entertaining.

2. The full details of these developments are outside the scope of this book. The interested reader should turn to Clive Beed's excellent paper, 'Philosophy of Science and Contemporary Economics: An Overview', in the *Journal of Post Keynesian Economics*, Summer, 1991, as well as the other excellent contributions to the Symposium on Postmodernism, Economics, and Canon Creation.

"absolute certainty or validity of its results, could no longer be claimed" and "this turn of events is not far short of an intellectual disaster"' (Kline quoted in Beed 1991, p. 468).[3] Not only have we discovered that the Emperor has no clothes, he is also a commoner.

This brings us to the third objection to an economic theory based on the natural sciences. The use of models in explaining actual phenomena must be based on one of two types of analogies, either an analogy of structure or a material analogy. In the former analogy the formal structure of the model, in this case the concept to be displaced, must correspond in some meaningful way with the structure of the phenomena to be explained, to which the concept is being displaced. Mary Hesse gives an example of this from the natural sciences: a 'swinging pendulum and an oscillating electric circuit, ... are analogous by virtue of the formal relations described in a wave equation satisfied by both' (Hesse 1967, p. 355). Meaningful material similarities would be based on a shared characteristic between the phenomena the concept (metaphor) explained before displacement and the phenomena to be explained by the displacement. For the Enlightenment, the material similarity between social and natural phenomena is that all phenomena were naturally determined, that is determined by natural laws. Thus concepts which were well defined and developed in the natural sciences could be justly displaced on to social phenomena.

As should be quite clear, economic theory started with the assumption of both material and formal analogies between the natural universe and the social. The basis of the material analogy, which still persists today, as the quotation from Allais demonstrates, is the assumption of a uniform human nature. In fact, it seems that the whole enterprise of a science of society rests on this issue, for it is only a universal human nature which can provide the invariants in time and space necessary in order to adopt the natural law approach. Even with the axiomatic method of analysis there is still a need for invariants in order for the formal analogy to hold up, for it is the existence of such invariants that has given the natural sciences the successes for which they are rightly celebrated. Since few would make the claim that there are invariants in any other aspect of the social universe (social institutions, government, customs, culture, religion, values, the list is endless) the crux of the argument is a universal human nature. As R. G. Collingwood (1946, p. 224) has noted: 'establishing the permanent and unchanging laws of human nature, is ... possible only to a person who

---

3. I am here reminded of the Calvin and Hobbes cartoon in which Calvin is telling Hobbes that in the final analysis mathematics has to be taken on faith, and is therefore a religion. Calvin, being a math atheist, thus feels that he should be exempted from math homework.

mistakes the transient conditions of a certain historical age for the permanent conditions of human life. It was easy for men of the eighteenth century to make this mistake, because their historical perspective was so short, and their knowledge of cultures other than their own so limited, that they could cheerfully identify the intellectual habits of a western European in their own day with the intellectual faculties bestowed by God upon Adam and all his progeny.' There is no justification for twentieth-century social theorists making the same mistake.

The universal human nature assumption, besides laying the basis for the invariants needed for either material or structural analogies between the social and natural sciences, also promotes the exclusion of that factor in human activity which makes social phenomena fundamentally different from natural phenomena, that is, the mind. If an event occurs repeatedly science attempts to explain it through the least number of general theories. Yet detached observation is not a sufficient basis for understanding and explaining social phenomena. Any attempt to understand the regularities and uniformities observed in social phenomena must concentrate on the meaning of the activity to the actor, for 'it is the purposive aspect of behavior, not its physical aspects, that constitutes the unity of an action' (Lessnoff 1974, p. 37). As Michael Lessnoff (Ibid. p. 47) has asserted, the 'model of physics is inapplicable in the social sciences because the existence of social facts always implies the existence of mental states - intentions, purposes, beliefs, expectations, awareness of rules - which are not observable by empirical methods.'

A successful case has not yet been made that there exists either material or formal correspondences between natural and social phenomena to justify the social sciences using the natural sciences as a model to emulate and as a source of concepts to be displaced. Walras (1909) made an attempt to argue that the similar structure of the equations used in economics and astronomy and mechanics was justification for treating economics as a physio-mathematical subject. Yet the similarities Walras found were there because he put them there, that is, because he developed equations in economics based on those found in astronomy and mechanics. What Walras did not do, which cannot be done, is to show that the economy operates in a manner similar to the mechanical universe, or heavenly bodies, without reconstructing the economy based on concepts displaced from these two fields. Furthermore, his reconstructed economy bears very little resemblance to any actual economy. Societies are not natural phenomena ruled by natural laws, nor created by natural forces. They are the creation of humans, as are their institutions, culture, and history. Particular societies and particular individuals in a society are bound by the history and social institutions they coexist with, not by the forces of nature. The basic difference is that which Werner Stark stated; the natural sciences study that which man finds, the social sciences study that which man creates.

The desire to explain regularities and uniformities starts, as we have seen in the previous chapter, which the a priori assumption of an underlying order which produces such reoccurrences. Yet what phenomena are we to investigate? Most economists have concentrated on the phenomena of prices, the explanation of which is in the field of the theory of value. Economists have typically held the view that the market brings order to the economy by sending price signals. Their apparent importance thus deserved investigation. The two broad traditions in value theory, the classicals' objective theories of value, and the neoclassicals' subjective theory of value, are in many ways expressions of the visions of society, organic and mechanical, respectively, held by each school. Both approaches are natural value theories, holding that the forces which determine natural values are natural laws, laws which are universals. One can read into Smith a social value theory, as we have done in Chapter 4, yet this is finding in Smith something Smith would not.

Yet prices are only the surface phenomena of economic activity, reflecting activities which are not as easily observed, much less catalogued and quantified. The basis of economic phenomena is the economic actions of humans, not prices and quantities. Prices and quantities are only significant in that they might reflect such activities, or at least give us a glimpse of some aspect of such activities, or because individuals give them significance, but they should not be given independent significance beyond their due. Economic theory studies how humans carry out the task of material reproduction, and the emphasis should be on humans and their actions, not the by-products. If one focuses attention on prices alone then one could easily draw false conclusions on the meaning and significance of economic activity and phenomena. One could look at the stability of relative prices in the middle ages and in the 1950s and conclude that such regularities and uniformities (stable relative prices) reflect universal laws, yet the significance of prices in the two epochs is quite different. Similarly, the act of exchange in two different cultures could easily have different meaning and significance. Similar physical actions, such as extending one's hand to greet someone, can very easily have significantly different meanings in different cultures or at different times. The methods of the physical sciences are of little help here.

Once attention is centered on human actions, the natural law approach to economics begins to break down, for humans do not have enough natural programming to generate regularities and uniformities in the carrying out of economic tasks. One could agree with David Hume on the universality of human nature only if all the attributes applied to human nature have been eliminated. Contrary to the view of the Enlightenment, society is not the natural result of human passions and interests. At birth, humans have the possibility of sociality, but not the actuality, and the difference between these is similar to the difference between being pregnant and the possibility of becoming pregnant. Nature gives us an instinct of self-preference and physical desires for food, clothing, shelter and sex. However, how these natural desires or drives are satisfied is determined by history and culture and our ability to satisfy successfully these desires in society comes from the suppression of our animal instincts. Both our actions, and the meaning of our actions, in every realm, are shaped, molded and to a large degree determined by society and not by nature, thus it is there that all attempts to comprehend human behavior must start. This is as true for the archeologist studying some ancient civilization, the anthropologists studying a newly discovered archaic society and most importantly for our purpose, for the modern economist attempting to understand our economy and the economic actions which comprise it. As Peter Berger and Thomas Luckmann (1966, pp. 46-7) have noted:

> Despite the obvious physical limits ... Humanness is socio-culturally variable. In other words, there is no human nature in the sense of a biologically fixed substratum determining the variability of socio-cultural formations. There is only human nature in the sense of anthropological constants (for example, world-openness and plasticity of instinctual structure) that delimit and permit man's socio-cultural formations. ... While it is possible to say that man has a nature, it is more significant to say that man constructs his own nature, or more simply, that man produces himself.

The main thesis of this book, to reiterate, is that in the pursuit of an economic theory modeled after the natural science, economists eliminated history and society from having any meaningful role. Yet by eliminating history and society from the process of explaining the economy and economic phenomena, we have excluded the only tools we have for such knowledge. For it is from society that the regularities and uniformities stem. To quote Collingwood once again (1946, p. 223), 'In order that behavior-patterns may be constant, there must be in existence a social order which recurrently produces situations of a certain kind.' Collingwood also argues that the most important aspect of humans, the mind, is understandable only with the methods of history. 'I shall maintain', he writes (Ibid. p. 209), 'that the science of human nature was a false attempt - falsified by the analogy of natural science - to understand the mind itself, and that, whereas the right way of investigating nature is by the methods called scientific, the right way of investigating mind is by the methods of history.' Furthermore, our understanding of social institutions, the efficient causes of the regularities and uniformities in social phenomena, is through history. As Berger and Luckmann (1966, p. 54-5) contend:

> Institutions ... imply historicity and control. ... Institutions always have a history, of which they are the products. It is impossible to understand an institution adequately without an understanding of the historical process in which it was produced. Institutions also, by the very fact of their existence, control human conduct by setting up predefined patterns of conduct, which channel it in one direction as against the many other directions that would theoretically be possible.

One of the most important points of the Berger and Luckmann study is that society is the active force in social phenomena, and that the objective reality of such phenomena is society, not nature or its surrogate, technology.

In the attempt to construct a science of society on a par with the natural sciences, economics has withdrawn history and society from having any meaningful role. Yet the phenomena we wish to understand are the result of history and society and little else. This is as true for the capitalist allocating his capital to maximize his profits as it is for the medieval landlord's use of his estate. Both actors' behavior is the result of their particular socialization by specific social institutions, and, as such behavior exhibits regularities and uniformities, it can only be the result of such a process. Thus our understanding of these activities is best served by starting our analysis with history and society.

The damaging effects of the displacement of concepts from the natural sciences on to the social stems from both the radical and the conservative effects of the displacement of concepts. The radical aspect of such displacements has been the concentration on discovering universal laws, based on natural foundations, which will explain the regularities of human activity. Metaphors from the natural sciences put the attention properly on the regularities, yet placed the source of these regularities incorrectly in natural laws. But it is the conservative aspect where most of the damage has come from, for by concentrating exclusively on the search for natural laws, understanding of social rules has been neglected. Furthermore, by adopting the metaphor of equilibrium, questions of process, developmental change, expectations, and many of the institutions which are problematic for equilibrium analysis, such as money, are excluded from the analysis, or reconstructed so as to give them meaning different from their actual significance. Our understanding of the economy thus becomes distorted.

The most damaging effect of viewing the social universe as analogous to the natural is that it has allowed the social theorist, as well as political leaders, to escape from taking responsibility for society's problems, and to allow economic actors to escape responsibility for their actions. As William Dugger (1989, p. 607) has observed: 'The simple observation that the market is an instituted process rather than a natural equilibrium takes on great significance because it makes accountable men and women who exercise power behind the protection of the market myth. That simple observation eliminates their protection. When the market is understood as an instituted process, those who institute it can be held responsible.' Rejection of natural law economics will allow economy theory to go beyond myths and allow it to focus on an understanding of the economy and its place in society.

References

Allais, Maurice. (1990) 'My Conception of Economic Science' *Methodus*, Vol. 2, June, pp. 5-7.

Allen, James Sloan. (1967) 'Adam Smith's Theory of Knowledge and his Conception of Natural Law' unpublished M.A. thesis, Columbia University.

Appleby, Joyce Oldham. (1978) *Economic Thought and Ideology in Seventeenth-Century England*, Princeton University Press, Princeton.

Arrow, Kenneth J. (1969) 'Economic Equilibrium' *International Encyclopedia of the Social Sciences*. Vol. 4, Macmillan, New York.

-----. and Hahn, Frank. (1971) *General Competitive Equilibrium*, North-Holland, New York.

Ayres, C. E. (1944) *The Theory of Economic Progress*, University of North Carolina Press, Chapel Hill.

Barnes, Barry. (1974) *Scientific Knowledge and Sociological Theory*, Routledge & Kegan Paul, London.

Becker, Carl C. (1934) *The Heavenly City of the Eighteenth Century Philosophers*, Yale University Press, New Haven.

Becker, James F. (1961) 'Adam Smith's Theory of Social Science' *Southern Economic Journal*, Vol. 28, July, pp. 13-21.

Beed, Clive. (1991) 'Philosophy of Science and Contemporary Economics: An Overview' *Journal of Post Keynesian Economics*, Vol. 13, Summer, pp. 459-94.

Bentham, Jeremy. (1982) *An Introduction to the Principles of Morals and Legislation*, edited by J. H. Burns and H. L. A. Hart, Methuen, London.

Berger, Peter L. and Luckmann, Thomas. (1966) *The Social Construction of Reality*, Anchor Books, New York.

Berry, Christopher J. (1974) 'Adam Smith's Considerations on Language' *Journal of the History of Ideas*, Vol. 35, pp. 130-38.

Bitterman, Henry J. (1944) 'Adam Smith's Empiricism and the Law of

Nature, I & II' *Journal of Political Economy*, Vol. 48, pp. 487-520, 703-34.

Black, Max. (1962) *Models and Metaphors*, Cornell University Press, Ithaca, New York.

Black, R. D. C., Coats, A. W. and Winch, C. D. W. (1973) *The Marginal Revolution in Economics*, Duke Unversity Press, Durham, North Carolina.

Black, Robert R. (1963) *A Comparison of Classical English Economic Thought with Newtonian Natural Philosophy,*. Ph.D. Dissertation, University of California, Berkeley.

Blaug, Mark. (1978) *Economic Theory in Retrospect*, 3rd. ed., Cambridge University Press, Cambridge.

-----. (1990) 'On the Historiography of Economics' *Journal of the History of Economic Thought*, Vol. 12, Spring, pp. 27-37.

Bonar, James. (1893) *Philosophy and Political Economy*, Swan Sorrenschein & Co., London.

-----. (1966) [1894] *A Catalogue of the Library of Adam Smith*, 2nd ed., Augustus M. Kelley, New York.

Bousquet, G. H. (1927) *Essai sur l'Evolution de la Pensée Economique*, Paris.

Brown, Robert. (1984) *The Nature of Social Laws*, Cambridge University Press, Cambridge.

Brown, S. C. ed. (1979a) *Philosophers of the Enlightenment*, Harvester Press, Sussex.

-----. (1979b) 'The "Principle of Natural Order": Or What the Enlightenment Sceptics Did Not Doubt' in Brown 1979a.

Bryson, Gladys. (1968) [1945] *Man and Society: The Scottish Inquiry of the Eighteenth Century*, Augustus M. Kelley, New York.

Burrow, J.W. (1966) *Evolution and Society*, Cambridge University Press, Cambridge.

Campbell, T. D. (1971) *Adam Smith's Science of Morals*, George Allen & Unwin Ltd, London.

-----. (1975) 'Scientific Explanation of Ethical Justification in the Moral Sentiments' in Skinner 1975.

Chalk, Alfred F. (1951) 'Natural Law and the Rise of Economic Individualism' *Journal of Political Economy*, Vol. 59, Spring, pp. 332-47.

Chipman, John S. (1965) 'The nature and meaning of equilibrium in economic theory' in *Functionalism in the Social Sciences: The Strength and Limits of Functionalism in Anthropology, Economics, Political Science and Sociology*, edited by D. Martingale, pp. 35-64, American

Academy of Political and Social Science, Philadelphia.

Clark, Charles M. A. (1987-88) 'Equilibrium, Market Process and Historical Time' *Journal of Post Keynesian Economics*, Vol. 10, Winter, pp. 270-81.

-----. (1989) 'Equilibrium for What?: Reflections on Social Order in Economics' *Journal of Economic Issues*, Vol. 23, June, pp. 597-606.

-----. (1991) 'Naturalism in Economics: the use of "State of Nature" in the History of Economic Thought' in *Perspectives on the History of Economic Thought*, Vol. 6, edited by William J. Barber, Edward Elgar, Cheltenham.

Clark, John Bates. (1894) 'A Universal Law of Economic Variation' *Quarterly Journal of Economics*, Vol. 8, April, pp. 261-79.

-----. (1965) [1899] *The Distribution of Wealth*, Augustus M. Kelley, New York.

Cohen, Ted. (1979) 'Metaphor and the Cultivation of Intimacy' in *On Metaphor*, edited by Sheldon Sacks, The University of Chicago Press, Chicago.

Colander, David and Klamer, Arjo. (1987) 'The Making of an Economist' *Journal of Economic Perspectives*, Vol. 1, Fall, pp. 95-111.

Collingwood, Robin G. (1945) *The Idea of Nature*, Oxford University Press, London.

-----. (1946) *The Idea of History*, Oxford University Press, London.

Cossa, Luigi. (1880) *Guide to the Study of Political Economy*, MacMillan, London.

Davis, John B. (1989) 'Axiomatic General Equilibrium Theory and Referentiality' *Journal of Post Keynesian Economics*, Vol 11, Spring, pp. 424-38.

Debreu, Gerard. (1959) *The Theory of Value: An Axiomatic Analysis of Economic Equilibrium*, Yale University Press, New Haven.

DeVroey, Michael. (1975) 'The Transition from Classical to Neoclassical Economics: A Scientific Revolution' *Journal of Economic Issues*, Vol. 9, pp. 415-39.

Dow, Sheila C. (1990) 'Beyond Dualism' *Cambridge Journal of Economics*, Vol. 14, pp. 143-57.

Downey, E. H. (1910) 'The Futility of Marginal Utility' *Journal of Political Economy*, pp. 253-68.

Dugger, William. (1989) 'Instituted Process and Enabling Myth: The Two Faces of the Market' *Journal of Economic Issues*, Vol. 23, June, pp. 607-16.

Durkheim, Emile and Mauss, Marcel. (1963) [1903] *Primitive Classification*, Translated and Introduced by Rodney Needham, The

University of Chicago Press, Chicago.

Edgeworth, F. Y. (1925) *Papers Relating to Political Economy*, Vol. II, Burt Franklin, New York.

-----. (1967) [1881] *Mathematical Psychics*, Augustus M. Kelley, New York.

Edwards, Charles S. (1981) *Hugo Grotius: The Miracle of Holland*, Nelson-Hall, Chicago.

Evensky, Jerry. (1987) 'The Two Voices of Adam Smith: Moral Philosopher and Social Critic' *History of Political Economy*, Vol. 19, Fall, pp. 447-68.

Everett, John R. (1982) [1946] *Religion in Economics*, Porcupine Press, Philadelphia.

Fisher, Robert M. (1986) *The Logic of Economic Discovery*, New York University Press, New York.

Foley, Vernard. (1976) *The Social Physics of Adam Smith*, Purdue University Press, West Lafayette, Indiana.

Friedrich, Carl J. (1963) *The Philosophy of Law in Historical Perspective*, 3rd ed., The University of Chicago Press, Chicago.

Gardiner, Patrick. ed. (1959) *Theories of History*, The Free Press, Glencoe, Illinois.

George, Donald. (1981) 'Equilibrium and Catastrophes in Economics' *Scottish Journal of Political Economy*, Vol. 28, pp. 43-61.

Gide, Charles and Rist, Charles. (1909) *A History of Economic Doctrines*, D. C. Heath and Company, New York.

Gordon, Scott. (1991) *The History and Philosophy of Social Science*, Routledge, London.

Grotius, Hugo. (1901) [1625] *The Rights of War and Peace*, M. Walter Dunne, London.

Hahn, Frank H. (1982) 'On the Notion of Equilibrium in Economics' in *Macroeconomics and Equilibrium*, by Frank Hahn, Cambridge University Press, Cambridge.

Halevy, Elie. (1972) [1928] *The Growth of Philosophical Radicalism*, Faber and Faber, London.

Hamilton, David. (1970) *Evolutionary Economics*, University of New Mexico Press, Albuquerque.

Harpham, Edward J. (1984) 'Natural Law and Early Liberal Economic Thought: A Reconsideration of Locke's Theories of Value' *Social Science Quarterly*, Vol. 65, pp. 966-74.

Hauser, Arnold. (1957) *The Social History of Art*, Vintage Books, New York.

Heilbroner, Robert L. (1975) 'The Paradox of Progress: Decline and Decay in the Wealth of Nations' in *Essays on Adam Smith*, edited by Andrew S. Skinner and Thomas Wilson, Oxford University Press, London.

-----. (1979) 'Modern Economics as a Chapter in the History of Economic Thought' *History of Political Economy*, Vol. 11, pp. 192-8.

-----. (1982) 'The Socialization of the Individual in Adam Smith' *History of Political Economy*, Vol. 14, Fall, pp. 426-39.

-----. ed. (1984) *The Essential Adam Smith*, Norton, New York.

-----. (1986) *The Nature and Logic of Capitalism*, Norton, New York.

-----. (1988) *Behind the Veil*, Norton, New York.

Henry, John F. (1982a) 'On Equilibrium' *Journal of Post Keynesian Economics*, Vol. 5, Winter, pp. 214-25.

-----. (1982b) 'The Transformation of John Bates Clark: An Essay in Interpretation' *History of Political Economy*, Vol 14, pp. 166-77.

-----. (1983) 'John Bates Clark and the Marginal Product: An Historical Inquiry into the Origins of Value-free Economic Theory' *History of Political Economy*, Vol. 15, pp. 375-89.

Hesse, Mary (1967) 'Models and Analogies in Science' in *The Encyclopedia of Philosophy*, Vol. 5, edited by Paul Edwards, Macmillan Publishing Co., New York.

Hetherington, Norriss S. (1983) 'Isaac Newton's Influence on Adam Smith's Natural Laws in Economics' *Journal of the History of Ideas*, Vol. 44, pp. 497-505.

Hirschman, Albert O. (1977) *The Passions and the Interests*, Princeton University Press, Princeton.

Hobbes, Thomas. (1964) [1651] *Leviathan*, Washington Square Press, New York.

Hollander, Samuel. (1973) *The Economics of Adam Smith*, University of Toronto Press, Toronto.

-----. (1985) *The Economics of John Stuart Mill*, University of Toronto Press, Toronto.

Hont, I. and Ignatieff, M. eds (1983) *Wealth and Virtue. The Shaping of Political Economy in the Scottish Enlightenment*, Cambridge University Press, Cambridge.

Hume, David. (1902) [1777] *Enquiries Concerning the Human Understanding and Concerning the Principles of Morals*, edited by L. A. Selby-Bigge, Clarendon Press, Oxford.

Hutchison, T. W. (1962) [1953] *A Review of Economic Doctrines*, Oxford University Press, Oxford.

-----. (1965) [1938] *The Significance and Basic Postulates of Economic Theory*, Augustus M. Kelley, New York.

-----. (1973) 'Some Themes from Investigations into Method' in *Carl*

Menger and the Austrian School of Economics, edited by J. R. Hicks and W. Weber, Oxford Univesity Press, London.

Hymer, Stephen. (1980) 'Robinson Crusoe and the Secret of Primitive Accumulation' in Nell 1980, pp. 29-40.

Ingrao, Bruna and Israel, Giorgio. (1985) 'General Economic Equilibrium Theory. A History of Ineffectual Paradigmatic Shifts' *Fundamenta Scientiae*, Vol. 6, pp. 1-45, 89-125.

-----. (1990) *The Invisible Hand*, Translated by Ian McGilvray, The MIT Press, Cambridge.

Jaffe, William. (1935) 'Unpublished Papers and Letters of Leon Walras' in Jaffe (1983).

-----. (1976) 'Menger, Jevons and Walras Dehomogenized' in Jaffe (1983).

-----. (1977) 'The Normative Bias of the Walrasian Model: Walras Versus Gossen' in Jaffe (1983).

-----. (1983) *William Jaffe's Essays on Walras*, edited by Donald Walker, Cambridge University Press, Cambridge.

Jevons, William S. (1879) [1871] *The Theory of Political Economy*, 2nd ed. Macmillan, London.

-----. (1882) *Money and the Mechanism of Exchange*, D. Appleton and Company, New York.

-----. (1890) *Pure Logic and Other Minor Works*, Macmillan, London.

-----. (1965) [1905] *The Principles of Economics*, Augustus M. Kelley, New York.

-----. (1981) *Papers and Correspondence of William Stanley Jevons*, Vol. 7, edited by R. D. C. Black. Macmillan, London.

Kauder, Emil. (1957) 'Intellectual and Political Roots of the Older Austrian School' *Zeitschrift Fur Nationaleconomie*, pp. 411-25.

Klamer, Arjo and Colander, David. (1990) *The Making of an Economist*, Westview, Boulder.

Kornai, Jonas. (1971) *Anti-Equilibrium*, North-Holland, Amsterdam.

Knight, Frank H. (1931) 'Marginal Utility Economics' in Spengler 1960.

Krupp, Sherman R. (1965) 'Equilibrium Theory in Economic and in Functional Analysis as Types of Explanations' in *Functionalisn in the Social Sciences: The Strengths and Limits of Functionalism in Anthropology, Economics, Political Science and Sociology*, American Academy of Political and Social Sciences, Philadelphia.

Kuznets, Simon. (1930) 'Equilibrium Economics and Business Cycle Theory' *Quarterly Journal of Economics*, Vol. 44, May, pp. 381-415.

Leibniz, G.W. (1972) [1706] 'Opinion on the Principles of Pufendorf' in *The Political Writings of Leibniz*, translated and edited by Patrick Riley, Cambridge University Press, Cambridge.

Leslie, T. E. C. (1969) [1888] *Essays in Political Economy*, 2nd ed. Augustus M. Kelley, New York.

Lessnoff, Michael. (1974) *The Structure of Social Science*, George Allen & Unwin Ltd, London.

Letwin, William. (1965) *The Origins of Scientific Economics*, Doubleday & Company, Garden City, New York.

Levy, David. (1978) 'Adam Smith's Natural Law and Contractual Society' *Journal of the History of Ideas*, Vol. 34, Oct., pp. 665-74.

Lindgren, J. Ralph. (1969) 'Adam Smith's Theory of Inquiry' *Journal of Political Economy*, Vol. 77, Nov., pp. 897-915.

-----. (1973) *The Social Philosophy of Adam Smith*, Martinus Nighoff, The Hague.

Locke, John. (1960) [1690] *The Second Treatise on Civil Government*, Basil Blackwell, Oxford.

Lovejoy, Arthur O. (1936) *The Great Chain of Being*, Harvard University Press, Cambridge.

Lowe, Adolph. (1951) 'On the Mechanistic Approach in Economics' *Social Research*, Vol. 18, pp. 403-34.

-----. (1965) *On Economic Knowledge*, Harper & Row, New York.

-----. (1967) 'The Normative Roots of Economic Value' in *Human Values and Economic Policy*, ed. by S. Hook. New York University Press, New York.

-----. (1988) *Has Freedom a Future?*, Praeger Press, New York.

Lowry, S. Todd. (1974) 'The Archaeology of the Circulation Concept in Economic Theory' *Journal of the History of Ideas*, Vol. 35, pp. 429-44.

Macfie, A. L. (1955) 'The Scottish Tradition in Economic Theory' *Scottish Journal of Political Economy*, Vol. 2, June, pp. 81-103.

-----. (1967) *The Individual in Society*, George Allen & Unwin, London.

-----. (1971) 'The Invisible Hand of Jupiter' *Journal of the History of Ideas*, Vol. 33, pp. 595-9.

MacIntyre, Alasdair. (1984) [1981] *Against Virtue*, 2nd ed., University of Notre Dame, Notre Dame, Indiana.

Malynes, Gerard de. (1973) [1623] *The Center of the Circle of Commerce*. Augustus M. Kelley, New York.

Marshall, Alfred. (1898) 'Distribution and Exchange' *The Economic Journal*, Vol. 8, pp. 37-59.

-----. (1920) *Principles of Economics*, 8th ed., Macmillan, London.

Mauss, Marcel. (1967) [1906] *The Gift*, Translated by Ian Cunnison, W.W. Norton, New York.

McCulloch, J. R. ed. (1856) *A Select Collection of Early English Tracts on Commerce*, Macmillan, London.

Meek, Ronald. (1971) 'Smith, Turgot, and the 'Four Stages' Theory' *History of Political Economy*, Vol. 3, Spring, pp. 9-27.

Menger, Carl. (1981) [1871] *Principles of Economics*, New York University Press, New York.

-----. (1985) [1883] *Investigations into the Method of the Social Sciences*, New York University Press, New York.

Milgate, Murry. (1987) 'Equilibrium: Development of the Concept' in *The New Palgrave*. edited by J. Eatwell, M. Milgate and P. Newman, New York: The Stockton Press, Vol. 2, pp. 179-83.

Mill, John Stuart (1868) *Dissertations and Discussions: Political, Philosophical, and Historical*, Vols 1 and 2, William V. Spencer, Boston.

-----. (1874) *A System of Logic, Ratiocinative and Inductive*, 8th ed., Harper & Brothers, New York.

-----. (1924) *Autobiography of John Stuart Mill*, Columbia University Press, New York.

-----. (1958) *Nature and Utility of Religion*, Bobbs-Merrill Company, Indianapolis.

-----. (1962) *Utilitarianism*, New American Library, New York.

-----. (1974) [1874] *Essays on Some Unsettled Questions of Political Economy*, 2nd ed., Augustus M. Kelley, Clifton.

-----. (1987) [1848] *Principles of Political Economy*, edited with an introduction by William Ashley, Augustus M. Kelley, Fairfield.

Mini, Piero. (1974) *Philosophy and Economics*, University Press of Florida, Gainesville.

Mirowski, Philip. (1984a) 'Physics and the "Marginalist" Revolution' *Cambridge Journal of Economics*, Vol. 8, pp. 361-79.

-----. (1984b) 'The Role of Conservation Principles in Twentieth-Century Economic Theory' *Philosophy of Social Science*, Vol. 14, 1984b, pp. 461-73.

-----. (1986) 'Mathematical Formalism and Economic Explanation' in *The Reconstruction of Economic Theory*, edited by Philip Mirowski, Kluner-Nighoff, Boston.

-----. (1988) *Beyond Mechanism*. Rowman and Littlefield, Totawa, New Jersey.

-----. (1989) *More Heat than Light*, Cambridge University Press, Cambridge.

-----. and Cook, Pamela. (1990) 'Walras' Economics and Mechanics: Translation, Commentary, Context' in *Economics as Rhetoric*, edited by Warren Samuels, Kluwer, Norwell.

Misselden, Edward. (1971) [1623] *The Circle of Commerce*, Augustus

Kelley, New York.

Mitchell, Wesley C. (1918) 'Bentham's Felicific Calculus' *Political Science Quarterly*, Vol. 33, pp. 161-83; reprinted in Mitchell 1950.

-----. (1929) 'Postulates and Preconceptions of Ricardian Economics' in *Essays in Philosophy*, edited by T. V. Smith and W. J. Wright, Open Court Publishing Co., Chicago; reprinted in Mitchell 1950.

-----. (1950) [1937] *The Backward Art of Spending Money and Other Essays*, Augustus M. Kelley, New York.

-----. (1967) *Types of Economic Theory*, edited with an Introduction by Joseph Dorfman, Augustus M. Kelley, New York.

Montesquieu, Charles Baron de. (1949) [1748] *The Spirit of the Laws*, Hafner Press, New York.

Moore, James and Silverthorne, Michael. (1983) 'Gershom Carmichael and the Natural Jurisprudence Tradition in Eighteenth-Century Scotland' in Hont and Ignatieff 1983.

Morrow, Glen R. (1969) [1923] *The Ethical and Economic Theories of Adam Smith*, Augustus M. Kelley, New York.

Mun, Thomas. (1664) *England's Treasure by Forraign Trade*, in McCulloch, 1856.

Myers, Milton L. (1975) 'Adam Smith as Critic of Ideas' *Journal of the History of Ideas*, Vol. 36, pp. 281-96.

-----. (1976) 'Adam Smith's Concept of Equilibrium' *Journal of Economic Issues*, Vol. 10, Sept., pp. 560-75.

-----. (1983) *The Soul of Modern Economic Man*, The University of Chicago Press, Chicago.

Myrdal, Gunnar. (1954) [1929] *The Political Element in the Development of Economic Theory*. Simon and Schuster, New York.

-----. (1958) *Value in Social Theory*, edited by Paul Streeten, Routledge & Kegan Paul, London.

-----. (1973) *Against the Stream*. Vintage Books, New York.

Nell, Edward. ed. (1980) *Growth, Profits, & Property*. Cambridge University Press, Cambridge.

-----. (1984) 'Structure and Behavior in Classical and Neoclassical Theory' *Eastern Economic Journal*, Vol. 11, pp. 139-53.

Newton, Isaac. (1934) [1686] *Mathematical Principles of Natural Philosophy and His System of the World*, Translated by Andrew Motte, revised translation by Florian Cajori, University of California Press, Berkeley.

-----. (1953) *Newton's Philosophy of Nature: Selections From His Writings*, edited by H. S. Thayers, Hafner Press, New York.

Nojiri, Taketoshi. (1972) 'Political Economy and the Law of Nature' *Kobe*

University Economic Review, pp. 41-61.

North, Douglas. (1691) *Discourses Upon Trade*, in McCulloch, 1856.

O'Brien, D. P. (1975) *The Classical Economists*, Oxford University Press, Oxford.

O'Dea, Thomas F. (1955) 'The "Residues" of Pareto: An Operational Definition of Natural Law' *American Catholic Sociological Review*, Vol. 16, Oct., pp. 170-82.

Ortony, Andrew, ed. (1979) *Metaphor and Thought*, Cambridge University Press, London.

Pareto, Vilfredo. (1935) [1916] *The Mind and Society*, Dover Publications, New York.

-----. (1966) *Sociological Writings*, Translated by Derick Mirfir, Praeger, New York.

-----. (1971) [1909] *Manual of Political Economy*, Translated by Ann S. Schwier, edited by Ann S. Schwier and Alfred N. Page, Augustus M. Kelley, New York.

Parson, Talcott. (1931) 'Economics and Sociology: Marshall in Relation to the Thought of his Time' *Quarterly Journal of Economics*, Vol. 46, pp. 316-47.

Passmore, John. (1967) 'Logical Positivism' in *The Encyclopedia of Philosophy*, Vol. 5, edited by Paul Edwards, Macmillan Publishing Co., New York.

Pokorny, Dusan. (1978) 'Smith and Walras: Two Theories of Science' *Canadian Journal of Economics*, pp. 387-403.

Pribram, Karl. (1951) 'Prolegomena to a History of Economic Reasoning' *Quarterly Journal of Economics*, Vol. 65, pp. 1-37.

-----. (1953) 'Patterns of Economic Reasoning' *American Economic Review*, Vol. 44, pp. 243-58.

Punzo, Lionello F. (1991) 'The School of Mathematical Formalism and the Viennese Circle of Mathematical Economists' *Journal of the History of Economic Thought*, Vol. 13, Spring, pp. 1-18.

Rambaud, Joseph. (1899) *Histoire des Doctrines Economiques*, Paris and Lyons.

Randall Jr., John Herman. (1976) [1926] *The Making of the Modern Mind*, Columbia University Press, New York.

Raphael, D. D. (1979) 'Adam Smith: Philosophy, Science, and Social Science' in Brown 1979.

Raynaud, Barthélemy. (1936) *Le Loi Naturelle en Economie Politique*, Editions Domat-Montchrestien, Paris.

Ricoeur, Paul. (1977) *The Rule of Metaphor*, Translated by Robert Czerny, University of Toronto Press, Toronto.

Robinson, Joan V. (1963) *Economic Philosophy*, Aldine Publishing Company, Chicago.

-----. (1980) *Collected Economic Papers*, Vol. 5, MIT Press, Cambridge, Mass.

Rosenberg, Nathan. (1960) 'Some Institutional Aspects of the Wealth of Nations' *Journal of Political Economy*, Vol. 68, Dec, pp. 557-70.

Rosenstein-Rodan, Paul. (1960) 'Marginal Utility' *International Economic Papers*, Vol. 10, pp. 71-106.

Routh, Guy. (1975) *The Origins of Economic Ideas*, Vintage Books, New York.

Ryan, Alan. (1970) *John Stuart Mill*, Pantheon Books, New York.

Schmitt, Bernard. (1986) 'The Process of Formation of Economics in Relation to Other Sciences' in *Foundations of Economics*, edited by Mauro Baranzini and Roberto Scazzieri, Basil Blackwell Ltd., Oxford.

Schneider, Louis. (1979) 'Adam Smith on Human Nature and Social Circumstance' in *Adam Smith and Modern Political Economy*, edited by Gerald P. O'Driscoll, Iowa State University Press, Ames, Iowa.

Schon, Donald A. (1967) *Invention and the Evolution of Ideas*, Tavistock Publishing, London.

Schumpeter, Joseph. (1954a) *History of Economic Analysis*, Oxford University Press, New York.

-----. (1954b) [1914] *Economic Doctrine and Method*, Oxford University Press, New York.

Scott, William R. (1965) [1937] *Adam Smith as Student and Professor*, Augustus M. Kelley, New York.

Sebba, George. (1953) 'The Development of the Concept of Mechanism and Model in Physical Science and Economic Thought' *American Economic Review*, pp. 259-68.

Shackle, G. L. S. (1972) *Epistemics and Economics*, Cambridge University Press, Cambridge.

-----. (1973) 'Marginalism: The Harvest' in Black 1973.

Shove, G. F. (1965) 'The Place of Marshall's Principles in the Development of Economic Theory' in James A. Gherity, ed. *Economic Thought A Historical Anthology*, Random House, New York.

Skinner, A. (1965) 'Economics and History - the Scottish Enlightenment' *Scottish Journal of Political Economy*, Vol. 12, Feb., pp. 1-22.

-----. (1972) 'Adam Smith: Philosophy and Science' *Scottish Journal of Political Economy*. Vol. 19, Nov., pp. 307-19.

-----. (1979) *A System of Social Science*. Clarendon Press, Oxford.

-----, and Wilson, Thomas, eds. (1975) *Essays on Adam Smith*, Clarendon Press, Oxford.

Small, Albion W. (1972) [1907] *Adam Smith and Modern Sociology*. Augustus M. Kelley, Clifton.

Smith, Adam. (1976) [1776] *An Inquiry into the Nature and Causes of the Wealth of Nations*, edited by R. H. Campbell and A. S. Skinner, Clarendon Press, Oxford.

-----. (1977) *The Correspondence of Adam Smith*, edited by Ernest Campbell Mossner and Ian Simpson, Clarendon Press, Oxford.

-----. (1978) *Lectures on Jurisprudence*, edited by R. L. Meek, D. D. Raphael and P. G. Stein, Clarendon Press, Oxford.

-----. (1979) [1759] *The Theory of Moral Sentiments*, edited by D. D. Raphael and A. L. Macfie, Clarendon Press, Oxford.

-----. (1980) [1795] *Essays on Philosophical Subjects*, edited by D. D. Raphael and A. S. Skinner, Clarendon Press, Oxford.

-----. (1983) [[1963] *Lectures on Rhetoric and Belles Lettres*, edited by J. C. Bryce, Clarendon Press, Oxford.

Solomon, Robert C. (1979) *History and Human Nature*, Harcourt Brace Jovanovich, New York.

Spengler, Joseph J. and William Allen. eds. (1960) *Essays in Economic Thought*, McNally & Company, Chicago.

Spiegel, Henry W. (1975) 'A Note on the Equilibrium Concept in the History of Economics' *Economie Appliqué*, Vol. 28, pp. 609-17.

-----. (1976) 'Adam Smith's Heavenly City' *History of Political Economy*, Vol. 8, pp. 478-93.

Stark, Werner. (1941) 'Liberty and Equality or: Jeremy Bentham as an Economist' *The Economic Journal*, Vol. 51, April, pp. 56-79.

-----. (1944) *The History of Economics in its Relation to Social Development*, Routledge, London.

-----. (1946) 'Jeremy Bentham as an Economist II' *The Economic Journal*, Vol. 56, Dec., pp. 583-608.

-----. (1947) 'Diminishing Utility Reconsidered' *Kyklos*, Vol. 11, pp. 321-44.

-----. (1950) 'Stable Equilibrium Re-examined' *Kyklos*, Vol. 14, pp. 218-32.

-----. (1958) *The Sociology of Knowledge*, Routledge & Kegan Paul, London.

-----. (1963) *The Fundamental Forms of Social Thought*, Fordham University Press, New York.

-----. (1966) 'The Sociology of Knowledge: A Guide to Truth' *Indian Sociological Bulletin*, pp. 3-6.

-----. (1976) [1943] *The Ideal Foundations of Economic Thought* Augustus M. Kelley, Fairfield, New Jersey.

-----. (1976-87) *The Social Bond*, Vol. 1-6. Fordham University Press, New York.

-----. (forthcoming) *History and Historians of Political Economy*, edited by Charles M. A. Clark, Transactions Press, New Brunswick.

Stein, Peter B. (1979) 'Adam Smith's Theory of Law and Society' in *Classical Influences on Western Thought, 1650-1870.* edited by R. R. Bolgar, Cambridge Uiversity Press, Cambridge.

-----. (1980) *Legal Evolution*. Cambridge University Press, Cambridge.

-----. (1982) 'From Pufendorf to Adam Smith: The Natural Law Tradition in Scotland' *Europaisches Rechtsdenken in Geschichte und Gegenwart: Restschrift fur Helmut Coing*. Munich, pp. 667-79.

Stewart, Dugald. (1829) *The Philosophy of the Active and Moral Powers of Man*. Vol 5 of *The Works of Dugald Stewart*. Hilliard and Brown, Cambridge.

Stigler, George. (1965) 'The Influence of Events and Policies on Economic Theory' in *Essays in the History of Economics*, University of Chicago Press, Chicago.

Tarascio, Vincent J. (1966) *Pareto's Methodological Approach to Economics*. University of North Carolina Press, Chapel Hill.

Taylor, O. H. (1929) 'Economics and the Idea of Natural Laws', in Taylor 1955.

-----. (1930) 'Economics and the Idea of Jus Naturale', in Taylor 1955.

-----. (1955) *Economics and Liberalism*. Harvard University Press, Cambridge, Mass.

Taylor, W. L. (1955) 'Gersham Carmichael: A Neglected Figure in British Political Economy' *South African Journal of Economics*, Vol. 23, pp. 251-5.

-----. (1965) *Francis Hutcheson and David Hume as Predecessors of Adam Smith*. Duke University Press, Durham.

Teichgraeber III, Richard. (1986) *'Free Trade' and Moral Philosophy*. Duke University Press, Durham.

Thomson, Herbert F. (1965) 'Adam Smith's Philosophy of Science' *Quarterly Journal of Economics*, Vol. 79, pp. 212-33.

Turgot, Ann Robert. (1973) *Turgot on Progress, Sociology and Economics*, Translated, edited and with an introduction by Ronald L. Meek, Cambridge University Press, Cambridge.

Van Melsen, Andrew G. (1954) *The Philosophy of Nature*, 2nd edition, The Ad Press, New York.

Vaughn, Karen I. (1980) *John Locke Economist and Social Scientist*, The University of Chicago Press, Chicago.

Veblen, Thorstein. (1898) 'Why is Economics not an Evolutionary

Science?' *Quarterly Journal of Economics*, Vol. 12, July, Reprinted in Veblen 1919.

-----. (1899-1900) 'The Preconceptions of Economic Science' *Quarterly Journal of Economics*, Vol. 13-14, Reprinted in Veblen 1919.

-----. (1908) 'Professor Clark's Economics' *Quarterly Journal of Political Economy*, Vol. 12, Feb., Reprinted in Veblen 1919.

-----. (1909) 'The Limitations of Marginal Utility' *Journal of Political Economy*, Vol. 17, Nov., Reprinted in Veblen 1919.

-----. (1919) *The Place of Science in Modern Civilisation and Other Essays*, Huebsch, New York.

-----. (1931) [1899] *The Theory of the Leisure Class*, Viking, New York.

Viner, Jacob. (1928) 'Adam Smith and Laissez Faire' in *Adam Smith, 1776-1926*, edited by John M. Clark, Chicago University Press, Chicago.

-----. (1972) *The Role of Providence in the Social Order: An Essay in Intellectual History*, American Philosophical Society, Philadelphia.

Walker, Donald (1984) 'Is Walras's Theory of General Equilibrium a Normative Scheme' *History of Political Economy*, Vol. 16, Winter, pp. 524-54.

Walras, Léon. (1860) 'Philosophie des Sciences Economiques' *Journal Des Economistes*, pp. 196-206.

-----. (1909) 'Économique et Mécanique' *Bullentin De la Societe Vaudoise des Sciences Naturalles*, Vol. 45, pp. 313-25. Reprinted in Walras (1987).

-----. (1954) [1874-77] *Elements of Pure Economics*, Translated by William Jaffe. Irwin, Homewood, Illinois.

-----. (1987) *Mélanges D'Économie Politique et Sociale*, edited by Pierre Dockes, Pierre-Henri Goutte, Claude Hebert, Claud Mouchot, Jean-Pierre Potier, and Jean-Michel Servet, Economica, Paris.

Walsh, Vivian and Harvey Gram. (1980) *Classical and Neoclassical Theories of General Equilibrium*. Oxford University Press, New York.

Weintraub, E. Roy. (1979) *Microfoundations*. Cambridge University Press, Cambridge.

-----. (1985) *General Equilibrium Analysis*. Cambridge University Press, Cambridge.

Whitehead, Alfred Noth. (1934) *Nature and Life*, Chicago.

Wightman, W. P. D. (1975) 'Adam Smith and the History of Ideas' in Skinner 1975.

Willey, Basil. (1961) [1940] *The Eighteenth Century Background*, Beacon Press, Boston.

Winch, Donald. (1973) 'Marginalism and the Boundaries of Economic Science' in Black 1973.

Wisman, Jon. (1979) 'Legitimation, Ideology-critique, and Economics' *Social Research*, Vol. 46, Summer, pp. 291-320.

Young, Jeffrey T. (1986) 'The Impartial Spectator and Natural Jurisprudence: An interpretation of Adam Smith's Theory of the Natural Price' *History of Political Economy*, Vol. 18, pp. 365-382.

Index